'this rugby spellbound pe

C000285967

Reviews of the First Editic

"...scrupulously researched [and] well written ...Gwyn Prescott has given [rugby in Wales] a history to be proud of."

Huw Richards, *scrum.com*

"Gwyn Prescott paints a meticulous picture of Welsh rugby's growth in Victorian Britain"

Rugby World

"It's a fascinating piece of research and a major contribution to the history of rugby, not just in Wales but generally."

Tony Collins, author of *A Social History of English Rugby Union*

"excellent"

Martin Johnes, author of *A History of Sport in Wales*

"If rugby is your thing...then get yourself a copy of Gwyn Prescott's account of the social, cultural and economical impact of rugby football on the people of South Wales...a detailed and fascinating study of the way in which rugby embedded itself in the fabric of Cardiff society and the villages and towns of South Wales, transforming itself from a fringe activity confined to the middle classes, to the mass-participation sport it became in the twentieth-century."

Gwladrugby.com

"the most assiduous archival research and rigorous command of the skills of the social historian...a book that also has significant implications for the historiography of rugby..."

Sport in History

"I knew immediately that I would enjoy Gwyn Prescott's account of how the game of rugby not only came to Cardiff but conquered it...The details are richly satisfying... The story is engrossing...If you have any nostalgia for those days when one eagerly crossed Westgate Street to get to a game this is the book for you."

Peter Stead

Front Cover Image

Cardiff Arms Park in 1903, when Wales overwhelmed Ireland 18-0. This wonderful action photograph may possibly record the first of Wales's six tries which was scored by Alf Brice. But it also superbly captures the atmosphere of the game that overcast day: the destruction of the Irish pack; the muddy "quagmire" of the pitch after heavy rain; the immediacy of the packed terraces with policemen patrolling the touch-lines; and the many spectators watching not only from the windows but also from the roofs of the buildings in Westgate Street. Of the Welsh team, only the diminutive Dickie Owen at half-back and the moustachioed Dai "Tarw" Jones in the forwards can be clearly identified.

Photograph courtesy of Daryl Leeworthy

'this rugby spellbound people'

The Birth of Rugby in Cardiff and Wales

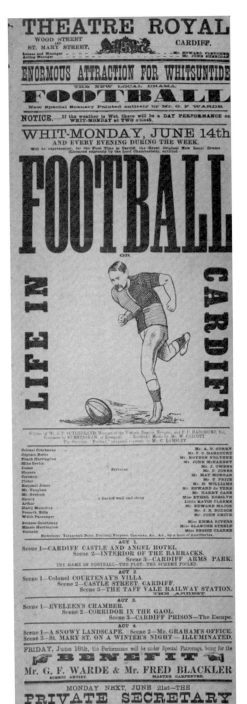

The playbill for the Theatre Royal's 1886 production, "Football or Life in Cardiff". Scene 3 was set at the Arms Park. The ground-breaking Cardiff team of 1885-6 played in quartered jerseys (see page 6). Courtesy of Glamorgan Archives.

'this rugby spellbound people'

The Birth of Rugby in Cardiff and Wales

Gwyn Prescott

ST DAVID'S PRESS

Cardiff

Published in Wales by St. David's Press, an imprint of

Ashley Drake Publishing Ltd
PO Box 733
Cardiff
CF14 7ZY

www.st-davids-press.com

Originally published, by Welsh Academic Press in 2011, as "This
Rugby Spellbound People": Rugby Football in Nineteenth-Century
Cardiff and South Wales

Second Edition – 2015

ISBN
978-1-902719-43-6

British Library Cataloguing-in-Publication Data.
A CIP catalogue for this book is available from the British Library.

Typeset by Replika Press Pvt Ltd, India
Printed by Akcent Press, Czech Republic

CONTENTS

FOREWORD

The title of this book derives from a report its author found in the *Irish Times* describing the crowd at the Wales v New Zealand game in December 1905 as 'this rugby spellbound people'. Throw 'spellbound' into a computer search engine and most likely it will cough up a film of that name. Gwyn Prescott, though, is more interested in Frank Hancock than Alfred Hitchcock. That's for the birds – though it seems that rugby already *was* in Cardiff when the first grandstand was erected at the Arms Park in 1881 'for the convenience of the spectators and the ladies in particular'. By 1898 there were complaints that they were monopolising it.

Some years ago I met Aeronwy Thomas, Dylan's daughter, at a concert at the London Welsh Centre in Gray's Inn Road given by the Pendyrus male choir (I was – am – a member and Aeronwy had married one). I told her I had once, with my friend Dai, written a book about Welsh rugby – a real conversation-stopper, this, when talking to the daughter of a famous poet, herself a writer – and we'd called it *Fields of Praise*. With just a flicker of a smile she replied, 'That's a good title', and moved on. How many times, I wondered, had Aeronwy read and recited her father's immortal lines '… how it must have been after the birth of the simple light/ In the first spinning place, the spellbound horses walking warm/Out of the whinnying green stable /On to the fields of praise'? Gwyn, whose daughter Sarah, he tells me, has been in love with 'Fern Hill' since childhood, was spellbound by the coincidence, though his Irish rugby correspondent can hardly have been aware of it, writing nine years before Dylan was born.

There weren't many green stables in late nineteenth-century Cardiff: that's what its explosive growth was all about, and Gwyn Prescott's study shows how rugby became a key component of the new urban culture that developed along with it. Fifty years ago a distinguished professor of Welsh history did indeed recognise that 'more organised sport was becoming popular' in Cardiff in the 1860s and '70s, providing as confirmation the death of two mountaineers on Mont Blanc. Fortunately sports history has developed apace since then. Prof William Rees can hardly be blamed for not knowing that by the 1890s there were over 200 rugby sides in Cardiff. I didn't either, until Gwyn Prescott's research unearthed and listed them. Clearly the clubs in formal membership of the WRU were only the tip of a much bigger iceberg, and Gwyn has blazed a trail for other pioneers to push on into the probably equally active conurbations of Newport and Swansea to enable us to further fill out the national picture.

It is unlikely that anyone who turns to this book needs persuading of the social significance of the history of sport. Academic snobbery about sports history may still linger in some of the mustier recesses of the ivory tower, but Gwyn Prescott, a university teacher, has never shared it: he well knows that sport generally – Welsh and therefore Cardiff rugby in particular – is socially and historically determined. Sports history, perhaps more than most comparable kinds of scholarly endeavour, can easily be reduced to the unimportant and the trivial, the anecdotal and anodyne, the stunningly statistical and the microscopically close reading where 'the alleged try scored by the New Zealander Deans in the historic Welsh victory over the All Blacks in December 1905 is described with the scholastic antiquarianism of an analysis of medieval commotes' (the historian Kenneth O., now Lord, Morgan reviewing *Fields of Praise* in the *Times Literary Supplement*).

Gwyn Prescott knows all this – though perhaps not that review (I never showed it to him). In this book he has brought off two major achievements. He recognises we need to know more facts, the raw data which only painstaking empirical research can uncover, because he is well aware that it is very often specific, even parochial, developments which determine the distinctive contours of sporting practice. He traces, from an exploration of a wide array of hitherto unused primary sources, the emergence and organisation of a robust infrastructure of socially inclusive teams and clubs in inner, dockside and suburban Cardiff; how many, where they played and how often. By the 1890s rugby football was contributing to an expressive local, civic, even national consciousness: Cardiffians, who have that endearing habit of equating Cardiff with Wales, were talking of rugby as 'the national game' as early as 1879. At the same time the author meticulously documents this unprecedented growth without losing sight of the wider context and culture of the teeming townscape of late Victorian Cardiff (we can only speak of a *city*scape from 1905), thereby placing his book on a par with the two other major studies of 'coal metropolis' in its heyday by Martin Daunton (1977) and John Davies (1994).

Neither neckless nor shaven-headed, a living refutation of the claim that the thinking prop is some fabulous beast, Gwyn Prescott also confirms that while one does not *have* to be a player, a spectator or even an armchair aficionado to appreciate that rugby football has been hardwired into the popular culture and urban life of Cardiff for over 130 years, it cannot be a disadvantage actually to have picked up the ball and run with it. The author, a product of Cardiff High School and the HSOB, has serious form in a playing career that spanned the sixties, extending from captaining the Welsh Secondary Schools to a near-Blue at Cambridge and playing for Glamorgan Wanderers and for Penarth against the Barbarians. His brother Colin also captained the Welsh Youth and played at prop for Cardiff, Newport and Penarth. Gwyn's interest in the history of the game was kindled by his father, an avid working-class rugby follower who was a schoolboy and District player in Cardiff before the war. Prescott senior had been taken to watch the Blue and Blacks in the early 1920s by his part-Irish grandfather who had himself watched and played in Cardiff from the 1890s. With his family thus steeped in the sport Gwyn has always been conscious of the city's rugby heritage whose historical undergrowth he here reveals and probes. And time and again we are reminded how the importance of rugby football within Cardiff's urban culture was physically symbolised by the strategically central location of the Cardiff Arms Park and the commercial and public benefits reaped because of its sheer accessibility. As the *Western Mail* remarked in 1896, 'the value of this piece of ground to the Cardiff Football Club is really untold, and they will never rightly value it till they have to shift!'

How the late, great Bleddyn Williams of Cardiff and Wales, a relative of the author's, would have savoured those prophetic words. The incomparable Bleddyn would have enjoyed reading Gwyn Prescott's book. So will you.

Gareth Williams
Pontypridd
November 2010 & August 2015

ACKNOWLEDGEMENTS

Both the first and second edition of this book could not have been written without the help of numerous others. In particular, I have to thank Professor Gareth Williams of the University of Glamorgan (now renamed the University of South Wales) who supervised the research on which these books are based. Like all good coaches, he always managed to keep me focused on getting the ball across the try line, not the easiest of achievements when dealing with a former prop-forward not used to handling the ball. Without his guidance, support and encouragement, my studies would never have been completed. Whether it was providing sources, or drawing on his unrivalled expertise to comment on all aspects of the work, his help was invariably given freely and with his customary good humour. The happiest outcome of the research is that he is now a valued friend.

There are many others who, in a variety of ways, also helped me to conceive, develop and produce these publications and to them all I offer my sincere thanks. They include Professor Dai Smith, Dr. Andy Croll, Professor David Hillier and Professor Chris Williams, all former colleagues at the University of Glamorgan and Professor Martin Johnes of Swansea University; Bryn Jones, Katrina Coopey, Tony Davidson, Peter Evans and colleagues in Local Studies, Cardiff Library; Michael Rowe and Jed Smith (World Rugby Museum, Twickenham); Martin Davies and Peter Owens (Welsh Rugby Union); and Dr. Mike Bassett (Barry RFC), Charles Brain (SA Brain and Co.), Terry Budd and Ivor Rodway (Canton RFC), the late Peter Cronin, Richard Daglish, Mike Dams (Newport RFC), David Dow (Swansea RFC), Angus Evans, Howard Evans, Amanda Gillard, Roger Goode, Robert Gould, Bernard Green (Llandaff RFC), Gareth Harvey, Dr. Andrew Hignell (Glamorgan County Cricket Club), Professor Mike Huggins, John Jenkins, Lindsay Jenkins, Dylan Jones (St. Fagans National History Museum), Gaynor Jones, Dr. Daryl Leeworthy, Dr. Julie Light, John Lyons, Rusty MacLean (Rugby School), Rupert May-Hill, Gareth Morgan, John Owen, Rhian Phillips (Glamorgan Archives), James Prescott, Mike Price, Jack Rickus, Gareth Thomas (Cardiff and District RU), Terry Thompson (St. Peter's RFC), the late Bleddyn Williams (Cardiff RFC), Dick Williams (Gloucester RFC), Tudor Williams, Viv Williams (Tongwynlais RFC) and Martin Wills. I am also especially grateful to David Hughes, secretary of one of my old clubs,

Penarth RFC, for allowing me to make use of the club archive and collection of handbooks. I apologise if I have inadvertently omitted to acknowledge anyone's assistance throughout the long period of my research.

I am also indebted to the following for their kind and generous permission to use their illustrations in this book: Canton RFC; Cardiff RFC; Cardiff and District RU; Cardiff Council Library Service; David Dow; Howard Evans; Glamorgan Archives; Gloucester RFC; Gloucestershire Archives; Dr. Andrew Hignell; Lindsay Jenkins; Gaynor Jones; Dr. Daryl Leeworthy; Llandaff RFC; Newport RFC; Penarth RFC; Rugby School Collections; SA Brain and Co.; St. Fagans National History Museum; St. Peter's RFC; Swansea RFC; John Taylor; Tongwynlais Community Council; Tongwynlais RFC; Webb Ellis Rugby Museum; Welsh Rugby Union; and World Rugby Museum Twickenham. Whilst every reasonable effort has been made to obtain copyright clearance for all the images used in this book, I would be delighted to hear from the small number we have been unable to identify.

I am also grateful to Ashley Drake, my publisher, for giving me the opportunity to produce this updated and revised edition. He has enthusiastically supported the project throughout and guided me with care and consideration at all times.

Finally, of course, I have to thank my family. Sarah, Anna and Siân all provided their father – a product after all of the pre-computer age – with much help in the book's preparation. Sarah also gave immeasurable assistance in arranging for its publication, while Siân took some of the photographs which illustrate this revised edition. I also thank my wife Catherine for her patience and invaluable help and advice at all times. This book is as much theirs as it is mine.

Gwyn Prescott
Cardiff, August 2015

PREFACE

Given the popularity which rugby has always enjoyed in Wales, it is strange that there has been no detailed historical study of the sport at a local level. This book aims to remedy that with an investigation of nineteenth-century Welsh rugby which concentrates on the nature of the game in one urban area. It sets out to argue that from the earliest days Cardiff was at the centre of rugby in Wales and that rugby was also at the heart of the Victorian town's popular culture. It is, therefore, the first in-depth study of its kind. The absence of any detailed research at this level has provided an opportunity to make a contribution to our knowledge, not only of the history of sport in Wales but also of nineteenth-century rugby and sport in general. Drawing on previously unused sources, it provides some fresh insights into the origins and early years of the game in Wales. It also throws new light both on the significance of Cardiff to Welsh rugby in the nineteenth century and on the importance of rugby in Cardiff.

In seeking to achieve this, the early chapters set out the context for the game in Cardiff by exploring the origins of rugby in Wales and its subsequent development as a popular sport, up to and including the formation of the Welsh Football (Rugby) Union in 1881. The following three chapters then concentrate on Cardiff, examining the extent and nature of the club game, how it was organised, who played and administered it and the impact which rugby had on the town and its popular culture.

The final chapter concludes that rugby very rapidly became the main sporting interest in Cardiff and it experienced very little serious competition from other sports until the end of the century. For many newly arrived citizens, therefore, rugby was an easily accessible and speedy route into the social life of the community. Cardiff's distinctive economic and social structure influenced the particular way in which the game evolved in the town. At the grass roots, the game was dominated by neighbourhood clubs, largely involving working-class and lower middle-class players and administrators, rather than by institutional teams organised by social improvers. At the highest level of competition, an emphasis on civic pride meant that success on the field was more important than social exclusivity. The game was played and supported, therefore, by representatives of all classes within the town.

Because more information on these topics has become available since the first edition was published in 2011, various updates, additions and revisions have been incorporated throughout the original text. In particular, the account of early "football" has been extended with new material, much of it relating to Wales. This new edition also includes many more illustrations and an expanded appendix. However, my main arguments and conclusions remain unaltered.

A range of sources was used in the research. In the absence of any of relevant club records from the nineteenth century, the main primary source was the local press, in particular hardcopy versions of the *South Wales Daily News* and the *Western Mail* held at Cardiff Library. These morning daily newspapers were published in Cardiff and circulated throughout south Wales. Therefore, as their coverage of rugby had both a Welsh and a Cardiff dimension, they were especially relevant to the study and so they were both thoroughly investigated from the late 1860s to 1900.[1] No previous study of rugby of this period has made use of this particular source in such depth. Other newspapers were also consulted where necessary.

As a research source, newspapers have their weaknesses and they have to be used with a degree of caution. They are written for a particular audience, time and locality. Sports coverage in the two Cardiff dailies was frequently variable and selective, leaving many topics unresolved, whilst reports may have suffered from uncorrected errors, bias and falsehoods. Nevertheless, they do provide, by far, the most comprehensive record we have of Welsh rugby during the period. Increasingly they came to articulate the local sporting culture and in doing so they helped to construct both a local and a national identity. However, they did not merely reflect the sporting context: they also contributed to it. Without this significant resource, the record of the personalities, clubs and institutions of Victorian Welsh rugby would have been largely lost forever. Thanks to our ancestors who read, wrote and published their newspapers with such vigour, a great deal of that record is still accessible to us, if we are prepared to look for it and use it critically. There is a huge amount of valuable evidence about the game in Wales still waiting to be discovered in the many newspapers of the time, particularly with regard to other parts of the country. Undoubtedly, the National Library of Wales's recently established resource, Welsh Newspapers Online, will greatly assist future research into the game.[2]

---

1   The *Western Mail* was published from 1869 and the *South Wales Daily News* from 1872.

2   National Library of Wales, Welsh Newspapers Online: http://newspapers.library.wales/

Contemporary football handbooks also proved to be very informative, as were copies of Alcock's *Football Annual,* another previously underused source for Welsh rugby. Other primary material included RFU and WFU minute books, as well as census returns, directories and biographical compilations which were used to identify individuals and their social background.

A wide range of books and articles and several academic theses were consulted, though there has been surprisingly little detailed and academic research on nineteenth-century Welsh rugby. Of course, David Smith and Gareth Williams's brilliant tour de force, *Fields of Praise,* was not only the inspiration for this book but was also a constant and invaluable reference. It would be hard to disagree with Geoffrey Moorhouse's view that *Fields of Praise* may well be the finest history written on any sport. However, a special mention should also be made of CS Arthur's remarkable and highly informative 1908 history of Cardiff RFC.[3]

A Note on Terminology

Contemporary sources invariably refer to "football" clubs rather than "rugby" clubs, so this style is consistently adopted throughout the book when discussing rugby clubs and unions in the nineteenth century, for example, Cardiff Football Club and Welsh Football Union. These, after all, are the names they called themselves and by which they were always referred to in the press at the time, so usages such as "Glamorgan RFC" and "South Wales Rugby Football Union" are simply anachronisms. All rugby clubs in Victorian Cardiff called themselves "football clubs". The only exception discovered in this research was "Cardiff YMCA Wednesday (Rugby) Football Club" and, interestingly, the Cardiff YMCA soccer club included "Association" in their title *without* the brackets.[4] In addition, following the practice in south Wales during the nineteenth century, all references in the book to the round ball version of football are qualified as "association" or "soccer". The word "football" is, however, also sometimes used here as a generic term describing all varieties of football. Finally, as Cardiff did not receive city status until 1905, it is described as a town in any reference before then.

---

3   David Smith and Gareth Williams, *Fields of Praise: The Official History of the Welsh Rugby Union 1881-1981* (Cardiff, 1980); Geoffrey Moorhouse, *At the George And Other Essays on Rugby League* (London, 1989), p.84; C.S. Arthur, *The Cardiff Rugby Football Club: History and Statistics, 1876-1906* (Cardiff, 1908).

4   *SWDN* 19 Sept. 1895.

ABBREVIATIONS

AFC	Association Football Club
C&DFU	Cardiff and District Football Union
C&DRU	Cardiff and District Rugby Union
CDFU	Cardiff District Football Union
FA	Football Association
FAW	Football Association of Wales
FC	Football Club
FU	Football Union
GAV	Glamorgan Artillery Volunteers
GRV	Glamorgan Rifle Volunteers
GWR	Great Western Railway
IJHS	International Journal of the History of Sport
IRB	International Rugby Board (World Rugby)
IRFU	Irish Rugby Football Union
NU	Northern Union
RFC	Rugby Football Club
RFU	Rugby Football Union
RMA	Royal Military Academy
RU	Rugby Union
RWF	Royal Welch Fusiliers
SFU	Scottish Football Union (Scottish Rugby Union)
SWDN	South Wales Daily News
SWFC	South Wales Football Club
SWFU	South Wales Football Union
WFU	Welsh Football Union
WM	Western Mail
WMC	Working Men's Club
WRU	Welsh Rugby Union

Dedicated to the memory of my father Jim Prescott
(St. Peter's School, Cardiff Centrals and Grange Baptists)
and my mother Maud Prescott,
who both loved rugby football

1

INTRODUCTION:
'The contagion will spread'

In December 1905, *The Irish Times* despatched a reporter to cover the All Blacks game in Cardiff. Only a little over thirty years earlier, apart from a few young middle-class blades who occasionally took exercise by playing with an oval ball on what was then still sometimes referred to as the "Cardiff Arms Hotel Park", the game of rugby was barely known in the town.[1] Yet following the historic Welsh victory over New Zealand, that Irish journalist memorably described the excited, good humoured and wildly enthusiastic crowds he witnessed that day in and around the Arms Park as "this rugby spell-bound people". He went on to declare that the Welsh were "undoubtedly the best exponents of the game."[2]

The south-east corner of the walled Arms Park around 1870. It was at this time, "when Cardiff was merely aping a large town", that local pioneers began playing rugby here.
Courtesy of Cardiff Council Library Service

---

1   *Western Mail* (hereafter *WM*) 21 Sept. 1878 (Cardiff Arms Hotel Park).
2   *Irish Times*, 18 Dec. 1905.

How did this come about? How did a game which elsewhere was played predominantly by public schools and largely middle-class clubs become within a few years such a passion for people of all classes in Wales and in Cardiff in particular?

By the early 1880s, as will be shown, rugby was already putting down strong roots in south Wales. But a series of events in the middle part of that decade was to establish Cardiff as one of the aristocrats of the club game and, in so doing, permanently embed rugby football into the popular culture and the very lifeblood of the town.

During miserable weather in February 1884, a decision was made by a selection committee in a hotel room in the centre of Cardiff which was to lead eventually to profound changes in the way rugby has been played ever since. In their previous fixture, Cardiff had played at Cheltenham College but, owing to the torrential conditions, only a few players bothered to turn up at the station. So a team was hurriedly cobbled together using some of the Second XV who were also meeting at the station travelling to an away fixture at Chepstow. Despite these changes, Cardiff won the match at Cheltenham, partly due to the play of Frank Hancock, who was making his First XV debut at three-quarter. This new recruit was a highly talented player. Within two months, and after only five games for Cardiff, he won the first of his four international caps when he played for Wales against Ireland.[3]

When Frank Hancock came from Wiveliscombe in Somerset to manage his father's new brewing interests in south Wales, he was already an accomplished club and county footballer, and he would shortly captain the town's rugby club in its most successful ever season. It was a fortunate set of circumstances which brought him to Cardiff at a time when his leadership and tactical skills could be used to lasting benefit for the game.[4]

Impressed with his performance at Cheltenham, the Cardiff selectors decided to keep him in the side for the following fixture with Gloucester. Perhaps not wishing to upset their fellow club-mates, they were reluctant to

---

3   For an account of Frank Hancock, see Andrew Hignell and Gwyn Prescott, *Cardiff Sporting Greats* (Stroud, 2007), pp. 163-4.

4   Remarkably, the Hancocks were not the only English brewing family to contribute to the sporting heritage of Cardiff. Joseph Brain helped to elevate Glamorgan County Cricket Club to first-class status, while other members of the Brain family have supported the Cardiff and District Rugby Union over the years. S.A. Brain and Co. still sponsor the District Union today as well as the Glamorgan County RFC. They are also past sponsors of the Welsh Rugby Union. For an account of Joseph Brain, see Hignell and Prescott, *Cardiff Sporting Greats*, pp. 41-3.

drop any of the regular three-quarters for a newcomer, so they came up with the inspired solution of selecting four, and thus a new system was born. The Cardiff selectors continued to experiment with four three-quarters during the rest of the 1883-4 season and the following year. They sometimes reverted to three players, but settled on the new formation by the end of 1884-5. By this time, other teams like Llanelli, Neath and Swansea were also occasionally selecting four three-quarters, demonstrating that Welsh clubs were already prepared to experiment with promising new ideas.[5] Less senior teams too were willing to innovate at this very early stage: when Penarth played Canton in March 1885, both employed four three-quarters.[6] Clearly the idea was catching on. Hancock is often credited with "inventing" the system but Henry (Joe) Simpson, his captain in those two seasons, and another Englishman incidentally, was the first to adopt it.[7] It was Frank Hancock, however,

Henry Simpson, captain 1883-5, when Cardiff first experimented with four three-quarters.

who worked out the best method of applying the new four three-quarter formation and, in doing so, he produced a tactical advance which helped to transform the game.

In August 1885, he was unanimously elected captain to replace Simpson. Hancock had a reputation for being a disciplinarian and his impact on the club was immediate. Up to that season, Cardiff had enjoyed success, but lacked consistency. The chaotic circumstances surrounding his introduction to the club eighteen months earlier must have made him realise that a dramatic change in organisation was required if Cardiff were to achieve their potential.

After the four three-quarter system had eventually become universally accepted, other clubs began to claim that they had played four three-quarters before Cardiff and therefore had "invented" the system. Writing in 1948, WJ Townsend Collins, the highly regarded rugby correspondent of the *South Wales Argus*, and whose own playing career went back to 1876, identified two such clubs. He astutely added, however, "What is certain is that to Cardiff belongs the credit of having perfected the system."[8] Searching

---

5   *South Wales Daily News* (hereafter *SWDN*) and *WM* Sept. 1884 to Apr. 1885 passim.

6   *SWDN* 17 Mar. 1885.

7   In 1884, Durham-born Simpson became the first man without an Oxbridge background to captain Wales.

8   W.J. Townsend Collins, *Rugby Recollections* (Newport, 1948), p. 13.

Frank Hancock, who perfected the four three-quarter passing game in 1885-6.

for some solace in England's defeat by Wales in 1899, *The Sunday Special* even claimed that it was an English invention. "The Welshmen ... have done splendid work in making Rugby football popular – even if they did obtain the system from the West of England clubs".[9] But, in any case, such claims entirely miss the point. It wasn't so much the mere placing of four men in the line-up which mattered: rather it was what was done with the new formation which was revolutionary. This was Hancock's – and Cardiff's – great legacy to the game. One hundred and twenty-five years later, this was acknowledged by the International Rugby Board (rebranded World Rugby in 2014), who inducted Frank Hancock and Cardiff RFC into their Hall of Fame in 2011.[10]

Reducing the pack from nine to eight was potentially a great risk and initially it was strongly criticised and resisted by many pundits and clubs, even those in the generally more progressive north of England. For Cardiff, this reduction was particularly risky because they did not possess big forwards. Hancock's solution was to encourage them to concentrate on winning and transferring the ball to the half-backs as quickly as possible, rather than engaging in prolonged scrums and mauls, which was then the conventional role for the forwards. Though this may not appear particularly innovative today, it certainly was so in the 1880s. For some, it represented nothing less than the emasculation of rugby football. Even as late as 1899, Arthur Budd, a former international and president of the RFU, was advising *Sporting Life* readers that English "decadence" began when they tried to imitate the Welsh three-quarter game and abandoned old-style forward play.[11]

At this time, both half-backs "fed the scrum" and there was no specialised outside-half. Instead of kicking or running with the ball, which was the usual practice, under Hancock the half-backs' responsibility was to move it quickly and accurately from the scrum to the three-quarters. Cardiff were lucky here since they possessed one of the finest passing half-backs of the era in William "Buller" Stadden, described as "brilliant" even by the largely Anglo-centric *Football Annual*.[12] The role of the centre three-quarters was to

9   Quoted in *SWDN* 9 Jan. 1899.
10   WRU website: http://www.wru.co.uk/eng/news/19258.php#.VKwWo9hF2M8 (accessed 6 Jan. 2015).
11   Quoted in *SWDN* 21 Mar. 1899.
12   *Football Annual* 1887 p. 168.

feed the wings as quickly as possible with low, accurate passing. Facing only three opponents, the wings invariably had a clear overlap by the time they received the ball and the tries flowed easily. Hancock also stressed the importance of correct alignment and insisted the backs took their passes on the run. Simple ideas perhaps but somebody had to be the first to practise them.

The speed and accuracy of the passing of the ball confounded opponents whose own attempts at passing in response were feeble in comparison, often amounting to no more than lobbing the ball in the hope that someone would catch it. Only three teams managed to score against Cardiff all season. Used to a more sluggish style of play in which the ball was often tied up for minutes in mauls and in which combined passing amongst the backs was a relatively rare event, spectators are recorded as being

William (Buller) Stadden, the first working-class player to be capped by Wales in 1884.

bewildered by the speed of the play; some even had difficulty following the ball. On their way to their match at Stradey Park, the team were "saluted with a few stones and handfuls of mud".[13] However, after their comprehensive ten try victory, they were greeted with cheers as they drove back through the streets of Llanelli. Even local journalists were impressed with Cardiff. "Llanellyite" perceptively wrote:

> fifteen [Cardiff] players worked with a perfection of combination unexampled in the annals of Welsh football. Selfishness, that bane of good play, was never once perceptible ... the victorious team, not only should be the pride of Cardiff, but of the whole Principality, and strange it will be if their success does not stimulate to more scientific play the other teams of Wales, and operate to improve the exposition of the Rugby game generally.[14]

The "passing game" had arrived.

The results *were* astonishing. Of twenty-seven games played, only the last against Moseley was narrowly lost when it seems that nerves finally got the better of the players. An even more remarkable statistic is that while 131 tries were scored, only four were conceded. Gareth Williams has described the new system as "a concept as enterprising and innovative as

---

13   *SWDN* 16 Nov. 1885.
14   *WM* 16 Nov. 1885.

The Cardiff team of 1885-6, inducted into World Rugby's Hall of Fame in 2011.
Back: A Duncan, A Bland, A Hybart, J Sant, A Emery, G Young, AF Hill, HJ Simpson,
W Treatt; Middle: W Jones, H Hughes, CS Arthur, FE Hancock (captain), W Douglas, QD
Kedzlie, AJ Stuart; Front: D Lewis, J Mahoney, W Jarman, W Stadden.　　Cardiff RFC

the brash, self-confident society that invented it."[15] It is no surprise then that in such an enterprising society, other Welsh clubs quickly responded to the new system by adopting it themselves, some before the end of the season. Thus, as "Llanellyite" accurately predicted, before very long, the "Cardiff game" became the "Welsh game". English clubs like Gloucester, with regular fixtures against Welsh teams, also switched, but in the main it was initially resisted by many die-hards of the game elsewhere in the British Isles. A not untypical response was that of *Pastime*'s rugby "expert" who wrote in 1885, "There is really not room for four three-quarter backs on an ordinary ground. In Jemmy [sic] Stokes's day the post used to be taken with some ease by *one*."[16] Players outside Wales seemed to struggle with the new system. Even as late as 1897, following Wales's 11-0 victory over England,

---

15　Gareth Williams, *1905 and All That: Essays on Rugby Football, Sport and Welsh Society* (Llandysul, 1991), p. 19.

16　Quoted in *SWDN* 30 Mar. 1885.

"Old Stager" was able to boast about "swift, sharp, low passing, which seems easy to crack local players, as it is pleasing to the eye of the spectator, and which is so difficult for the premier backs in the three sister countries to acquire."[17]

One of the most common descriptions of the play of Hancock's team was its "machine-like"

The ball used in the Welsh 26-3 victory over England at Swansea in 1899.
Swansea RFC

quality. To modern ears this may sound rather negative, conveying a sense of the mundane, the mechanical and the repetitive. However, at the high summer of Britain's industrialisation, which had so transformed the lives of Victorians, the analogy was both valid and complimentary. Combination, precision, speed and practice were the keys to the system's success. Unfortunately, the "scientific attack" theory initially proved difficult to transfer successfully to the international level, where teams were assembled at short notice with little opportunity for practice. In addition, in the early years, Wales simply did not have strong enough forwards to compete with the bigger nine-men packs of the other nations.

However, by the end of the 1890s, the problem was finally cracked, when the four three-quarter game was at last hitched to a powerful, well-drilled pack of so-called "Rhondda" forwards. Two days before the crushing 26-3 defeat which Wales inflicted on England in January 1899, the team had assembled to practise, though they were criticised for their "serious and business-like" approach which was "not quite in keeping with the traditions of amateur football".[18] Even so, the *Daily Mail* described the victory as:

the vindication, long expected, of the Welsh system ... Experience has shown over and over again, that granted forwards of sufficient strength and skill, the scientific style developed by Welsh backs is much more

17   *SWDN* 11 Jan. 1897.
18   *SWDN* 13 Jan. 1899.

productive of free scoring than the older and more haphazard methods adopted by English players.[19]

At last Wales were now able to prove conclusively the superiority of their system and to silence the critics for ever. After the 1899 match, the *Morning Leader* ran up the white flag and conceded defeat:

> Our methods, like our "rulers", are antiquated … After Saturday's lesson the contagion will spread, and in a few years' time we will doubtless see the "Welsh game" played throughout England. We are a proud, if not pig-headed nation, but we will show wisdom even at this late hour by copying the superior method of our conquerors.[20]

The *Morning Leader* was right. That contagion was the basis of Wales's great successes in the first "Golden Era" of 1900 to 1911, which included six Triple Crowns – the last three of which were converted into Grand Slams after France joined in – and the historically significant victory over the first All Blacks. And the contagion *did* eventually spread, not just to England but throughout the rugby world. This, therefore, is arguably Cardiff's greatest contribution to the game.

It is no exaggeration to claim that these events in Cardiff ultimately brought about a revolution in the way rugby was played. It led to the demise of the forward-dominated mauling game in which passing movements were made only infrequently. For the first time, it handed the main attacking thrust to the backs, who previously – apart from an occasional individual run – had played a largely defensive tackling or kicking role. Some historians have suggested that one of the reasons why in the late nineteenth century association football eventually began to eclipse rugby – at least in England – was its greater fluidity compared to the more static handling code.[21] But this ignores how dramatically rugby changed after 1885. It was in Wales, and in Cardiff in particular, that these changes were first put into practice and exploited so well. There is no doubt that, in Cardiff *and* throughout south Wales, this new and exciting playing style contributed greatly to the enormous growth in the popularity of rugby, both as a game to play and to watch. Within four years of Hancock's ground-breaking season, the number of teams in the immediate Cardiff area alone rose from sixty to well over

---

19   Quoted in *SWDN* 10 Jan. 1899.
20   Quoted in *SWDN* 10 Jan. 1899.
21   Dave Russell, *Football and the English: A Social History of Association Football in England, 1863-1995* (Preston, 1997), p. 20.

200. Certainly for the next fifteen years, it far outstripped soccer in the locality.

Cardiff's Gwyn Nicholls, the captain of the Welsh team which defeated the All Blacks and regarded by many as the greatest player of his era, wrote about its impact in 1908:

> [Rugby's] process of evolution has been very marked during the last twenty years. ... all clubs nowadays *combine* more or less ... The new idea was originated and its virtues first demonstrated by the Cardiff team, which, under the captaincy of ... F.E. Hancock, originated the four three-quarter game ... [it requires the] total merging of the player in the team. He is no longer even an [sic] unit, but rather an integral part of the whole.[22]

Forty years later in 1948, Townsend Collins – he was after all a Newport man – generously acknowledged:

Gwyn Nicholls depicted on a pirate programme for the Wales v New Zealand match 1905.

> The "Cardiff tradition" has persisted till this day. No other club have played the four three-quarter game with such consistent success. Theory has been handed on from generation to generation ... players have been found to illustrate anew the value of judgement, unselfishness and accuracy in the combined game with eight men in the scrummage and four in the threequarter line.[23]

22   E. Gwyn Nicholls, *The Modern Game and How to Play It* (London, 1908), pp. 9-11.
23   Townsend Collins, *Rugby Recollections*, p.13.

Both the success and the playing style of the club became matters of great pride for Cardiff's sports-loving citizens and so rugby became an important feature of the popular culture of the town. It was, after all, the "Cardiff game". It is interesting too to note the extent to which Hancock's team mirrored the character of the fast growing town. Though all of the seventeen leading players lived and worked in Cardiff, only nine were born in the locality. One came from Pembrokeshire and another from north Wales. Two were Scots, while one Cardiff-born player was a member of the town's very large Irish community. Four team members were English and it should not be forgotten that the four three-quarter system was both introduced and developed at the club by two of them. A third of the team was working class. The players were also substantially products of a local club system which flourished spectacularly during the late nineteenth century. The composition of Hancock's team was, then, a reflection of Victorian Cardiff society and as such it was a team with which the town's citizens could easily identify and proudly share in its success.

This book is concerned with many of the themes highlighted here: the extraordinary growth in the number of clubs in late nineteenth-century Cardiff; the take-up of the game by working-class players and its socially inclusive nature there; civic pride and the popularity of rugby; the wider impact of the game; and its contribution to local, civic and national consciousness. Referring to Cardiff City's success in the First Division and FA Cup in the 1920s, Neil Evans has suggested that "the popular dimension of Cardiff's civic pride was mainly expressed in [association] football" at this time.[24] This book demonstrates, however, that the citizens of Cardiff were already celebrating their civic pride through rugby football several decades earlier.

The story begins, however, with the arrival of "football" in south Wales in the 1860s.

---

24   Neil Evans, "Regions, Nations, Globe: Roles, Representations and Urban Space in Cardiff, 1839-1928", in Andreas Fahrmeir and Elfie Rembold (eds.), *Representation of British Cities: Transformation of Urban Spaces, 1700-2000* (Berlin/Wien, 2003), p.126.

2

FROM FOOTBALL TO RUGBY:
'Neither dribbling fish nor handling fowl'

The remarkable popularity of rugby in Victorian Cardiff did not occur in isolation. It is necessary, therefore, to establish the context for this by exploring the introduction and consolidation of the game in Wales up to 1881, when the Welsh Football Union (WFU) was founded. In so doing, the hitherto unrecognised contribution which the town made to the earliest days of rugby football in Wales will be demonstrated.

Within a few years, the rapid expansion of the coal industry transformed nineteenth-century Welsh society. It also dramatically changed the country's sporting culture, for it was during this period of massive population growth – mainly the result of inward migration – that rugby football became the dominant sport in the south. In so doing, it helped to bind newcomers not only to their communities but also to their nation.

The arrival of rugby in Wales coincided with a period of extraordinary economic change. Between 1870 and 1914, south Wales became a centre of heavy industry of global significance. At no other time in its history was Wales more important to the British economy.[1] Though the expansion in steel and tin-plate production contributed to the spectacular growth experienced in this period, its main cause was the dramatic increase in the export-driven demand for Welsh coal. In 1840, Wales was producing four and a half million tons. By the 1870s, this had risen to sixteen million and by 1913 coal output reached fifty-seven million. The exploitation of steam coal in the Glamorgan and Monmouthshire valleys was well advanced by the 1880s but the continued expansion, largely due to the seemingly insatiable demand from the world's steamships, was especially pronounced in the Rhondda. The anthracite areas of west Wales also saw an unprecedented expansion, though mainly to meet domestic and commercial demands. By 1913, over half of all British coal exports passed through the ports of south

---

1   Kenneth O. Morgan, *Rebirth of a Nation: Wales 1880-1980* (Oxford, 1982 edn.), p. 59.

The Close, Rugby School.   *David Dow. Courtesy of Rugby School*

Wales and there were over a quarter of a million men – almost one in three of the total labour force – employed in the industry.[2]

Initially, demand for labour was largely met from Wales itself, mainly by migration from the depressed countryside. Between 1851 and 1911, rural Wales experienced a net loss of population of 338,000: this was balanced by an inward migration into the south Wales coalfield of 366,000. From the 1890s, however, the migrants came increasingly from outside Wales, particularly from the west of England and the border counties.[3] By 1911, a fifth of Glamorgan's population and a quarter of Monmouthshire's had been born outside Wales, mainly in England.[4]

During every decade after 1850, there was a net gain through migration in the populations of Glamorgan and Monmouthshire. As David Smith and Gareth Williams argue, the massive migration into the area was highly significant as far as Welsh rugby is concerned. The industries of south Wales

---

2   Morgan, *Rebirth*, pp. 60-7; D. Gareth Evans, *A History of Wales 1815-1906* (Cardiff, 1989), pp. 177-189; Chris Williams, *Capitalism, Community and Conflict: The South Wales Coalfield, 1898-1947* (Cardiff, 1998), p. 11.

3   Morgan, *Rebirth*, p. 7.

4   Williams, *Capitalism, Community and Conflict*, p. 69, 86.

were labour intensive. Not only did coal have to be cut and steel and tin-plate manufactured, they also had to be carried to the ports and transferred onto ships, while their export had to be arranged through coal and shipping companies. Railway lines and port facilities had to be constructed. This all required a new workforce which had to be housed and serviced and, as a consequence, new urban communities sprang up in the valley areas, while port towns like Swansea, Newport and particularly Cardiff expanded dramatically. This newly urbanised population also had to be entertained and it was here that rugby football had a special contribution to make.[5]

Rugby came late to Wales. By the 1860s, clubs playing according to rules based on those deriving from Rugby School had been established not only in England but also in Scotland, Ireland and even Australia. While there is simply no evidence to support Guy's Hospital's claim of an 1843 foundation date, England's oldest club, Liverpool, was in existence by the 1857-8 season. The title of the oldest club in the world, though, is claimed by Trinity College Dublin and this is supported by a newspaper report from as early as 1855.[6] However, it was only during the early 1870s that the Rugby School code began to have any noticeable impact in Wales, although there is evidence that sporadic games of hybrid "football" were being played across south Wales before then.

The game which eventually arrived in Wales had evolved considerably from the version of football which had been played at Rugby School in the early decades of the nineteenth century. Described as "spontaneous and uncomplicated" by Jennifer Macrory, the Rugby game then had no written rules and, when required, changes could be easily implemented following discussions held at the completion of play. Handling *was* allowed, but running with the ball was not permitted. But, as the 1897 Old Rugbeian Society report *The Origin of Rugby Football* pointed out, "*Some* one must have broken through the rule against running with the ball." Of course, in 1876 Matthew Bloxham had claimed that it was William Webb Ellis who had broken through. After assessing the testimonies of fifteen Old Boys from

---

5   David Smith and Gareth Williams, *Fields of Praise: The Official History of the Welsh Rugby Union 1881-1981* (Cardiff, 1980), pp. 28-9.

6   Adrian Harvey, "The Oldest Rugby Football Club in the World?", *Sport in History*, 26, 1 (2006), pp. 150-2. Harvey reveals that the Guy's 1843 claim originates in an 1883-4 fixture card which alleged that the club was in its fortieth season, though there is no evidence to support this. Guy's first appear in the records in 1867 when the club is stated as having been formed in 1866; J.R.A. Daglish, *Red, Black & Blue: The First 125 Years of Liverpool Football Club (Rugby Union)*, Manchester, 1983, pp. 2-4.

The 1845 handwritten rules.   *Courtesy of Rugby School Collections*

the 1820s and 1830s – none of whom corroborated Bloxham's account – the report concluded that, although William Webb Ellis *may* have picked up the ball and run with it in 1823, he did not create a brand new game:

at some date between 1820 and 1830 the innovation was introduced of running with the ball, [and] … this was in all probability done in the latter half of 1823 by Mr. W. Webb Ellis ... To this end we would add that the innovation was regarded as of doubtful legality for some time, and only gradually became accepted as part of the game, but obtained customary status between 1830 and 1840, and was duly legalized first ... in 1841-2 ... and finally by the [written] Rules of 1846.[7]

Macrory reveals that, because of the increasing numbers of pupils attending Rugby School by the 1840s, the customary practice of disseminating the rules by word of mouth could no longer be relied upon.[8] The Rugbeian Society's report referred to the "1846" rules but there was an earlier printed version, Rule 8 of which allowed "running in". For it was in August *1845* – and some eighteen years *before* the Football Association game was codified – that the Rugby boys wrote the "Rules for Football"; and shortly after they produced a printed booklet containing the earliest written rules of football of any kind: the "Laws of Football Played at Rugby School".

According to Jed Smith, it was this, and "not the mythical William Webb Ellis action", which was "the truly revolutionary act at Rugby School ... The composition of the first ever written rules ... enabled their game to survive, flourish and ultimately overshadow all competitors" from other schools.[9] Unlike soccer, which was a compromise game invented in 1863, rugby was (and remains) a continually evolving sport, so the 1845 rules were regularly updated. Adrian Harvey has revealed that they were made available to outsiders in 1859 when they were published in *Lillywhite's Guide to Cricketers*.[10] The revised rule book of 1862 was the first actually written for the benefit of *all* players, whether at Rugby School or not. This had been produced because, by the early 1860s, the handling game was expanding and demand for the rules

Rule 8: *"Running in is allowed to any player on his side, provided he does not take the ball off the Ground, or take it thru' Touch."*   Courtesy of Rugby School Collections

---

7   Jennifer Macrory, *Running with the Ball: The Birth of Rugby Football* (London, 1991), pp. 18-51; Old Rugbeian Society, *The Origin of Rugby Football* (Rugby 1897), pp.11 (italics added), 22-3.

8   Macrory, *Running with the Ball*, pp. 92-3.

9   Jed Smith, *The Original Rules of Rugby* (Oxford, 2007), p. 15. See also pp. 9-37 for an account of the rules of rugby from 1845 to 1871, including the 1845 laws.

10   Adrian Harvey, *Football: The First Hundred Years: The Untold Story*, (London, 2005), p. 49.

The Webb Ellis commemorative tablet at Rugby School, the misleading wording of which helped to create a myth.

David Dow. Courtesy of Rugby School

was coming from emerging clubs like Liverpool, Blackheath, Richmond, and Manchester; from the universities; and from other public schools like Marlborough, Cheltenham, Clifton, Haileybury and Wellington.[11] In Ireland, laws were drawn up at Trinity College Dublin by an Old Rugbeian, while in Scotland, public schools and clubs were also playing a form of rugby by the 1850s. In 1868 Edinburgh Academy produced the "Laws of Football As Played by the Principal Clubs in Scotland". The official historian of the Scottish Rugby Union claims that the first Scotland v England international match in 1871 may have been played under these laws.[12]

This illustrates that it would be a mistake to assume that all clubs and schools in the 1860s played to a common set of laws. Even teams in England favouring the handling game did not necessarily follow Rugby School's rules exactly. Blackheath, for instance, produced their own modified set of laws in 1862.[13] As Adrian Harvey points out, some clubs "were very catholic in their adoption of rules" and used elements of both rugby and

11   Macrory, *Running with the Ball*, pp. 86-101; Tony Collins, *A Social History of English Rugby Union*, (London, 2009), p. 12; Graham Curry, Eric Dunning and Kenneth Sheard, "Sociological Versus Empiricist History: Some Comments on Tony Collins's 'History, Theory and the Civilizing Process' ", *Sport in History*, 26, 1 (2006), p.116.
12   Edmund Van Esbeck, *Irish Rugby 1874-1999: A History* (Dublin, 1999), pp. 10-12; A.M.C. Thorburn, *The Scottish Rugby Union: Official History* (Edinburgh, 1985), pp. 1-3; Sandy Thorburn, *The History of Scottish Rugby* (London, 1980), pp. 9-16.
13   Collins, *Social History*, p.13; see F. Marshall (ed.), *Football: The Rugby Union Game* (London, 1894 edn.), pp. 335-6 for the 1862 Blackheath laws.

association football in their games.[14] The *Football Annual* of 1868 lists the differences between fifteen varieties of football being played at that time and it is clear that there were many variations, even between those playing a broadly similar game.[15] Harvey usefully identifies five main categories of football which were played at this time. At the two extremes were those teams which only played a "pure" form of either association or rugby. Then there were those who played games which were *based* on one of these two codes but with some variations. Finally, some teams played a version of football which adopted rules from both codes.[16] Nevertheless, for those who preferred a handling game, it was the Rugby School rules which provided the substance and much of the terminology for the first set of laws drawn up by the RFU in 1871 and which became universally adopted soon after. The RFU minutes of 1871 confirm this in their description of the laws as "Football Rules ... based upon the Rugby system of play".[17]

It has to be borne in mind in the following discussion, therefore, that before the mid-1870s clubs did not *necessarily* adhere to any single set of unified rules. It was common practice to adopt local variations, or compromise on rules, or even play under a variety of codes. Harvey has discovered, for example, that during a remarkable five week period in 1863-4, Richmond first played Forest FC under Cambridge Rules, the code most distinct from rugby, then Barnes under the new FA rules and finally Blackheath under rugby laws.[18] It should also be pointed out that up to the 1880s, it was by no means certain that association would eventually become the dominant version of football in Britain. Of the clubs listed in the 1873 *Football Annual*, 114 played rugby, while 93 adhered to the rules of the Football Association or the Sheffield Association. Five played both.[19] In the north of England in the 1870s, rugby "towered" over soccer, according to Tony

---

14   Harvey, *Football: The First Hundred Years*, p. 130.

15   *Football Annual* 1868, pp. 55-75. The rules investigated included those of the Football Association, Sheffield Football Association, Cambridge, Rugby School, Eton, Winchester, Cheltenham, Marlborough, Haileybury, Brighton, Harrow, Charterhouse, Rossall, Shrewsbury and Uppingham.

16   Harvey, *Football: The First Hundred Years*, p.159.

17   RFU minutes 26 Jan. 1871; see Smith, *Original Rules of Rugby*, pp. 57-88 for the 1871 laws.

18   Adrian Harvey, " 'An Epoch in the Annals of National Sport': Football in Sheffield and the Creation of Modern Soccer and Rugby", *International Journal of the History of Sport*, 18, 4 (2001), p. 69; E.J. Ereaut, *Richmond Football Club: From 1861 to 1925* (London, 1926), pp. 8-12, 193.

19   *Football Annual* 1873, pp. 62-80.

A Bronze Age burial mound, known as "The Island", where the Rugby boys debated the rules after their matches.   *David Dow. Courtesy of Rugby School*

Collins.[20] It should not be a matter of any surprise, therefore, that rugby took root so strongly in Wales at that time.

David Smith and Gareth Williams argue in relation to the origins of the game in Wales:

> Bloodhounds roaming the centuries on the scent of the pedigree of Welsh rugby ... have detected a number of exciting aromas, but they have managed to establish little more than that ball games have been a feature of the Welsh countryside for well over a millennium.[21]

Drawing on George Owen's 1603 account of the game in Pembrokeshire, they refer to cnapan as the most plausible forebear of Welsh rugby. This was a "carrying" game, which shared some "striking similarities [with rugby] ... It engendered a vigorous community involvement and fierce inter-village rivalry; it was a game of throwing, tackling and kicking". Particularly popular

---

20   Tony Collins, *Rugby's Great Split: Class, Culture and the Origins of Rugby League Football* (London, 2006 edn.), p. 30; Tony Collins, "History, Theory and the 'Civilizing Process' ", *Sport in History*, 25, 2 (2005), pp. 291-6.

21   Smith and Williams, *Fields of Praise*, p. 17.

in west Wales, Owen claimed cnapan contests could sometimes involve over a thousand participants.[22]

Owen, who played the game himself, also reveals that cnapan participants possessed similar qualities to their nimble-footed and innovative Welsh rugby descendants:

> [the players] shew such agillite in runninge, such actyvitie in leaping, such strength and skillfull deliverance in hurleinge [the ball], such boldness in assaultinge, such stoutness in resisting, such policie in inventing ...

It seems the rolling maul has an ancient heritage too:

> ... one [player] happenninge on the Knappan clappeth the same against his bellye, holding it fast with bothe his hands, another of his companie, clapeth him about the middle, turning face to face, so then is the Knappan in fastness between both their bellies, and then cometh more of the same side and layeth gripes on and rounde aboute them bothe, so that you shall see a hundred [or 120] thus clustered together as Bees, when they swarme, are knitte together (the bowle beinge in middest of them)

Foot-ball "THE ROSH."

Military cadets in 1857 play a version of "Foot-Ball", which George Owen would have found familiar.   *Courtesy of World Rugby Museum, Twickenham*

---

22   Smith and Williams, *Fields of Praise*, p. 18; George Owen, (ed. Henry Owen), *The Description of Penbrokeshire* [1603] (London, 1892), pp. 270-282.

which the other partie seeketh to open or undoe, by haleinge [hauling] and pulling, but in vaine ...

It was a rough game, "troublesome to discribe, and painfull to practice ... not without resemblance to warlicke [warlike] providence". However, it was played in a spirit not unlike rugby, for we learn that:

> ... gamesters retorne from this playe with broken heads, black faces, brused bodies, and lame legges, yet laughing and merylie jesting at their harmes, telling theire adversaries how he broke his heade, to another that he strake him on the face, and how he repaied the same to him againe, and all this in good mirthe, without grudge or hatred, and if anye be in arrerages [arrears] to the other they skore it upp till the next plaie, and in the meane tyme will continue loveinge frindes ...[23]

As elsewhere in the British Isles, the existence of an earlier popular tradition of such mass "folk" football may partly explain why rugby was eventually adopted readily and widely in Wales, particularly by the working class. Tony Collins refers to this as a "residual consciousness of older forms of football".[24] However, John Gouldstone argues that more sophisticated versions, some involving handling, were *already* being played by the working class in the first half of the nineteenth century; while research by Adrian Harvey also demonstrates that, even at that time, varieties of organised football with rules, referees and fixed teams were taking place *outside* the influence of the public schools.[25] There has consequently been some debate in academic circles about the significance of such early, non-public school football.[26] It

---

23 Owen, *Description of Penbrokeshire*, pp. 275 (skills), 278 (maul), 277 (injuries).

24 Collins, *Rugby's Great Split*, p. 3.

25 John Gouldstone, "The Working-Class Origins of Modern Football", *IJHS*, 17, 1 (2000), pp. 135-147; Harvey, *Football: The First Hundred Years*, p. 91.

26 See Harvey, "An Epoch in the Annals of National Sport", *IJHS*, 18, 4 (2001), pp. 53-87; Eric Dunning, "Something of a Curate's Egg: Comments on Adrian Harvey's 'An Epoch in the Annals of National Sport' ", *IJHS*, 18, 4 (2001), pp. 88-94; Adrian Harvey, "The Curate's Egg Put Back Together: Comments on Eric Dunning's Response to 'An Epoch in the Annals of National Sport' ", *IJHS*, 19, 4 (2002), pp. 192-9; Eric Dunning and Graham Curry, "The Curate's Egg Scrambled Again: Comments on 'The Curate's Egg Put Back Together'!", *IJHS*, 19, 4, (2002), pp. 200-204; Adrian Harvey, "Curate's Egg Pursued by Red Herrings: A Reply to Eric Dunning and Graham Curry", *IJHS*, 21, 1 (2004), pp. 127-131; Peter Swain, "The Origins of Football Debate: The 'Grander Design and the Involvement of the Lower Classes', 1818-1840", *Sport in History*, 34 (4), (2014), pp. 519-543.

is possible that the eventual adoption of rugby in Wales was the result of a convergence of such working-class football with the public school game, though little firm evidence for it has so far emerged. However, the rapidly increasing availability of digitised newspapers may yet reveal that forms of organised, small-sided, working-class football – separate from mass "folk" or "public school" football – also existed in mid nineteenth-century Wales.

So it is certainly quite possible that some of the young men who took up rugby in Wales in the 1870s and 1880s had previously experienced a variety of "football" which had nothing to do with the public school game. Adaptations of cnapan may possibly have been practised in Victorian times; and Shrove Tuesday football was certainly still played until well into the nineteenth century. Local newspapers record mass Shrovetide games in the streets of Haverfordwest, Narberth, Pembroke, Laugharne, Tenby and elsewhere.[27] In 1835 in Haverfordwest, for instance, the "ancient custom" involved "kicking and catching the football … from noon to dark" and it

Shrove Tuesday football at Kingston-Upon-Thames, 1846.
Courtesy of World Rugby Museum, Twickenham

27   *Welshman* 6 Mar. 1835 (Haverfordwest), 18 Feb. 1842 (Narberth), 23 Feb. 1849 (Pembroke), 18 Feb. 1853 (Laugharne); *Tenby Observer* 28 Feb. 1884 (Tenby).

forced shop-keepers to suspend business, and householders to barricade their windows. However, the "disgraceful practice" was stopped in the town the following year following the passing of the 1835 Highways Act which banned football from the public highway.[28] By 1842 it was proclaimed that "the barbarous practice" of Shrove Tuesday football had been extinguished throughout Pembrokeshire. Not quite. In 1849, "hundreds of persons of all ages" kept up the tradition at Pembroke and, as a result, six footballers were fined at the subsequent petty sessions.[29] By 1858, some control was effected, when a Pembroke resident "with his usual kindness", presented a ball to the participants and allowed them to play in his field just outside the town, "where several well-contested matches came off ... without any fighting or the disgraceful conduct which so frequently characterize similar sports." However, disorder had returned to Pembroke by 1865, when twenty-two of the eighty Shrove Tuesday celebrants were summonsed, after gas lamps were damaged, vehicles stopped and passers-by crushed against walls. While the magistrates deliberated, they were intimidated with cries of "football for ever!" from the crowds outside the court. As late as 1884, a correspondent to *The Red Dragon* recorded that, in Narberth, Shrovetide football was still "played in the streets, all the shutters are put up, and the principal thoroughfare is given over to the players."[30]

Of course, street football wasn't necessarily restricted to the celebration of Shrove Tuesday. In January 1846, two unnamed men were charged with playing football with many others in Crockherbtown (today's Queen Street) in Cardiff. A week later, one Jerry Neil achieved the distinction of becoming the first-ever named Cardiff footballer, when he was charged with committing the same offence at the same place, presumably a popular venue for early Cardiff footballers. Twelve years later, there were complaints about the large numbers of young men who regularly played impromptu "foot-ball" in the evenings in the main streets of Cardigan.[31] These are just glimpses, of course, of what must have been a common occurrence. No doubt many similar events went unrecorded or still await discovery in the archives of the Welsh press.

---

28 *Welshman* 6 Mar. 1835; *Cambrian* 27 Feb. 1836.

29 *Welshman* 18 Feb. 1842; 2 Mar. 1849; *Pembrokeshire Herald* 23 Feb. 1849; *Principality* 2 Mar. 1849.

30 *Pembrokeshire Herald* 19 Feb. 1858, 17 Mar. 1865; *Welshman* 17 Mar. 1865; Martin Johnes, *A History of Sport in Wales* (Cardiff, 2005), p. 9; *The Red Dragon*, Vol. VI, 1884, p. 284. In some accounts, these events in Narberth are mistakenly reported to have taken place in Neath.

31 *Cardiff and Merthyr Guardian* 24, 31 Jan. 1846; *Welshman* 29 Jan. 1858 (Cardigan).

Another way in which early Welsh rugby players might have first experienced "football" occurred in rather different circumstances. During the nineteenth century, it was customary for Welsh newspapers to report – sometimes in great detail – the many festivals, fêtes, outings, picnics, treats, tea parties, celebrations and other social gatherings organised by a wide variety of employers, churches, Sunday schools, charities and community groups.[32] These numerous accounts demonstrate that games, or "rustic recreations", were frequently part of the entertainments, with football, cricket, rounders, quoits and foot races being popular. Where the sports were provided for youngsters, the football may have been an informal kick-about. However, occasionally, it is evident that the participants in these games were youths or adults and so perhaps they were contested more seriously. Some of the seventy workers, for instance, at a Haverfordwest factory outing to Broad Haven in 1852, took part in "football kicking", as well as other sports, on the beach and drinking a "plentiful supply of ale and porter" was part of the day-out. In Kilvert's account of the Harvest Festival just over the border at Whitney in 1871, he noted that "After dinner all the men played or rather kicked football at each other ... till it grew dark, when the game ended in a general royal scuffle and scrummage."[33] None of the

The William Webb Ellis statue in the centre of Rugby. However, some early footballers may never have been influenced by the public school game.   *David Dow*

---

32   These were identified by searching for "football" and "foot ball" on the NLW Welsh Newspapers Online website from 1850 to 1870 in August 2014.

33   *Pembrokeshire Herald* 3 Sept. 1852; William Plomer (ed.), *Kilvert's Diary, 1870-1879*, (London, 1973), p. 149.

many accounts of such events give any indication of rules or organisation and only one case was found when a result was recorded, when Nevern, Beifil and Moylegrove parishes defeated Newport and Dinas parishes at "foot ball" during the Newport (Pembrokeshire) Races in 1859. (Does George Owen's 1603 reference to Nevern and Newport being annual rivals at cnapan two and half centuries earlier hint that this may have been a variation of an old tradition?)[34] However, the evident popularity of "football" at these outings suggests that even before the introduction of codified versions of the game, it was already part of the popular culture of Wales. So although some of the first club players may never have been near a private or public school, they may nevertheless have already come into contact with some form of football, either as a participant or spectator.

However, according to the official historians of rugby in Scotland and Ireland, though there may have been a tradition of earlier folk football involving handling in those countries too, it was predominantly pupils and masters – both returning locals and newcomers – from English rugby playing schools who introduced the codified handling game there. In addition, it was through the public schools and universities, crucially located in the main urban centres, that rugby was eventually introduced to a wider Scottish and Irish public.[35]

The comparatively late arrival of rugby in Wales may, therefore, be partly explained by the absence of any large public schools and universities in the main centres of population at this time. The three south Wales public schools were all located in rural areas – Llandovery, Brecon and Monmouth – and they were small compared to their English and Scottish counterparts. Between the founding of Llandovery in 1848 and 1875, for instance, there were never more than eighty boys at the school. By 1875 the numbers had declined to forty, whilst Christ College Brecon had fewer than a hundred boys in the years before 1881.[36] Cheltenham, on the other hand, had over 600 pupils as early as 1858.[37]

---

34 *Potter's Electric News* 24 August 1859; Owen, *Description of Penbrokeshire*, p. 271.

35 Thorburn, *Official History*, pp. 1-4; Thorburn, *History of Scottish Rugby*, pp. 6-16, 323-6; Van Esbeck, *Irish Rugby*, pp. 1-24.

36 D.I. Gealy, 'Sport at Llandovery: Rugby Football' in R. Brinley Jones (ed.), *Floreat Landubriense: Celebrating a Century and a Half of Education at Llandovery College* (Llandovery, 1998), p. 242; Danny James and P.O.J. Rowlands, *Brecon Rugby Football Club: One Hundred Years of Rugby Football 1879-1979* (Brecon, 1979), p. 15.

37 Timothy J.L. Chandler, "Games at Oxbridge and the Public Schools, 1830-1880: The Diffusion of an Innovation", *IJHS*, 8, 2 (1991), p. 181.

Whilst these three Welsh public schools are regularly credited, somewhat simplistically, with being the main conduits through which rugby entered south Wales, the reality is rather more complicated.[38] Though rugby *was* introduced early at Llandovery College around 1868, it was not adopted at Monmouth and Brecon until 1873 and 1875 respectively, by which time the game was already starting to take hold in Wales. Indeed, rather than initiating rugby in Wales, these two schools may have embraced it because it was already beginning to be played locally. The contribution of the Welsh public schools to the *introduction* of rugby, therefore, may not have been quite so crucial as is customarily claimed. At the same time, the influence of local private and grammar schools to this process is often over-looked. On the other hand, as will be shown, all three south Wales public schools were playing *forms* of football before the 1870s and this perhaps matters more in terms of their influence than their formal adoption of a specific code. For instance, several prominent members of the highly successful Newport XV of the late 1870s had played a hybrid game, perhaps closer to association, at Monmouth before that school adopted rugby.

There were no universities in Wales until Aberystwyth was founded in 1872 – again a small institution located well away from the main urban centres – and Cardiff in 1883. The only higher education establishments which did contribute to the early game in south Wales were St. David's College Lampeter and Carmarthen Training College, both situated in rural west Wales. There were no large urban equivalents of Edinburgh

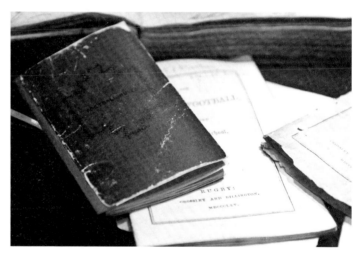

Copies of the earliest printed rules booklets, which helped to disseminate the game to other schools, universities and the first clubs. They were small so they could be carried in players' pockets during matches.

David Dow. Courtesy of Rugby School Collections

---

38 For two recent popular examples which give primacy to the Welsh public schools, see Owen Sheers, *Calon: A Journey to the Heart of Welsh Rugby* (London, 2013), p. 10; and Bill O'Keefe and Emyr Young, *The Arms Park: Heart of a Rugby Nation*, (Talybont, 2012), pp. 21-2.

and Glasgow Universities, founder members of the Scottish Football Union, or of Trinity College Dublin (1855) and Sydney University (1864), both of which were the first clubs in their respective countries.[39]

That Wales had a smaller middle and upper class was another contributory factor. There were relatively fewer former public school and university men returning home bearing rugby balls and printed copies of the laws. Nevertheless, it would appear that it *was* these men, together with similarly educated newcomers, who were eventually instrumental in bringing the codified game to Wales. As Jennifer Macrory puts it:

> Young men from South Wales, the sons of industrialists and clergymen, were anxious to continue playing football when they returned home from school or university and followed the example of their schoolfellows in England by setting up clubs.

And this happened not only across Britain but also throughout the rugby world.[40] It is no co-incidence that a swathe of rugby-playing public schools is found in and around the west of England and many affluent south Wales families sent their sons to institutions such as Marlborough, Cheltenham, Hereford, Clifton, Sherborne and Blundell's. Old boys from these, as well as from Rugby School itself, of course, were closely involved in early Welsh rugby, and they provide an example of what Neil Tranter terms the "proximity to the culture hearth".[41] A similar process appears to have happened in north-east Wales, where, as Martin Johnes and Ian Garland demonstrate, it was old boys of Shrewsbury School who played a key role in introducing soccer there.[42] This is consistent with David Russell's work on the spatial differences in the preference for rugby or soccer in Yorkshire and Lancashire, where he found that this depended at least partly on the schools which the local elite attended.[43]

It was probably rugby-playing public school men who were responsible for an intriguing account in the *Cambrian* in November 1864, which announced

---

39 Thorburn, *Official History*, p. 4; Van Esbeck, *Irish Rugby*, pp.15-16; Jack Pollard, *Australian Rugby: The Game and the Players* (Chippendale, Australia, 1994), pp. 21-5.

40 Macrory, *Running with the Ball*, pp. 192, 197-205.

41 Neil Tranter, *Sport, Economy and Society in Britain, 1750-1914* (Cambridge, 1998), p. 30.

42 Martin Johnes and Ian Garland, " 'The New Craze': football and society in north-east Wales, c1870-90", *Welsh History Review*, 22, 2 (2004), pp. 279-280.

43 David Russell, "Sporadic and Curious: The Emergence of Rugby and Soccer Zones in Yorkshire and Lancashire, c 1860-1914", *IJHS*, 5, 2 (1988), p. 194.

the formation of a club at Neath which adopted the rules "as played at Rugby". This is a remarkable report because it is, by some years, the earliest reference to "rugby" being played in Wales. That the Eton and Oxford educated JTD Llewelyn had been invited to become the club president suggests a public school connection. The article reveals: "On Thursday a game was played in a field near Court-Herbert though the number of players was not so large as may be expected when the Club becomes more fully formed." Perhaps attracting sufficient members continued to be a problem as there are no further reports of its activities and this early attempt to establish rugby in Wales appears to have been stillborn. It cannot be convincingly argued, therefore, that 1864 marks the foundation of Neath RFC.[44]

Jennifer Macrory shows that west-country public schools were "sending out players in force by the 1870s" and she argues that the subsequent popularity of rugby in that region is attributable to this.[45] It is now widely accepted that the Welsh game was stimulated by an influx of rugby playing migrants from the west of England.[46] With regard to public school men, there is much truth in this and, indeed, Macrory agrees: "The west-country schools supplied much of the early support for the game in South Wales".[47] But as far as ordinary *club* players are concerned, this may need qualification. A study of the founding dates of west of England clubs reveals that very few were formed before the early 1870s.[48] Therefore, there is some doubt about the extent to which many experienced *club* players from that region were involved in the early *introduction* of rugby to Wales. On the other hand, there is absolutely no question that from the later 1870s onwards their contribution to the *evolution* of the Welsh game was significant.[49]

The official historians of the WRU place the first incursion of rugby into Wales in the rural west, following the arrival from Cambridge of Rowland Williams as vice-principal at St. David's College Lampeter in 1850. He had been a contemporary at Cambridge of Albert Pell, the Rugbeian who

---

44   *Cambrian* 11 Nov. 1864. I am very grateful to David Dow and Jack Rickus who both drew my attention to this important article.
45   Macrory, *Running with the Ball*, pp. 183.
46   For example, Martin Johnes, History of Sport in Wales, p. 24.
47   Macrory, Running with the Ball, pp. 192-3.
48   Uel A. Titley and Ross McWhirter, *Centenary History of the Rugby Football Union* (London, 1970), pp. 202-4. This lists the foundation dates of all the clubs in membership of the RFU in 1970. In the west of England, only Bath (1865), Cirencester (1866) and Cirencester College (1868) claim to have been formed before 1870. References to clubs in early RFU minutes and editions of the *Football Annual* confirm the general point.
49   See Smith and Williams, *Fields of Praise*, p. 33.

Believed to be the earliest of its kind, and rather more plum-shaped than oval, this rugby ball was made by William Gilbert of Rugby. It won first prize in its category at the Great Exhibition of 1851.
David Dow. Courtesy of Webb Ellis Rugby Museum

first attempted, unsuccessfully, to introduce rugby at the university in 1839. Initially Pell managed to persuade a dozen Cambridge undergraduates (who were "objects of wonder and at first contempt") to take part in six or seven a-side "puntabouts" on Parker's Piece. Though there were a few more participants the following year, Pell's Cambridge initiative soon fizzled out amid disputes over the many different rules which individual public schools then practised. A few years later in 1848, a compromise code at the university was eventually agreed, known as the "Cambridge Rules" but it was not rugby. These rules were much closer to what later became "association" football.[50]

Williams's influence at Lampeter may have been immediate because a college rule of 1850 urged students to spend their spare time in "healthful exercise rather than in clownish lounging about the shops or market place". In 1851, he apologised for the poor sporting facilities at Lampeter compared to those at Cambridge and Williams may well have been responsible for the introduction of cricket there (first recorded in 1852) and football. However, whether he "introduced" rugby, a restricted version of which he can only at best have witnessed briefly over ten years earlier, is questionable. Undoubtedly, though, he was responsible for encouraging a sporting environment at the college in which rugby would certainly flourish. Initially, the Lampeter students played internal games against each other but, as *Fields of Praise* demonstrates, from the mid-1860s, "foreign" matches of an "undefined football nature" under local rules took place against school teams, in particular Llandovery. It is likely that the students at Lampeter College had formally adopted rugby laws by the late 1860s. Kenneth Evans claims that a college club was formed as early as 1866, but unfortunately he provides no source. Soon afterwards, Lampeter College became one of the strongest teams in Wales, reaching the final of the South Wales Challenge

---

50   Smith and Williams, *Fields of Praise*, pp. 20-3; Albert Pell, *The Reminiscences of Albert Pell* (London, 1908), pp. 69-72; Macrory, *Running with the Ball*, p. 142-144.

Cup on one occasion. The College were also founder members of the WFU in 1881.[51]

An account of rugby at Llandovery College, published in the *Western Mail* in 1949, maintained that "football of a sort" was "probably" played there in the 1850s. A recent history of the school refers to a claim that the first game between Llandovery and Lampeter College was played as early as 1856, though there is no contemporary evidence for this. It also mentions an account by a Breconian, probably JA Parry-Price referred to below, who recalled playing against Llandovery at some time between 1864 and 1867. David Smith and Gareth Williams's suggestion that these early matches were "a hybrid game" is confirmed by the following evidence in the school history relating to the introduction of formal rugby rules at Llandovery. [52]

After teaching at Merchiston Castle School in Edinburgh, Watkin Price Whittington took up a post at Llandovery in 1868. In a letter written thirty years later, he described how he introduced rugby there soon after arriving. He referred to the game it replaced as "a *sort* of Association without definite rule", though the *Llandovery School Journal* in 1926 confusingly claimed that rugby was "easily adopted"

From left, Thomas Judson (Llandovery College) seated on the floor, George Lockwood Morris (Swansea) and Charles Prytherch Lewis (Llandovery College) in the Welsh team, 1882.

---

51 D.T.W. Price, *A History of Saint David's University College Lampeter, Volume One: To 1898* (Cardiff, 1977), p. 152; Kenneth Evans, *A Historical Study of the Formative Years of the Welsh Rugby Union 1870-1900* (M.Ed. thesis, University of Liverpool, 1981), p. 73.

52 *WM* 1 July 1949; Gealy, 'Sport at Llandovery', pp. 241-3; see also H.A. Harris, *Sport in Britain: Its Origins and Development* (London, 1975), pp. 132-3; Smith and Williams, *Fields of Praise*, p. 23.

in the 1870s "because the old Rugby game had for years been played". Since Whittington arrived at Llandovery before the RFU's codification of the laws in 1871, it is possible that the version of rugby that he brought to the college was based on the 1868 "*Laws of Football As Played by the Principal Clubs in Scotland*".[53]

The evidence provided by Whittington, then, appears to confirm that Llandovery College were perhaps the first rugby playing organisation – or, if not, certainly one of the first – in Wales. They were founder members of the WFU and competed in the early years of the South Wales Challenge Cup until 1881. Llandoverians were frequently found in the ranks of many of the first Welsh clubs and international teams. As was common practice in schools at the time, the College XV regularly included masters, like Charles Prytherch ("CP") Lewis and Thomas Judson, both of whom were capped by Wales as adult players of the college (and not as members of Llandovery RFC as usually claimed). In one game in 1882, the Llandovery College team included six current and future internationals.[54] However, an even stronger influence on the early game may have been the college's ability to provide good regular opposition for newly emerging teams.

Jonathan Harris's study of soccer in Breconshire notes a very early mention of football at Christ College Brecon in 1861, when six schoolboys challenged any six "gentlemen" from the town to a game. It would be some years yet, however, before the college would formally adopt rugby. JA Parry-Price, who had been at Christ College in the second half of the 1860s, recalled in 1931 that "Our football was somewhat feeble, the game played being a kind of soccer, but with no very stringent rules with regard to hands or offside."[55] Swansea Grammar School played matches with Kilvey

53   Jones, *Floreat Landubriense*, p.48 (letter); *WM* 28 July 1898 (Whittington introduces rugby); W. Gareth Evans, *A History of Llandovery College* (Llandovery, 1981), p. 70 (1926 Journal).

54   *WM* 5 Dec. 1882. CP Lewis had already been capped and TH Judson won his first cap two weeks after this match. The other college players (all pupils) who later became Welsh internationals were EP Alexander, EH Bishop, AA Mathews and RL Thomas. See also: Bob Harrigan and Andrew Hignell, *C.P. Lewis: The Champion Cricketer of South Wales*, (Cardiff, 2009), pp. 76-85 which confirms Lewis and Judson played for the college when capped.

55   Jonathan Harris, "The Early History of Association Football in Breconshire", *Brycheiniog*, XXVII, (1996), p. 128. Harris quotes the *Brecon Journal* of 28 Mar. 1861, drawing on the earlier work of J.R. Boulton, *Brecon Football 1860-1880* (Brecon, 1969).

in March 1865 and with twelve Swansea "gentlemen" in 1871.[56] Another early game took place between a Bridgend School XIV and R. Randall's VIII in 1866. The school won by 3 goals to 1:

> due in great measure to the general good play and "charging" of Messrs Green, E.S. Thomas and W.W. Thomas. Messrs. E.F. Blosse, T.A. Rees and A.W. Stockwood also contributed ... For the "eight", Messrs. R. Randall, R.C. Blosse, T.J. Morgan and P. Llewellin, worked hard and well; the first gentleman distinguishing himself in the "squashes". The disparity of numbers was counterbalanced by the prestige of the public school men playing with the "eight."[57]

The mention of "public school men" playing football in south Wales at this early time is instructive. Robert Blosse of the public school "eight" was at Marlborough at the time. His younger brother, Edward Blosse also attended this prominent rugby school soon afterwards, and he later became a member of the Cardiff club.[58] The references to "charging" and "squashes" may also imply that the game was a version of rugby, but it cannot be claimed that this provides conclusive proof. It *is* known, however, that Bridgend School had adopted rugby by the early 1870s. Welsh international, WD (Bill) Phillips, learned the game there possibly as early as 1871-2 because, when he retired in April 1885, he claimed to have played for fourteen years.[59] Newspaper reports confirm the school was playing rugby by 1872.[60] Bridgend was a boarding and day school which prepared boys for the public schools, professions and commerce. Sport was an important part of the curriculum. The boys received "every encouragement in Manly Exercises" and were provided with a gymnasium and "a large ground for cricket and football."[61] If most of the boys being prepared for public school went on to those in

---

56 A.L. Evans, "Some Reflections on Local Sport", *Port Talbot History Society Transactions*, 13, 2 (1981), pp. 22-49 (Kilvey); David Farmer, *The Life and Times of Swansea R.F.C.: The All Whites* (Swansea, 1995), p. 1 (town gentlemen).

57 *Bridgend Chronicle* 26 Jan. 1866.

58 Anon, *Marlborough College Register From 1843 to 1904 Inclusive*, (Oxford, 1905), pp. 169, 205; W.T. Pike (ed.), *Glamorgan Contemporary Biographies: Pike's New Century Series No. 20* (Brighton, 1907), p. 156 (R. Blosse); C.S. Arthur, *The Cardiff Rugby Football Club: History and Statistics, 1876-1906* (Cardiff, 1908), p. 21 (E. Blosse).

59 *South Wales Daily News* 13 Apr. 1885.

60 *SWDN* 29 Nov. 1872.

61 *Webster and Co.'s Postal and Commercial Directory of the City of Bristol and Counties of Glamorgan and Monmouth* (London, 1865), p. 40; *Cardiff and Merthyr Guardian* 11 Dec. 1863.

An early version of a scrummage at Rugby School, 1845.
Courtesy of World Rugby Museum, Twickenham

the west of England, then it would be reasonable to suppose that rugby became the preferred sport at Bridgend from an early date.

In November 1867, the *Monmouthshire Merlin* carried an announcement that a football club had just been formed in Newport and local "gentlemen" were invited to join. One who did was Oxfordshire-born Joseph Gould, six of whose sons would later play rugby for Newport and three of them – Arthur, Bert and Bob – for Wales. Weekly scratch matches at the Marshes (later Shaftesbury Park) were planned though the new club enjoyed only a short life. During 1913, WJ Townsend Collins, ("Dromio"), wrote a series of articles in the *South Wales Argus* about the history of Newport rugby club (founded in 1874). In these, he drew on accounts in the *Merlin* of three football matches arranged with Abergavenny by this earlier Newport club between November 1867 and March 1868.[62] "Dromio" was initially convinced that the game played in this series of matches was a close relative of rugby, citing fifteen a-side teams and references to "dodging" and "running". There is also a mention in one of the match reports of Abergavenny forcing "the Newport side to touch the ball behind their own goal".

Townsend Collins was able to speak to several players who had participated in these contests. Two assured him that the game they played *was* rugby. Conversely, however, another player informed him that it was "chiefly a dribbling game, and that the players were not allowed to pick up the ball

---

62 *Monmouthshire Merlin* 9, 30 Nov. 1867, 29 Feb., 14 Mar. 1868.

on the run; but that they *could* run from a catch from an opponent's kick, or from a pass by the foot to the hands on the part of a fellow player ... a player could be tripped or hacked over." "Dromio" was later contacted by an old Newport RFC player, who said that he had played a hybrid game himself at Monmouth School, before they adopted rugby. He did not participate in the Newport-Abergavenny matches, so therefore cannot have been an authority on them, but he suggested that the game may have been more closely related to association and that it was essentially football "without a qualifying title" (i.e. neither rugby nor soccer). "The object of the game was to score a goal by kicking the ball between the posts and there was no cross bar. No try could be scored. But players could handle the ball *and run* if they could catch direct from an opponent's or a comrade's kick (without the ball touching the ground)." Reluctantly, Townsend Collins came to the conclusion that it was a hybrid game, with elements of both rugby and association.[63] With more rigour than some club historians, he later wrote in 1925 about these events:

> There is no special purpose in referring to this hybrid game except to indicate that in 1867-8 there was a football interest. So far as can be discovered, there is no record of continuous play, and we have to come down to 1874 for the foundation of the [Newport] Club.[64]

The 1867-8 Newport-Abergavenny matches, therefore, probably fall into Harvey's fifth category of football which adopted rules from both codes. So whilst it is not possible to argue with any conviction that these early Newport games were "rugby", neither can they be used as evidence that association pre-dated rugby in south Wales, as claimed by one article on early Welsh soccer.[65] This contends that handling was not allowed in the 1867 Newport-Abergavenny game, but "Dromio" clearly established that running with the ball *was* allowed. The FA had abolished touch downs by this time, whilst running with the ball and hacking had been distinctly outlawed by the first FA laws of December 1863:

---

63 *South Wales Argus* 4, 11 Oct. 1913 (italics added). For a brief biography of Townsend Collins, see Meic Stephens (ed.), *New Companion to the Literature of Wales* (Cardiff, 1998), p. 117.

64 Townsend Collins, *Newport Athletic*, p. 10.

65 Harvey, *Football: The First Hundred Years*, p. 159; Brian Lile and David Farmer, "The Early Development of Association Football in South Wales, 1890-1906", *Transactions of the Honourable Society of Cymmrodorion*, (1984), p. 195.

Law 9. No player shall carry the ball.

Law 10. Neither tripping nor hacking shall be allowed, and no player shall use his hands to hold or push an adversary.

Whatever rules the games were played under, they were not those of the Football Association.[66]

There was military involvement in the last of these games, when three locally stationed officers of the Royal Welch Fusiliers (RWF) played for Newport, while Abergavenny included players from a local educational establishment preparing young men for the army and navy. Since the RWF arranged fixtures with Cardiff and Brecon at this time, it is quite likely that they also played Newport but, if so, these matches went unrecorded. The contribution of the military – through garrisons, Volunteers and military academies – in introducing the game to Wales has not previously been explored. Andrew Hignell reveals that the presence of military units helped to stimulate interest in cricket in south east Wales during the 1840s.[67] According to JD Campbell, the Royal Military Academy Woolwich was playing rugby by 1860 and the sport became popular in the Army during the 1870s.[68] The armed services were influential in spreading the game throughout the world, including Australia, Canada, New Zealand and South Africa and there is some, admittedly limited, evidence of their early involvement in Wales.[69] Between 1867 and 1869, the RWF were stationed at Newport, Brecon and Cardiff. As it happens, these were all centres of early Welsh football.[70]

On 19th March 1868, the RWF participated in perhaps the earliest ever organised football contest played at the Arms Park. According to the *Bristol Mercury*, "the first match [of the] old English game was played by the *new football club recently established in Cardiff*". Again, there is no certainty about

---

66   Geoffrey Green, *The History of the Football Association* (London, 1953), pp. 36-8 (FA laws 1863); Harvey, "An Epoch in the Annals of National Sport", p. 67; Macrory, *Running with the Ball*, pp. 171-180.

67   Andrew K. Hignell, *A 'Favourit' Game: Cricket in south Wales before 1914* (Cardiff, 1992), pp. 38-42.

68   J.D. Campbell, " 'Training for Sport is Training for War': Sport and the Transformation of the British Army, 1860-1914", *IJHS*, 17, 4 (2000), pp. 33-4.

69   Macrory, *Running with the Ball* , pp. 203-5; Titley and McWhirter, *Centenary History Rugby Football Union*, p. 94; Pollard, *Australian Rugby*, p. 21.

70   Rowland Broughton-Mainwaring, *Historical Record of the Royal Welch Fusiliers* (London, 1889), pp. 259-261; A.D.L. Cary and S. Stouppe McLance, *Regimental Records of the Royal Welch Fusiliers Volume II 1816-1914* (London, 1923), pp. 137-9.

Sheep grazing on the north-west corner of the Arms Park around 1870. Cricket was played at this northern end, so it is possible the 1868 matches took place here. The entrance to Sophia Gardens is amongst the trees on the far side of the river Taff.

Courtesy of Cardiff Council Library Service

the form of football adopted, but perhaps "scrimmages" suggests that it might have been a more robust version.

> The match consisted of a picked 15 of the Cardiff and Canton Cricket Club[s] and 15 of the Royal Welsh Fusiliers (now on detachment in this town) headed by Lieutenant Patterson and Ensign Gilbert. The Cardiff men won the toss, which gave them great advantage having both sun and wind in their favour. After two hours' play of the most exciting kind the match terminated in a draw, neither party being able to effect a goal, although the red coats had decidedly the better of the match. The gallant Lieutenant was very conspicuous in the scrimmages, and one or two of his men showed great skill and activity. Messrs Jones and Yorath, on the Cardiff side, did their party great service, as did Mr. Robinson, the Captain of the club.

The fifteen pioneering Cardiff footballers that day were: Philip Robinson, TE Heath, W Hutchins, EW Jones, R Rhys Jones, GC Thompson, Macbeth,

F Bell, J Bush, G Thomas, D Thomas, H Reece, W Jones, W Biggs and Yorath.[71]

Cardiff cricket club had been re-formed the previous year and this match provides a good example of cricket's influence on early football in Wales, which others have noted.[72] The fixture clearly aroused local interest, for another was immediately arranged for the 28th March and this too was duly reported:

> at the Cardiff Arms Park, the largest number of spectators we remember having seen present at any sports, watched the game throughout with unflagging interest … when time was called, the victory remained undecided, though, in the opinion of the majority of the spectators, the *Cardiff Football Club* might well have claimed Mr. Heath's first kick as a clear "goal" … For especially good play amongst the Fusiliers, we may mention Ensign Gilbert, Private Astbury, and Glass, each of whom gained a "touch down" … For the club, first praise is due to Mr. Bassett Jones, while the play of Messrs. Hutchins, Rhys Jones, and Bell, were deservedly admired. The "touch downs" for the club were gained by the last two players.[73]

The references to touch downs "gained" may provide a further clue about the type of football played. That the match attracted the largest ever sporting crowd to the Arms Park clearly anticipated the hold which rugby was to have in later decades on the public of both Cardiff and Wales.

The military were involved in Brecon too. In 1867-8, a "Town" team had lost to Christ College, while a Brecon twelve went down to thirteen Abergavenny "gentlemen", the winning score here coming from a drop kick, perhaps suggesting a version of rugby. So it may have been these defeats which motivated local footballers to establish the Brecon Football Club in October 1868. Their first opponents a month later were eleven officers of the RWF stationed in the town. There were also further newspaper references to the club in 1868-9, including a fixture with Crickhowell.[74] In November

---

71   *Bristol Mercury* 21 Mar. 1868 (italics added); *Cardiff Times* 21 Mar. 1868 (team); *Bridgend Chronicle* 20 Mar. 1868.

72   W. Alan Thomas, *Cardiff Cricket Club: 1867-1967* (Cardiff, 1967), p. 13; Gareth Williams, *1905 and All That: Essays on Rugby Football, Sport and Welsh Society* (Llandysul, 1991), p. 129 (cricket and football).

73   *Bridgend Chronicle* 3 Apr. 1868 (italics added).

74   *Brecon County Times* 9 Nov. 1867, 21 Mar., 24 Oct., 21 Nov. 1868, 16 Jan. 1869; see also James and Rowlands, *Brecon Rugby*, pp. 11-14 for quotes from the *Brecon County Times*.

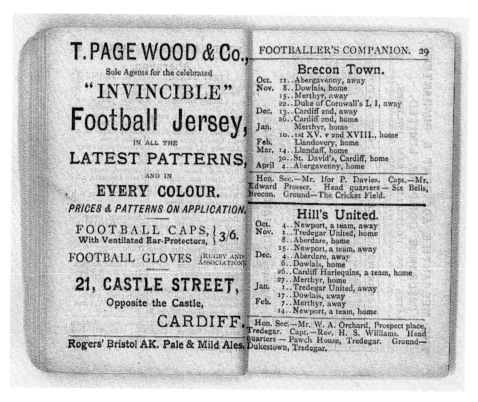

The 1890-1 fixture list of Brecon, one of Wales's oldest clubs.

1872, Brecon arranged a match with the 94th Regiment, though bad weather prevented it from being played.[75] That Brecon was a garrison town, as well as being the location of Christ College, may account for the early arrival of football there. However, the evidence for what version Brecon FC played in the very early years is unclear.

Local rifle and artillery volunteer corps were other military organisations which helped to spread rugby later during the 1870s and 1880s. Tony Collins notes the contribution which Volunteers made to early organised football in the north of England.[76] The Cardiff-based 10th Glamorgan Rifle Volunteers (GRV), for instance, were an early club which participated in the South Wales Challenge Cup and they were the first ever team to play against Newport at Rodney Parade.[77] Volunteers in Aberdare, Neath, Newport and Swansea all had

---

75   *SWDN* 23 Nov. 1872.

76   Collins, *Rugby's Great Split*, p. 7.

77   W.J. Townsend Collins (ed.), *Newport Athletic Club: The record of half a Century 1875-1925* (Newport, 1925), p. 14; *SWDN* 17 Oct. 1877 (GRV).

A well-dressed Victorian official oversees a match.

rugby teams from time to time, while in rural Wales, both Breconshire and Builth Volunteers played occasional games. It seems that a good number of the first players in Wales were also Volunteers and there are a number of reports of matches between Volunteers and "Civilians". When Cardiff drew the 10th GRV in the 1878-9 South Wales Challenge Cup, they refused to allow any of their Volunteer members to play for their opponents in the match.[78]

The Pontypool RFC history, drawing on reports from the *Pontypool Free Press*, shows that at the end of their 1868 season, local cricketers discussed "taking up physical activities during the winter months to keep fit". Two of the main proponents were Arthur and Herbert James, the sons of the Rector of Panteg. Herbert later became headmaster of Rugby School. By October 1868, the cricketers had formed a football club, drawn up their own rules – which were a mixture of rugby and association – and played their first match. The club history suggests that Pontypool's early matches were closer to association. This was confirmed during this research with the discovery of the club's entry in the 1871 *Football Annual* which describes Pontypool as playing a "modification of association". It is tempting to speculate whether this modification might have involved *some* handling, particularly as a report of a fixture against Panteg in the *Free Press* in January 1870 criticised the Pontypool players for frequently using their hands to stop the ball and push it along the ground before kicking it. In October 1871 a fixture with the Tredegarville club of Cardiff was announced in the press, but unfortunately no report of the match appears to have survived. Since, as will be shown, Tredegarville played both association and rugby at this time, it is not known which version was played in this fixture. Pontypool did not formally *adopt* rugby union laws until 12th October 1875, though that is not to say, of

---

78   *WM* 2 Dec. 1878.

course, that they did not experiment with rugby before that date and the likelihood is that they did.[79]

The history of Trinity College Carmarthen reveals that the vice-principal and acting principal between 1868 and 1870 was Reverend Francis Marshall, the well-known rugby author and administrator. Without providing any evidence, the college history suggests that he was instrumental in bringing rugby to Carmarthen. Given Frank Marshall's influential place in early rugby football, this seems credible.[80] At a college alumni dinner in Leeds in 1892, one speaker referred to Marshall having taken "a very active part in cricket, forming a college club which has existed ever since". Unfortunately, however, no reference was made to his setting up a rugby club.[81] Carmarthen Training College was indeed one of Wales's earliest rugby clubs but it was not regularly mentioned in the Cardiff press until 1876-7, several years after Marshall had left.

Reverend Francis Marshall, author of Football: The Rugby Union Game.

The sporadic, casual and hybrid nature of football in the 1860s in south Wales – "neither dribbling fish nor handling fowl" in David Smith and Gareth Williams's memorable phrase[82] – gradually began to give way during the following decade to a more organised version. Football was now played according to a recognised and unified set of rules, in particular those of the RFU, which became standard in south Wales from the early 1870s. It was during this decade that Wales began to undergo the transformation in sporting culture which was experienced by the whole of Britain in the second half of the nineteenth century. This was partly the result of improved transport and communications, shorter working hours and higher wages.[83] In south Wales, the 1870s was a period of significant growth in organised rugby. By the end of the decade, not only were many members of the Welsh public playing and watching the game regularly, but the social background of the sport's participants was beginning to widen.

79   Edward Donovan, Arthur Crane, Allan Smith and John Harris, *Pontypool's Pride: The Official History of Pontypool Rugby Football Club 1868-1988* (Abertillery, 1988), pp. 28-31; *Football Annual* 1871 p. 66, 1872 p. 65, 1873 p. 77.

80   Russell Grigg, *History of Trinity College Carmarthen 1848-1998* (Cardiff, 1998), pp. 197-8.

81   *WM* 5 Mar. 1892.

82   Smith and Williams, *Fields of Praise*, p. 30.

83   Tranter, *Sport, Economy and Society*, pp. 13, 32-6.

The 1871 *Football Annual* provides the first conclusive *contemporary* evidence of an established club playing according to rugby laws anywhere in Wales. This lists "Tredegarville (Cardiff)" as having been founded in 1870 with a membership of fifty and playing at Sophia Gardens. It may be significant that the club took the name of a small exclusive area of high status housing rather than that of Roath, the suburb in which it was situated. The secretary was listed as C Prior of "Lansdowne", Tredegarville. Twenty years later, he was referred to as a university man who was "a thorough exponent" of rugby and "under whose tuition the game was fostered" in Cardiff". He is also mentioned in Charles Arthur's 1908 history of Cardiff RFC, where he is described as a teacher at Monkton House. This was a private school (also known as "Shewbrooks") which was located in "Lansdowne House" in The Parade. Arthur adds that the Tredegarville club was comprised mainly of old boys of that school. According to the *Football Annual*, the club played in an outfit of blue and white jerseys, white flannel trousers and blue velvet cap with white silk tassel. The *Football Annual* records Tredegarville as playing *both* rugby and association. Such an arrangement was not at all unusual at the time and several clubs were listed in early editions of the *Football Annual* as playing under a variety of rules.[84]

An intriguing report in the *Western Mail* records Tredegarville's match with the "Cardiff Club" at Sophia Gardens on 21st December 1870, which they won by two goals and four rouges. "Rouges" refers to touch downs and since they had been abolished in association football for over three years, this brief report may perhaps record one of the very earliest club rugby matches played in Wales.[85] The teams met again at Sophia Gardens exactly a week later when Prior kicked the winning goal:

Charles Arthur, club historian, captain of Cardiff in 1889-90 and Welsh international.

[The] match between the Tredegarville Football Club and Cardiff Club ... resulted in a victory for the Tredegarville team by 1 goal and 13 points, the goal being kicked by C. Prior. ... The Cardiff Club were beaten through their not being well-up in the game. In the Cardiff team E.W. Jones, for the brilliant and effective manner in which he defended his goal, was especially distinguishable, being ably seconded by J. Jones, R.P. Thomas, Crick and

---

84   *Football Annual* 1871 p. 69, 1872 p. 66, 1873 p. 80; *Evening Express* 27 Aug. 1892 (Prior); Arthur, *Cardiff Rugby*, p. 9.

85   *WM* 22 Dec. 1870; Harvey, "An Epoch in the Annals of National Sport", p. 78 (rouges).

Bell. On the Tredegarville side, R. Evans ... [made] some neat runs, as also did W. Evans, A.E. Evans, H. Jackson, and C. Prior. H. Shewbrooks was of good service as a forward player, being nearly always "on the ball." C. Alexander, H. Fisher, Williams, J. Bush, Insole and B. Vachell were indefatigable in their play.[86]

The "13 points" presumably refers to the touch downs conceded by Cardiff.

The club's listing in the 1871, 1872 and 1873 editions of the *Football Annual* not only shows that Tredegarville had some degree of permanence but also provides the earliest contemporary evidence of an established club playing rugby in Wales. The discovery of the existence of Tredegarville at such an early time throws an entirely fresh light on the importance of Cardiff as a potential crucible for the early game in Wales; though whether a "Cardiff Club" had been formed by 1868 or 1870 is a question which still has to be resolved.

The Cowbridge Grammar School history is vague about exactly when rugby was introduced there.[87] *Fields of Praise* says it happened in the early 1870s and this may well be confirmed by a press report of a football match played on 26th October 1871 between a Grammar School XV and a team of twelve Cowbridge "gentlemen".[88] However, this wasn't the first appearance of football in the locality. In 1867, the "Town" had played and lost to the "Country"; while Christmastide inter-parish matches between Cowbridge and Penllyn continued well into the 1870s.[89]

A "hotly contested" match took place at the Arms Park on 8th November 1871 between the Science and Arts Club and Shewbrooks (Monkton House). While the report provides no indication of the type of football played, there is some circumstantial evidence to suggest that it may have been a form of rugby.[90] The headmaster of the Science and Arts School (later to evolve by many steps into Cardiff University) was James Bush, who also taught at Monkton House, and who was the father of the famous Welsh international Percy Bush.[91] Henry Shewbrooks was the headmaster of Monkton House

---

86 *Cardiff Times* 31 Dec. 1870.

87 Iolo Davies, *"A Certaine Schoole"*: A History of the Grammar School at Cowbridge Glamorgan (Cowbridge, 1967), p. 126.

88 Smith and Williams, *Fields of Praise*, p. 23; *WM* 28 Oct. 1871.

89 *Cardiff and Merthyr Guardian* 8 Feb. 1867; *WM* 30 Dec. 1875, 30 Dec. 1879.

90 *WM* 9 Nov. 1871; *Cardiff and Merthyr Guardian* 11 Nov. 1871.

91 Venessa Cunningham and John Goodwin, *Cardiff University: A Celebration* (Cardiff, 2001), pp. 16, 156-174.

Henry Shewbrooks, headmaster of Monkton House and pioneer of the game.

school, which was often referred to by his name during the 1870s. Both are known to have played rugby and, indeed, James Bush had also participated for Cardiff in the 1868 matches at the Arms Park against the Royal Welch Fusiliers.[92] Contemporary press match reports show that both men turned out regularly for the Monkton House school rugby team. Shewbrooks, whose contribution to Welsh rugby has been largely over-looked, was born in Taunton, was a graduate of London University and was probably already a rugby player when he came to Cardiff to open his school in 1870. Described on a number of occasions as "the father of South Wales football", he was so keen on the game that he would punish pupils who were reluctant to play by giving them lines.[93] His obituary in 1905 claimed that he "was largely instrumental in introducing rugby into South Wales" which appears to confirm the importance of Monkton House in the establishment of rugby in Cardiff at the very least, if not in the whole of Wales.[94]

These events in Newport, Abergavenny, Cardiff, Brecon, Cowbridge, Pontypool and elsewhere all predate, therefore, the fixture between Neath and Swansea on the 3rd February 1872, which is widely accepted as the earliest press report of a Welsh rugby match. The centenary history of Neath RFC quotes the *Swansea and Glamorgan Herald* of 7th February:

> On Saturday a match was witnessed between Swansea and Neath clubs. The interest displayed was very great, although the result was undecided, both parties claiming to be victors.[95]

It is this very brief 1872 match report on which Neath base their claim of being the oldest rugby club in Wales and "the birthplace of Welsh rugby" with a foundation date of 1871. Neath neatly side-step their opponents that day by arguing that Swansea did not formally adopt rugby until several years later. According to a later club historian:

> As a result of that brief account, Neath are held to be the most senior of Welsh clubs ... because while the footballers of Swansea enjoyed a

---

92 *Cardiff Times* 21 Mar. 1868.
93 *Welsh Athlete* 19 Oct. 1891.
94 *WM* 2 Jan. 1905.
95 Quoted in T. Dargavel, *Neath R.F.C. 1871-1971 Centenary Year* (Neath, 1971), p. [2]

flirtation with the association game, the men of Neath stuck firmly with the rugger cause.[96]

This interpretation has never been seriously challenged and Neath's seniority and 1871 foundation date are unquestioningly accepted throughout the sport. But where is the evidence that the variety of football played that day was rugby? The game *could*, have been contested under hybrid or even association rules and so the *Herald* report provides no more convincing a case for the first ever rugby match in Wales than many of the earlier ones already discussed. Interestingly, Matthews' history of Swansea RFC claims that a later fixture against Neath in November 1872 *was* held under association rules, which means that the Neath players *also* continued to "flirt" with the round ball.[97] However, perhaps of even greater concern to Neath's seniority claim is the question of continuity. There are no reports in the *Western Mail* or the *SWDN* of matches involving Neath until 1875-6; while the club does not figure in *any* of the comprehensive early results lists of Llanelli and Swansea until 1877-8 or Cardiff and Newport until 1878-9. Moreover, neither of the Neath club histories refers to any subsequent matches involving Neath until 1876-7.[98] So, even if the 1872 match *was* played under rugby laws, there must be considerable doubt about whether the Neath "club" enjoyed a continuous existence thereafter. If Neath is the oldest rugby playing club in Wales, stronger evidence than one brief match report from 1872 is required to provide conclusive proof.

Whenever the club *was* formed, it is generally accepted that Neath's founders were members of the professional middle class. David Smith and Gareth Williams say they comprised, "a consortium of ten: a doctor, a surveyor, a mining engineer and a veritable plague of solicitors, in the chamber of one of whose number … the club's first meetings were held." These included Lewis Kempthorne, who had been at Llandovery and Thomas Whittington, who had been educated at Merchiston Castle

---

96   Mike Price, *Images of Sport: Neath RFC 1871-1945* (Stroud, 2002), pp. [7] -11.

97   Brinley E. Matthews, *The Swansea Story: A History of the Swansea Rugby Football Club 1874-1968* (Swansea, 1968), p. 10; David Dow has discovered that Matthews obtained his information on this match and on the foundation of the Swansea club from: J. Livingston, "Football", *St. Paul's Church Sketty: A Souvenir* (1910) pp. 22-24.

98   Gareth Hughes, *The Scarlets*: *A History of Llanelli Rugby Football Club* (Llanelli, 1986), p. 13; Arthur, *Cardiff Rugby* , p. 24 ; Jack Davis, *One Hundred Years of Newport Rugby 1875-1975* (Risca, 1974), p. 180; David Dow, *"White Gold": The Story of Swansea R.F.C. 1872-1914* (in preparation); Dargavel, *Neath RFC*, p. [4]; Price, *Neath RFC*, p. 11.

School in Edinburgh. He became the first Welshman to win international honours when he was capped by Scotland in March 1873 and it is often claimed that Whittington was playing for Neath at the time. However, he had been studying medicine at Edinburgh University for several years and qualified as a surgeon there in July 1873. While in Edinburgh, he played for Merchistonians and it was as a member of this club that he represented Edinburgh against Glasgow in the first Inter-Cities match in November 1872, and was selected two months later by Scotland. He was also a well-known Edinburgh cricketer.[99]

According to Matthews, the Swansea club was founded nine months after the *Herald* match on 26th September 1872. It seems that initially association matches were played, including one against Neath on 23rd November 1872. Following a proposal by Fred Meager, Swansea *formally* adopted the rugby code on 17th October 1874 but this does not necessarily mean, of course, that the club had not previously played some games of rugby. Indeed, an early history, published in the *Cardiff Times* only eighteen years after the event in 1892, claims that the Swansea club's first game of rugby took place seven months earlier on 28th February 1874. David Dow's recent research into the early history of Swansea RFC has revealed that their opponents that particular day were almost certainly Cowbridge Grammar School. Swansea's first match after they formally switched to rugby took place on 14th November 1874 against Llandovery College. The school had already featured on Swansea's fixture list before then and they continued to do so regularly for some years afterwards, suggesting that Llandoverians were closely involved in early days of the Swansea rugby club. This has recently been confirmed by David Dow, who has also discovered that several Old Cheltonians were prominent too. In their first official season of rugby, Swansea were assisted by Tom Whittington, by then a Scottish international, and CP Lewis who later played for Wales in the 1880s.[100]

In the same season that Swansea were formed (1872-3), other games were reported involving Cowbridge Grammar School, Monkton House and Brecon; while a match between Shewbrooks and Bridgend School resulted in a win for Bridgend by "2 goals and 4 points to nothing", the reference to points suggesting tries or touch downs.[101] By February 1873, a Llanelli club

---

99 Smith and Williams, *Fields of Praise*, p. 24; *Glasgow Herald* 23 Nov. 1873; *Morning Post* 3 Mar. 1873; Thorburn, *History of Scottish Rugby*, p. 27; *British Medical Journal* 2 Aug. 1873 p. 135.

100 Matthews, *The Swansea Story*, p. 10; Farmer, *Swansea R.F.C.*, p. 1; *Cardiff Times* 1 Oct. 1892; Dow, *"White Gold"* (in preparation).

101 *SWDN* 23 Nov. 1872 (Brecon), 29 Nov. 1872 (Shewbrooks), 6 Mar. 1873 (Cowbridge).

Llanelli's John Rogers and William Nevill, who attended Rugby School, would have been familiar with this scene of 1870.

Courtesy of World Rugby Museum, Twickenham

was in existence, playing internal matches at the New Park. The captain and founder was John Rogers, who had been educated at Rugby School and who was a manager at his family tinplate works; while the secretary, David Williams, was a solicitor's clerk.[102] However, this early team disbanded for, as the club historian Gareth Hughes has demonstrated, the modern club was re-founded in November 1875, when Rogers was elected the first captain. The new secretary was another Rugbeian, William Nevill, a member of a local family prominent in shipping and industry.[103]

During the 1873-4 season, games of an uncertain nature were reported involving Brecon, Roath, Pontypridd, Swansea, Christ College Brecon, Monmouth School, Swansea Collegiate School, Swansea Normal College and Arnold College Swansea. The Christ College matches were probably played

102 *WM* 12 Feb. 1873.
103 *Welshman* 3 Dec. 1875; Gareth Hughes (ed.), *One Hundred Years of Scarlet* (Llanelli, 1983), p. 1; Gareth Hughes, *The Scarlets*, pp. v-vi, 7; Macrory, *Running with the Ball*, p. 192; A.T. Michell (ed.), *Rugby School Register Volume II From August 1842, To January, 1874*, (Rugby, 1902), p. 226 (Rogers), p. 277 (Nevill).

Sexton Campbell Cory, captain of Glamorgan FC 1874-5.

under association type rules.[104] Monmouth had previously played a hybrid "dribbling game in a somewhat casual way," according to Henry Wilson Peill, the master who introduced rugby there in November 1873 and who turned out for them against adult teams. Peill had attended King William's College, a rugby school, and Cambridge University. This development was soon to have great significance for the game in Wales, as Old Monmothians were very prominent members of the highly successful Newport sides of a few years later.[105]

Though there is no conclusive evidence, when "Roath (Cardiff)", captained by SC Cory, met Pontypridd at Sophia Gardens in December 1873, they almost certainly played rugby. It is quite possible that this was the Tredegarville club, or at least an offshoot of it. The game was drawn with no goals but the match report refers to a touch down, not a feature of association football for over six years. Over half of those who took part can be identified as active in rugby in later years. At least eight became members of the Glamorgan club. It is probable, therefore, that the game was played under a version of rugby laws. Census returns indicate that the participants in the 1873 match were predominantly members of the professional and commercial middle class. Perhaps as a sign of the growing interest in football, the press also commented that "a goodly number of ladies honoured the players with their presence."[106] That a team existed in Pontypridd as early as 1873 seems to have previously gone unnoted. Pontypridd RFC celebrated their centenary in 1976, though a subsequent club history now firmly places the club's foundation as late as 1877-8.[107]

There is evidence that by 1873, if not earlier, the players who were to form the Cardiff Wanderers and Glamorgan clubs, the forerunners of Cardiff, were meeting at the Arms Park to play rugby. The precise origins of Cardiff's two predecessors have never been established. Surprisingly,

104 James and Rowlands, *Brecon Rugby*, p. 12; *SWDN* 13 Dec. 1873 (Brecon v Christ College); *WM* 20 Dec. 1873 (Roath v Pontypridd), 28 Feb 1874 (Swansea teams), 21 Mar. 1874 (Brecon v College).

105 H.C. Toulouse, *Monmouth School Rugby Football Club: One Hundred Years* (Newport, 1973), p. 9; J. A. Venn, *Alumni Cantabrigienses* Part II Vol. V p. 77 (Cambridge, 1940-1954). (HW Peill).

106 *WM* 20 Dec. 1873.

107 Desmond T. Jones (ed.), *Pontypridd Rugby Football Club 1876-1976* (Pontypridd, 1976), p. 1; Gareth Harris and Alan Evans, *The Butchers Arms Boys: The Early Years* (Neath, 1997), pp. 11-15.

historians of the club have shown no great interest in them, preferring to concentrate on 1876 as the club's foundation date. For this reason, a widely held misconception has taken hold that rugby came later to Cardiff than to other Welsh towns but, as has been shown, this was far from the truth. Unfortunately, the club's first historian is a little confusing in the matter of precise dates.

> It was in what I may call the *season of 1873-1874* that a number of young men … banded themselves together and formed the first real club in the town and called themselves the Glamorgan Football Club. Mr. S. Campbell Cory was the prime mover and early in the *autumn of 1874* he sent out a circular letter stating that it was intended to form a club, and giving the names of about fifty players who had already consented to join. Those to whom circulars were sent were invited to apply for membership to Mr. Henry White … Some of the players referred to in Mr. Cory's circular … had *in the preceding season* formed themselves into a club for the purpose of playing football in the Cardiff Arms Park.[108]

If Charles Arthur's account is correct – and he did speak to many of the pioneering Glamorgan players, including Cory, when researching his 1908 history – it appears then that a group had begun playing rugby amongst themselves at the Park by 1873-4. However, though they had given themselves a name, they did not get round to formally organising a club with officers and fixtures until 1874-5. Something very similar had happened at Richmond when they were formed a few years earlier.[109] It is significant that, in 1873-4, both Sexton Campbell Cory and Henry White played against Pontypridd for Roath, so there was probably a connection between that team and the personnel of the Glamorgan FC and conceivably with the earlier Tredegarville club. Glamorgan FC is the only Welsh rugby club listed in the 1875 *Football Annual* when its year of foundation is shown as 1873, (though an account published some years later even suggests 1872 for both Glamorgan and Cardiff Wanderers).[110] The *Football Annual* also records that Glamorgan played at the

Thomas Donaldson Selby, captain of Glamorgan FC 1875-6 and Cardiff 1876-7.

---

108 Arthur, *Cardiff Rugby*, p. 7 (italics added).
109 Arthur, *Cardiff Rugby*, pp. 3-5; Ereaut, *Richmond Football Club*, pp. 5-7.
110 *Football Annual* 1875, p. 149; *Cardiff Times* 3 Sept. 1892.

Arms Park, had a membership of 147, and wore dark blue jerseys with red collars and cuffs. Arthur relates that there were a number of Cheltenham College men amongst the first members. Solicitor's clerk Henry White, who was Glamorgan's secretary and treasurer, was born in Cheltenham and may have been a day boy at the college. Thomas Donaldson Selby was a sufficiently prominent player to be elected Cardiff's first captain in 1876-7. He is described in Cheltenham College's report in the 1874 *Football Annual* as "an honest player [who] makes good use of his strengths". An even more talented Old Cheltonian was William Grave, of whom more later.[111] The Cheltenham College connection is also confirmed by subsequent regular fixtures between the school and Glamorgan and later Cardiff.

Glamorgan FC are first mentioned in the local press in 1874-5. At around the same time, another separate group was also playing football at the Arms Park, and these men formed the Cardiff Wanderers club under the leadership of WD (Bill) Phillips.[112] There are many later references to his being only seventeen years old at the time, which would place the year of formation at around 1873. One of the pioneers of the Welsh game, Bill Phillips, the son of a public house licensee, was an accountant for a railway company. He founded the Wanderers shortly after leaving Bridgend School and was the club captain until the amalgamation of 1876. He later played five times for Wales, was an international referee and served on the WFU committee for many years. He also held many offices of the Cardiff club, including that of captain, and was generally referred to as "the father of the club".[113]

William David (Bill) Phillips, captain of Cardiff Wanderers 1874-6 and Cardiff 1879-81, 1882-3.

It is possible that the Wanderers were based around ex-pupils of Bridgend School. Though there is no hard evidence, the Glamorgan club may have initially enjoyed a slightly higher social status, perhaps drawing on a stronger public school contingent. Only a few of the Wanderers matches were recorded in the press and contemporary reports suggest that they concentrated

111 A. A. Hunter (ed.), *Cheltenham College Register 1841-1889*, (London, 1890), pp. 122 (White), 283 (Selby), 187 (Grave); *Football Annual* 1874, p. 24.

112 *SWDN* 23 Oct. 1874 (Glamorgan), 30 Oct. 1874 (Wanderers and Arms Park), 18 Jan. 1875 (Glamorgan and Arms Park).

113 For an account of Bill Phillips's career, see Andrew Hignell and Gwyn Prescott, *Cardiff Sporting Greats*, (Stroud, 2007), p. 129.

mainly, though not exclusively, on pick-up games, rather than playing many what were then termed "foreign matches".[114]

To summarise so far then, although there may have been an earlier version of folk or working-class football which subsequently converged with the public school game, it was predominantly the latter which was responsible for the eventual adoption of the handling code in south Wales. Though the Welsh public schools were small in size, there were several prominent rugby playing public schools in the west of England and it was old boys of these and their English and Welsh feeder schools who also helped to introduce the game to south Wales.

Football of an undefined nature was played from the 1850s at St. David's College Lampeter and from the 1860s at Llandovery College, Christ College Brecon and elsewhere. In the later 1860s, "clubs" at Neath, Newport, Abergavenny, Cardiff, Pontypool and Brecon emerged, though it seems they too played under a mixture of rules and were mostly short-lived.

Towards the end of the decade, as a result of the efforts of a master from a rugby playing Scottish public school, Llandovery College formally adopted the game, as Lampeter College probably did around the same time. By 1870, Tredegarville, the first recorded Welsh club playing under rugby rules, was in existence. Following the codification of the laws of the game by the RFU in 1871, schools and clubs throughout south Wales began to give up their earlier hybrid and compromise versions of football and play under a commonly accepted set of rules. Accounting for the take-off of rugby rather than soccer in the 1870s in south Wales, Martin Johnes argues that once a particular football code had gained an initial foothold in an area, then it was more likely that local sportsmen would take it up in preference to any rival.[115] It would appear that something like this did happen as, in the second half of the decade, the popularity of rugby increased dramatically, as we shall now see.

---

114 *Cardiff Times* 3 Sept. 1892.
115 Johnes, *Sport in Wales*, p. 18.

3

THE GAME IS ESTABLISHED:
'The running business'

Whatever versions of football had previously been played in south Wales, there can be no doubt that by 1874-5 rugby had become the overwhelming choice of players. This was a pivotal year in the history of Welsh rugby: new clubs were springing up, the organisation of the game was improving and interest was spreading beyond the participants.

Matches were reported this season involving Brecon, Bridgend School, Cambria (Swansea), Cardiff Wanderers, Cowbridge Grammar School, Glamorgan, Lampeter College, Llandovery College, Newport, Pontypridd, Swansea, Swansea Grammar School and University College Aberystwyth. There was also an attempt in December 1874 to form another club in Cardiff, when a meeting was convened to set one up in Canton, though this initiative seems to have been unsuccessful at first. Nevertheless, Canton – Cardiff's third oldest existing club – was eventually established only a couple of years later, following some scratch matches played at Leckwith Common in January 1877 between local lads and Cowbridge Grammar School boys who were at home on holiday. In 1989, Canton RFC returned to their place of birth when they took up residence at their Lawrenny Avenue ground, once part of Leckwith Common.[1]

For Glamorgan FC, 1874-5 was a successful and eventful first season, in which they remained undefeated, with victories over Cowbridge Grammar School and Swansea and draws with Newport and Swansea. The arrival of a lively new sports club in the town may not have been welcomed by everyone, however. Having celebrated well, after victory in their first ever fixture, the team were returning home from Cowbridge in a coach, when one of the players was forced to take over the horses' reins from an inebriated coachman. They then ran through the turnpike gate at Ely and, arriving at their destination in St. Mary Street, they collided with a street lamp in front of the old town hall. The volunteer driver was thrown into the road but unhurt. The street lamp, however, suffered terminal

---

1   *Western Mail* 30 Nov. 1874 (Canton); *Football Express* 19 Feb. 1927 (1877 matches).

The third oldest club in Cardiff, the ever-present Canton RFC, with the Mallett Cup in 1920-1.
                                                                            Canton RFC

injury. The Corporation demanded compensation and, since the new club had no funds, they were forced to hold a special concert to raise the money. The concert was apparently a great success, with "the pianoforte playing of [one of the miscreants] Mr. Trevor Thomas being a leading feature."[2]

Glamorgan even had a large enough playing membership in their first season to field two teams on that eventful day in November 1874; while an internal match held in January 1875 involved sixty players ("First Twenty v Next Forty").[3] The number of participants in club games still varied greatly, however. It is often asserted that rugby matches were contested by teams of

---

2   *WM* 23 Nov. 1874; C.S. Arthur, *The Cardiff Rugby Football Club: History and Statistics, 1876-1906* (Cardiff, 1908), pp. 8-9.

3   *WM* 24 Nov. 1874 (Cowbridge), 16 Dec. 1874 (Swansea), 30 Dec. 1874 (sixty players); *South Wales Daily News* 18 Jan. 1875 (Swansea); *Cardiff Times* 10 Apr. 1875 (Newport).

The old town hall in St. Mary Street, with fully restored street lamps.
Courtesy of Cardiff Council Library Service

twenty a-side until numbers were reduced to fifteen in 1876-7. However, the idea that because of a decision made that season by the RFU, Welsh clubs suddenly reduced their teams from twenty players to fifteen is simply to misunderstand the nature of the game at this time. It is quite evident that the usual practice was for clubs to compete with whatever number of players they had available. No single example of a Welsh twenty a-side club match was traced in the local press in this research. In only two reported games – Glamorgan Seconds against Cardiff Wanderers in 1874 and Swansea against Llandovery College in 1876 – were the sides initially made up of eighteen players. Other matches normally involved teams of around twelve to sixteen players.[4]

It was during 1874-5 that newspaper reports began to notice large attendances at matches. Several hundred spectators, for instance, turned up at the Arms Park to watch Glamorgan FC defeat Swansea in January 1875; while a similar number attended the same venue two months later when Cardiff Wanderers drew with Pontypridd. The novelty of the game to the public, however, was still apparent. In the Glamorgan-Swansea match:

> The game was so attractive that on several occasions the spectators passed through the bounds, and in one instance, there was a somewhat laughable spectacle presented by a scrimmage party becoming wholly surrounded by the general public, who, curious to see the mode in which the process was performed, closed round the opponents in scores.[5]

Within only a few years, as will be seen, Welsh spectators would sometimes be crowding onto the field of play with worse motives than mere curiosity.

A significant event took place in September 1874 with the foundation of the club, which was to become Cardiff's closest and fiercest rival. This appears to have been at least partly an initiative of the Phillips family who had recently moved their brewing operations from Northampton to Newport, bringing with them, it is alleged, one of the first oval balls seen in the town. The Newport club was founded at Thomas Phillips's Dock Road Brewery, by his two sons William and Walter Clifford, together with a group of Old Monmothians, including Charles Newman, later capped by Wales. As shown earlier, up to 1873, Monmouth School had played a hybrid football, closer perhaps to soccer, so it seems that association may have initially been adopted by the new club. However, no record of any association fixtures survives, so perhaps the players only experimented with a few "internal" kick-abouts. Presumably, the rugby playing Phillips family would not have been too happy with this and Newport soon switched permanently to rugby, playing their first fixture in a drawn match with Glamorgan on 5th April 1875. Henry Peill, who had introduced rugby to Monmouth and later played for Newport, is also believed to have been influential in the decision. Newport gained more than a brewery from the Phillips family, as Will and Clifford, together with their younger siblings Fred and Owen, all

---

4   *SWDN* 23 Nov. 1874 (Glamorgan), 7 Feb. 1876 (Swansea).
5   *SWDN* 18 Jan. 1875 (Swansea); 12 Mar. 1875 (Pontypridd).

William Gilbert's shop in Rugby, where the first rugby balls were manufactured. It is likely that the Phillips brothers' "first" Newport rugby ball came from here.   *David Dow*

became prominent members of the successful Newport teams of the 1870s and early 1880s.[6]

It was also during the 1874-5 season that the first description of a rugby match and the response of the spectators to it appeared in the Cardiff press. The account is very illuminating in several respects and it is worth quoting in full.

> [On] Saturday great interest was felt in a football match on Ynysangharad fields (kindly leant by Mr. Gordon Lennox) between the Cowbridge Grammar School and … Pontypridd … A commodious marquee had been erected on the ground for the convenience of the ladies. Soon after two o'clock the public began to arrive, and shortly afterwards the excellent

---

6   W.J. Townsend Collins (ed.), *Newport Athletic Club: The record of half a Century 1875-1925* (Newport, 1925), pp. 10-26; Jack Davis, *One Hundred Years of Newport Rugby 1875-1975* (Risca, 1974), pp. 60-70 ; Brian Glover, *Prince of Ales: The History of Brewery in Wales* (Stroud, 1993), pp. 124-5; Mike Brown, *Brewed in Northants* (Longfield, Kent, 1998), pp. 48-9; David Smith and Gareth Williams, *Fields of Praise: The Official History of the Welsh Rugby Union 1881-1981* (Cardiff, 1980), p. 25.

brass band of Treforest, comprised exclusively of working men, entered the field ... The game commenced about three o'clock ... and was watched with eager interest by the hundreds that were present, who appeared highly amused. It appears the play was in accordance with the Rugby rules, and by these rules carrying the ball is a prominent feature of the game. This was much oftener done on Saturday than kicking it ... But what afforded most amusement to lookers-on was *the running business*. A red striped Cowbridgian would succeed snatching the ball from the ground, and would then endeavour by his fleetedness of foot to carry it towards his party's goal [sic]. This was the signal for the "blues" to hurry from all parts of the field and fall on the "coch" [red] like an avalanche: Of course this would bring all the "reds" to the rescue of their colleague with the ball, and all would fall, blue and red "in one burial blent"[7], followed by roars of laughter from the spectators. These incidents frequently happened to both parties, and created much merriment. After an hour and a half the Pontypridd club was declared the victor, having won three goals. The Cowbridge boys struggled manfully, and the contest was of the hottest, but they did not succeed in sending the ball over to the goal. It should be stated, however, that [in] the preceding contests which took place between the parties at Cowbridge, the school was victorious, so that this victory places the two clubs on equal footing.[8]

Evidently the game was not the first between the teams, earlier ones having been won by the school. The importance of local schools in providing fixtures for the newly established clubs cannot be over-emphasised. One week later, for instance, Cowbridge were entertaining Glamorgan in their first match. During the following season, Swansea played Llandovery College no less than five times out of their eleven fixtures.[9]

"In one burial blent".

---

7   This is an allusion to a line in Byron's *Childe Harold's Pilgrimage*, where he refers to the Field of Waterloo: "Rider and horse, - friend, foe, - in one red burial blent!"

8   *WM* 16 Nov. 1874 (italics added).

9   Brinley E. Matthews, *The Swansea Story: A History of the Swansea Rugby Football Club 1874-1968* (Swansea, 1968), p. 11.

The match was actively supported by a prominent local industrialist, Gordon Lennox, who provided the field on land near his home at Ynysangharad House. A former player himself, he had captained the Pontypridd team which played Roath the previous season and he became president of the Pontypridd club in later years.[10] Census returns indicate that many of the town team and officials were drawn from the professional and commercial classes. There may be further evidence of this in the reporter's comment that the Treforest Band comprised only working men, while he makes no mention of any working-class players actually participating in the game. This suggests, therefore, that, even in the valleys, rugby was initially a middle-class pastime.

Perhaps of greatest interest, however, are what may be the earliest recorded references to the reactions of Welsh spectators to the game in which "carrying the ball is a prominent feature". The hundreds who attended were obviously enthralled and "highly amused" by this novel "running business". It is hard for us to imagine now what it must have been like to watch a colourful new ball game for the very first time but this account reveals something of the sheer thrill, excitement and enthusiasm it must have aroused. Comments such as: "what afforded most amusement to the lookers-on was the running business"; "roars of laughter from the spectators"; and "these incidents … created much merriment" anticipate the sense of boisterous, humorous spectacle and theatre which has characterised Welsh rugby ever since.

That rugby continued to grow in popularity is revealed by the establishment of the South Wales Football Club (SWFC) on 2nd September 1875 at Brecon. The first secretary was HW Davies of Brecon, confirming the key position this club held in the early days of Welsh rugby.[11] Cardiff was very well represented on the committee by Sexton Campbell Cory, Edward Fry, Thomas Donaldson Selby and Fleming Thomas, all members of the Glamorgan club. Though the SWFC could in no sense be described as a controlling body for the sport in Wales, it does mark an important step towards that goal. The club's initial objective was simply to provide members with an opportunity to play a better class of football against English teams.[12] This could be interpreted as an acceptance of the inferior status of Welsh rugby at this time: the only way Welsh players could compete well with English teams was to combine forces. However, another interpretation might be that, even at a very early stage in the development of Welsh rugby, and before

---

10   *WM* 20 Dec. 1873; *SWDN* 28 Aug. 1886 (president).

11   Smith and Williams, *Fields of Praise*, p. 44.

12   *Cambrian* 24 Sept., 1 Oct. 1875.

working men were taking up the game in numbers, there existed a strong desire *to* compete. It must be noted that the organisation was a "club" and members were individuals rather than clubs, so early South Wales teams were not truly representative. A subscription fee of five shillings guaranteed that membership was restricted to the better off. Six fixtures against English teams were arranged for the inaugural season though only two appear to have been played.[13] Nevertheless, the first match involving a nominally "representative" Welsh team took place on 27th November 1875 in Hereford. Despite having to borrow three "substitute" players (one of whom was a future captain of Wales, James Bevan, then a pupil at Hereford Cathedral School), South Wales won.[14] However, defeat followed in the fixture with Clifton, played in front of hundreds of appreciative spectators at the Arms

SOUTH WALES FOOTBALL CLUB.
President—Major T. CONWAY LLOYD.
Hon. Sec. and Treasurer—Mr. H. W. DAVIES.
COMMITTEE.

Mr. C. C. Chambers.	Mr. D R. Rees
Mr. S. C. Cory.	Mr. T. S. D. Selby.
Mr. F. C. Davies.	Mr. H. S. Sutton.
Mr. H. C. Davies.	Mr. F. Thomas.
Mr. E. C. Fry.	Mr. H. V. Thomas.
Mr. D. Jeffreys.	Mr. D. P. Warren.
Mr. C. P. Lucas.	Mr. T. P. Whittington.

Mr. R. D. G. Williams.
MATCH COMMITTEE.

Mr. C. C. Chambers.	Mr. T. S. D. Selby.
Mr. S. C. Cory.	Mr. H. V. Thomas.
Mr. H. C. Davies.	Mr. T. P. Whittington.

This club has been formed with the intention of playing Matches with the principal Clubs in the West of England and the neighbourhood.

All gentlemen wishing to join the Club are desired to send in their names to the Hon. Secretary, Brecon, for the approval of the Committee

A list of Matches will be published and sent to the principal Clubs in Wales as soon as the fixtures are complete.

Gentlemen desirous of playing in all or any of the Matches must send in their names, with the place they generally take, to the Hon. Secretary, at least a fortnight before the date fixed for the Match or Matches in which they wish to play.

The selection of the players in each Match will be left to the Match Committee.

Rules: Rugby Union. Colours : Black and white.

Costumes can be obtained through the Hon. Secretary, or by applying to any of the committee

Subscriptions, 5s per annum, payable by P. O Order to the Hon. Secretary, at Brecon.

H. W. DAVIES, Hon. Secretary.
Brecon, Sept 22nd, 1875.   10400kt

The formation of the South Wales Football Club in September 1875.

Park.[15] According to the Clifton club history, however, the return fixture was cancelled because South Wales were unable to raise a side.[16]

Another first was achieved in 1875-6 with the earliest mention in the local press of an Anglo-Welsh fixture. This took place on 13th November 1875 at Cheltenham College and it involved a Cardiff club. Though the 1876 *Football Annual* describes the team which played the College as "South Wales Ramblers", it is clear from the press report that their opponents were

---

13   *WM* 15 Oct. 1875. The fixtures arranged were Hereford (2), Clifton (2), Gloucester and West of England.

14   *WM* 30 Nov. 1875.

15   *SWDN* 24 Jan. 1876.

16   Frank C. Hawkins and E. Seymour-Bell, *Fifty Years with the Clifton Rugby Football Club 1872-1922* (Bristol, 1922), p. 8.

Glamorgan FC. Cheltenham won comfortably, not least because the Welsh club "had the disadvantage of not knowing the College rules", revealing that even at this late stage there might still be some variation in the rules adopted in matches. That the College had accepted this fixture, which was the forerunner of a long series of games with Cardiff, provides further evidence of the link between Cheltenham and the establishment of the Glamorgan club.[17]

New clubs such as those at Llandeilo, Neath, Panteg, Pontypool and Abergavenny (Vale of Usk) continued to emerge, or at least feature in the press for the first time. Llanelli re-formed in November 1875, with thirty members playing their first internal match at the People's Park.[18] Llandaff can claim to be Cardiff's oldest club still in existence, since they were formed in February 1876, (seven months before the merger which created Cardiff Football Club), though they appear to have played under the name of Ely before changing to Llandaff in 1878.[19] The founding of the Carmarthen town club this season has been attributed to the arrival from Cowbridge Grammar School of AF Laloe, who took up the headship of Carmarthen Grammar School in June 1874.[20] Schools rugby continued to flourish. When Llandovery College defeated Lampeter College, in front of "an unusually large number of visitors", they demonstrated that training and skill could still overcome size and age.

> [Llandovery] counterbalanced their opponents' superiority in weight by their skill in "dodging" and passing on the ball, in which the Lampeterians were deficient, trusting as they did more to "big" kicks.[21]

During this season, Llandovery College lost only one of their five matches with Swansea; while Christ College Brecon decided to adopt rugby, playing their first fixture against the town in December 1875.[22] In Cardiff, Monkton House and Cardiff Collegiate combined forces on several occasions as "United

---

17   *Football Annual* 1876, p. 50; *WM* 15 Nov. 1876. Cardiff Reserves were still playing the College in 1902.

18   *Welshman* 3 Dec. 1875.

19   *SWDN* 4 Feb. 1876. As Ely, the club drew with Newport in 1877 and lost to Cardiff in 1878.

20   T.L. Evans, *Carmarthen Rugby Football Club Centenary Year 1874-1974* (Llandeilo, 1974), p. 1.

21   *WM* 2 Dec. 1875.

22   Matthews, *The Swansea Story*, p. 11; Danny James and P.O.J. Rowlands, *Brecon Rugby Football Club: One Hundred Years of Rugby Football 1879-1979* (Brecon, 1979), p. 13.

Cardiff Schools" to play local men's teams, anticipating the Cardiff Schools Union by nearly thirty years.[23]

Suggesting that players and spectators were beginning to take the game rather more seriously, particularly in matches between close rivals, the first indications of disagreement appear in press reports and correspondence. For instance, disputes flared up in games between Glamorgan and Newport, Carmarthen and Llandeilo and Newport and a Cardiff scratch XV.[24]

Llandaff, technically Cardiff's oldest club, with the South Wales Challenge Cup in 1891-2. Jack Elliott (with the ball), later captained Cardiff in 1896-7 and won three Welsh caps.
Llandaff RFC

Nevertheless, the spectacle of the game continued to appeal to increasing numbers as evidenced by the 400 who attended this last match. When Newport later secured a home victory over Swansea, the *Western Mail* acknowledged the growing interest:

> A good deal of excitement prevailed among the spectators as the various movements of the contestants were executed, and great enthusiasm prevailed when Newport was declared the winner ... *a large company was present, including many ladies. The game is becoming very popular.*[25]

Towards the end of 1875-6, a dispute was aired in the columns of the *Western Mail* between the SWFC and the Football Association of Wales (FAW). This arose when the FAW announced that they had selected a team to play Scotland. SWFC officials protested that they knew nothing about this. The FAW reasonably replied that since Welshmen throughout England and Wales were aware of the arrangements, it was hardly their fault if the SWFC had failed to take notice of the announcements.[26] In their article on early Welsh soccer, Brian Lile and David Farmer refer to correspondence in *The Field*

---

23   *SWDN* 17 Dec. 1875; *WM* 29 Jan. 1876.
24   *WM* 20 Dec. 1875 (Glamorgan), 11, 13 Jan. 1876 (Carmarthen), 7, 8 Mar. 1876 (Cardiff XV); Townsend Collins, *Newport Athletic*, p. 12 (Cardiff XV).
25   *WM* 20 Mar. 1876 (italics added).
26   Smith and Williams, *Fields of Praise*, pp. 31-2; *WM* 2, 3, 10 Mar. 1876.

A contemporary representation of a tackle.

in 1876 which discussed the establishment of a national Welsh association team. They quote "Half-Back" who argued that association rules were those "chiefly adopted in the Principality". Lile and Farmer claim that this correspondence provides "confirmation of the early dominance" of soccer in Wales.[27] However, "Half-Back" evidently had little or no knowledge of what was happening in the south. As any close inspection of the Cardiff press will demonstrate, there were virtually no soccer clubs in south Wales at this time and certainly none at all of any standing. There can be absolutely no doubt about the dominance of rugby there by 1876.

Indeed, the SWFC secretary's response to the *Western Mail* confirms the extent of the spread of rugby in south Wales by this time. He wrote that it was unlikely that players would travel to trials in the north all the way from "Cardiff, Swansea, Neath, Merthyr, Pontypridd, Llanelly or even from Carmarthen or Brecon." The omission of Newport from his list is explained by the uncertainty over the sporting status of Monmouthshire at the time.[28]

This was addressed the following season by the SWFC, when in October 1876 it was agreed that Monmouthshire should be considered part of south Wales and, therefore, anyone in the county was eligible to join. At the same

---

27   Brian Lile and David Farmer, "The Early Development of Association Football in South Wales, 1890-1906", *Transactions of the Honourable Society of Cymmrodorion*, (1984), pp. 195-7.

28   *WM* 15 Mar. 1876.

meeting, it was also "unanimously resolved that the club should enter the Rugby Union challenge cup".[29] This resolution is highly significant, as it reveals that the club members – still overwhelmingly, if not wholly, drawn from the middle and upper classes – were keen to take part in competitive rugby and it is an early hint that Wales would travel a distinctly different path from that of the RFU. Unfortunately for the SWFC, events had already overtaken them. During 1875-6, the Royal Military Academy Woolwich had offered to present a cup for competition amongst RFU clubs. An RFU subcommittee drafted the rules but unfortunately the offer of the cup was then withdrawn by Woolwich and the competition was kicked into touch for a century.[30]

During 1876-7, the game continued to spread geographically in Wales and there were also signs that it was beginning to break out of its class boundaries. New clubs in Aberdare and Merthyr continued the expansion into the valleys. At first, these were probably mainly middle class in composition, however. The *Western Mail* reported that Aberdare included no fewer than six university men in a fixture with Roath in 1877; while Andy Croll's research on Merthyr reveals that players at this time were predominantly drawn from the commercial and professional classes.[31] Even in north Wales the game took root though it was short-lived. In December 1876, Bangor was formed with a decidedly middle-class committee, who resolved "that the game be played according to the rules of Rugby Football". Unfortunately, the club switched to soccer the following year.[32] However, in the south at this time, the first indications were emerging of developments which *were* to have a lasting effect on the Welsh game.

One such development was the fixture between Swansea Reserves and Swansea Working Men's Club (WMC) in December 1876.[33] It is likely that some Welsh working men had already begun playing before this date, either by joining existing clubs, or by taking part in informal matches amongst themselves. There are allusions to such games in several club histories and

---

29   *WM* 13 Oct. 1876.

30   F. Marshall (ed.), *Football: The Rugby Union Game* (London, 1894 edn.), p. 86; O.L. Owen, *The History of the Rugby Football Union* (London, 1955), p. 251. Unfortunately, the RFU minutes relating to the RMA Woolwich cup proposal have not survived, as there is a gap from 1872 to 1877.

31   *WM* 21 Dec. 1877 (Aberdare); Andrew J. Croll, *Civilizing the Urban: Popular Culture, Public Space and Urban Meaning, Merthyr c.1870-1914* (PhD thesis, University of Wales, Cardiff, 1997), pp. 222-3.

32   R. Wendell Edwards, *100 Years of Rugby Football in Bangor* (Bangor, 1980), pp. 1-3.

33   *WM* 13 Dec. 1876.

whilst in all probability this did happen, the only proof for it is usually anecdotal.[34] Though not everyone who belonged to the Swansea WMC was necessarily working class, this match nevertheless does provide some evidence of the early diffusion of the game beyond the middle class and it therefore marks a very important stage in the history of Welsh rugby. We can only speculate how this began to happen, but it is highly likely that an initial interest in watching the town team led to a desire to give the game a try. There appears to have been little resistance to this process and indeed, it is instructive that Swansea were prepared to offer the new club a fixture. Perhaps given the increasing keenness with which matches were being fought, they shrewdly recognised the potential advantage from doing so.

It was the desire to produce a team which would best represent the town in an increasingly competitive environment which led Glamorgan and Cardiff Wanderers to merge and form the Cardiff Football Club at the beginning of the 1876-7 season. Many accounts of this event incorrectly claim that the Tredegarville club was also a party to the merger. However, this club appears to have disbanded by 1876 and it is quite clear from the press reports that only Glamorgan and Cardiff Wanderers were involved.[35] Though described at the time, and indeed ever since, as a merger, in reality it was a take-over by the Glamorgan club. They had the much larger membership and stronger organisation. At the end of the previous season, the Wanderers were clearly struggling and may have been on the verge of collapsing judging by one contemporary account. Combining the playing strengths of the two clubs made obvious sense and it is evident that this had already been considered for, in March 1876, it was an unofficial "Cardiff XV" raised by Thomas Donaldson Selby which played Newport twice, confounding record keepers ever since.[36] Viewing the event as a take-over, therefore, in which Glamorgan absorbed the remnants of the Wanderers, reinforces the argument here that, effectively, the modern Cardiff club's formation predates September 1876.

Notwithstanding this, the new club decided to abandon Glamorgan's dark blue kit and replace it with a black jersey, at the centre of which

---

34   See, for example, Anthony J. Moses and Brenda C. Moses, *A History of Dinas Powys Rugby Football Club and its Associations with the Village, 1882-1982* (Risca, 1982), p. 1 which refers to young farm-workers and quarry workers playing in the village by 1882, though no records of this exist. The first reported game took place there in 1889.

35   *WM* 23 Sept. 1876; Arthur, *Cardiff Rugby*, pp. 9-10.

36   *WM* 6 Mar., 8, 14, 19 Sept. 1876. Selby was later elected captain of Cardiff the following season.

The Cardiff XV which lost at Sophia Gardens in the final of the 1878-9 Cup.

Back: WG Jones, AW Watts, PK Heard, AJ Evans; Middle: FS Thomas, BE Girling, RH Foa (captain), TW Rees, WD Phillips, JA Jones; Front: B Godfrey, ED Thomas, AR McDonald, WB Ferrier, F Perch, BB Mann.

This image not only records TW Rees's college jersey but also the wall which surrounded the Arms Park at this time. Only a small remnant now remains in Westgate Street/Castle Street.   *Cardiff RFC*

was a large skull and crossbones. This somewhat racy strip was changed shortly afterwards to a rather more sober outfit of blue and black hoops. The inspiration for this was a jersey worn in training by Thomas W Rees who had learned the game at Rugby School.[37] Though usually said to be Cambridge University colours (which are actually blue and white), they are, in fact, the colours of Gonville and Caius, the Cambridge college attended by Rees. He did not win a Blue at Cambridge and so it was his Caius *College* jersey which so excited the interest of his team-mates. In the Cardiff team photograph of 1878-9, the players can be seen in their new jerseys but Rees is wearing one with slightly broader hoops. This then must be the

---

37   Michell, A.T. (ed.), *Rugby School Register, Volume II, From August 1842, To January, 1874*, (Rugby 1902), p. 331.

very jersey which inspired Cardiff RFC's traditional blue and black strip, and without which – who knows? – the regional team of today might have been named Cardiff Pirates rather than Cardiff Blues![38]

Whilst Glamorgan and the Wanderers had originally been founded purely for the enjoyment of their members, the amalgamated club was now reconstituted to serve the interest of the town's honour. This was also happening in the north of England, where increasing inter-town rivalry meant that clubs were evolving into civic or community organisations rather than private institutions for young gentlemen.[39] A similar process was also at work in New Zealand, where – as in Wales – a significant expansion in the number of clubs, players and spectators was taking place.[40]

Before long, both playing and non-playing members of Cardiff would be drawn from a much wider spectrum of society and the club would give supporters a focus for deep pride in their home town. Richard Holt argues that whereas the working class were anxious to identify emotionally with their town (soccer) club, this was less important to the middle and upper classes, who had alternative ties to schools and professions.[41] However, in the socially inclusive version of rugby which was emerging in south Wales, it was evident that enthusiastic support for the town was not restricted to the working class by any means. Regional, if not national, pride was also becoming more apparent. Playing in front of a crowd of 500, probably the largest to watch a game in the locality so far, South Wales were able to gain revenge over Clifton with a comfortable two tries to nil victory at Newport.[42] Another development this season which signified the changing nature of the Welsh game was Newport's decision to charge for admission. The 200 spectators at Wales's most go-ahead club each handed over sixpence to watch them win their first ever fixture with Cardiff in December 1876.[43]

38 Arthur, *Cardiff Rugby*, pp. 10, 12, 22; J. A. Venn, Alumni Cantabrigienses Part II Vol. V p. 268 (Cambridge, 1940-1954) p. 331 (TW Rees).

39 Tony Collins, *Rugby's Great Split: Class, Culture and the Origins of Rugby League Football* (London, 2006 edn.), p. 15.

40 Geoffrey T. Vincent, " 'To Uphold the Honour of the Province': Football in Canterbury c.1854-c.1890", in Greg Ryan (ed.), *Tackling Rugby Myths: Rugby and New Zealand Society 1854-2004* (Dunedin, 2005), pp. 14-30. See also Greg Ryan, *The Contest for Rugby Supremacy: Accounting for the 1905 All Blacks* (Christchurch, 2005), pp. 13-51 for early rugby in New Zealand.

41 Richard Holt, 'Working-Class Football and the City: The Problem of Continuity', *British Journal of Sports History*, 3, 1 (1986), p. 10.

42 *WM* 22 Jan. 1877.

43 *WM* 5 Dec. 1876; Townsend Collins, *Newport Athletic*, p. 13.

Within two years, supporters at Sophia Gardens were complaining to the *SWDN* that Cardiff had followed suit.[44]

Newspapers were beginning to reflect the "edge" which was creeping into the game. When Cardiff defeated Swansea in December 1876, their supporters were criticised for their "repeated plaudits of their own party exclusively [which] scarcely constituted a fitting welcome to the Swansea team".[45] Hardly bad behaviour by today's standards, but it was a sign perhaps that some of those watching the game in Wales were now coming from a different social and sporting background from those who adhered to any "gentlemanly" code.

Ironically, it was an act by Welsh soccer authorities in 1877-8 which helped to stimulate the process by which rugby became deeply rooted in the popular culture of south Wales. When the FAW placed a notice in the *Western Mail* in September 1877 announcing the inauguration of a Welsh Cup, they did so in the hope of encouraging soccer in an area which was already becoming a rugby stronghold.[46] Martin Johnes and Ian Garland argue that the introduction of the cup was to have a significant influence on the development of soccer.[47] However, its initial effect in south Wales was to indirectly help the growth of rugby. An immediate retaliation came in the form of a letter to the *Western Mail* from "Half Back" from the Vale of Towy (probably CP Lewis) suggesting the introduction of a rugby cup for south Wales because "all of its leading football clubs play the Rugby Union rules and not that of association." He accurately predicted that it would stimulate rugby in south Wales, "which yearly increases in popularity ... [whilst] it is so evident that association rules are far from popular here." Enthusiastic support then came from Cardiff FC in the form of a letter from the secretary, Raoul Foa, who "strongly advocate[d] the establishment of a football challenge cup for South Wales". The SWFC secretary replied that the proposal had already been discussed in committee and, as a result, a special meeting had been convened to consider it. Perhaps appropriately, given the significance of the event, this meeting was held at the *Cardiff Arms Hotel*, the hostelry which gave its name to the Arms Park. On 22nd October 1877, the SWFC formally agreed to organise the competition. A fifty guinea

---

44   *SWDN* 12 Nov. 1878.
45   *WM* 19 Dec. 1876.
46   *WM* 12 Sept. 1877.
47   Martin Johnes and Ian Garland, " 'The New Craze': football and society in north-east Wales, c1870-90", *Welsh History Review*, 22, 2 (2004), p. 284. See also Peter Corrigan, *100 Years of Welsh Soccer: The Official History of the Football Association of Wales* (Cardiff, [1976]), pp. 4-5.

The Cardiff Arms Hotel, which gave its name to a world famous ground, c1870. It stood across what is now Castle Street and was demolished in 1878 to widen the road for traffic.   *Courtesy of Cardiff Council Library Service*

cup was to be presented to the winners and clubs were invited to send in their entries before 3rd November. The speed with which the competition was set up suggests that the SWFC were anxious not to be beaten to the goal-line once again by the FAW.[48]

The inspired decision to promote the cup probably ranks only second in importance, if that, to the founding of the Welsh Union in 1881 in confirming rugby as the main sporting pastime of the south Wales public. Although the major clubs competed for only ten years, it was during that crucial period that Welsh rugby took off both in popularity and in playing standards.[49] The cup greatly stimulated these processes and it was in these early cup ties that the Welsh public's passion for the game, accompanied by a deep desire for success, first emerged in a significant way. Its popularity was a reflection of the competitive nature of working-class culture which fueled the partisan nature of the Welsh game. In 1897, the *Western Mail* was certain about the significance of the cup to Welsh rugby: it had generated "intense partisanship" and "attracted a following for the various clubs that

---

48   *WM* 21 Sept. 11, 15, 24 Oct. 1877 (cup).
49   See Appendix 4 for the cup winners and runners- up from 1877-8 to 1913-14.

[has] never left since them."[50] The South Wales Challenge Cup was also the forerunner of numerous county and local cup competitions which sprang up over the following twenty years. For example, knock-out cups were subsequently organised for clubs in Monmouthshire, Pembrokeshire, Cardiff, Llanelli, Neath, Newport, Swansea, Aberavon, Blaenavon, Ebbw Vale, Morriston, Treherbert and elsewhere.

The introduction of a club competition is noteworthy, however, for another reason. The Welsh game was barely out of its infancy in 1877, but it was already sufficiently ambitious and self-confident to innovate, when administrators in older and more established rugby playing areas were reluctant to do so. As we have seen, two seasons earlier, the RFU missed the opportunity to introduce a national competition. Then again in 1878, the Calcutta Cup was *initially* offered for annual club competition. However, displaying a keen lack of enthusiasm, the Union rejected this proposal, according to RFU minutes, because of "difficulties of all clubs playing together", whatever that meant. The RFU did, however, inform the Calcutta club that the Union "would accept the cup as a gift to be played for annually by the representative teams of England and Scotland".[51] No difficulties there, then. The RFU minutes also reveal that the issue of a challenge cup was unsuccessfully raised again in 1881.[52] For the long-term interests of the game, the failure of English rugby officials to introduce a competition may have been a serious error of judgement. In Tony Collins's view, the lack of a national focus at club level was a major reason why soccer eventually overtook rugby in popularity in England.[53] The Scottish Union's original objectives included provision for a cup, but at their first AGM in 1873, they quickly dropped the proposal.[54] Similarly the Irish Union rejected a national cup competition in 1882, though the Leinster Senior Cup was introduced in 1881-2.[55]

50   *WM* 25 Oct. 1897. See also Smith and Williams, *Fields of Praise*, pp. 1-5 for an account of the cup's impact.

51   RFU minutes 22 Jan. 1878. See Uel A. Titley and Ross McWhirter, *Centenary History of the Rugby Football Union* (London, 1970), pp. 99-102 for a detailed account of the origin of the Calcutta Cup. The Hospitals Cup was introduced in 1874-5 but, of course, was not a competition for open clubs. See Owen, *History of the Rugby Football Union*, p. 251.

52   RFU minutes 10 Jan. 1881.

53   Collins, *Social History*, pp. 43-4.

54   A.M.C. Thorburn, *The Scottish Rugby Union: Official History* (Edinburgh, 1985), pp. 4-6.

55   Edmund Van Esbeck, *Irish Rugby 1874-1999: A History* (Dublin, 1999), pp. 32-3.

Attitudes to competition in England were different in the north, however. Tony Collins reveals that the Yorkshire Challenge Cup, involving sixteen invited clubs, was "hurriedly organised for December 1877".[56] As in Wales, improving the standard of play was an important motive. It is remarkable to note, though, that Wales introduced their cup before Yorkshire, where the game was much more advanced at the time. The first round in Wales was completed *before* 1st December, so it was only by a matter of weeks, but the South Wales Challenge Cup can claim seniority.[57] That it was in Wales that the first major rugby competition for open clubs in the British Isles took place is surely evidence that something different was stirring there.

Table 1: South Wales Challenge Cup 1877-8

First Round Draw
Carmarthen v Cardiff (at Swansea)
Merthyr v Talgarth
Brecon v Monmouth School (at Cardiff)
Cowbridge Grammar School v Llanelli (at Neath)
Carmarthen Grammar School v Lampeter College
10th Glamorgan Rifle Volunteers v Llandovery College (at Swansea)
Newport v Pontypool
Neath v Llandeilo
Swansea v Abergavenny (at Brecon)

The first competition did not proceed without difficulties, however. There were eighteen entrants but some teams withdrew without playing. Though some matches were held on neutral grounds, this did not necessarily obviate a long journey and this prospect still caused some teams to scratch. Match dates were left for clubs to arrange and Cardiff's first round defeat was blamed on Carmarthen for responding so late that the visitors only had one day's notice of the fixture, forcing them to take a weakened team. This tie also resulted in a dispute over a vital score, which Cardiff threatened to take to the RFU for resolution. These matters were fully played out in correspondence in the press.[58] Cardiff's experience of the competition over the years was an unhappy one, involving frequent disputes, crowd misconduct and foul play. As a result, after a particularly unpleasant local derby with

---

56   Collins, *Rugby's Great Split*, p. 20.
57   *WM* 7 Nov. 1877. The draw for the first round is accompanied by the statement that the "ties must be played off on or before the 1st of December."
58   *WM* 29 Nov., 1, 3, 12 Dec. 1877.

a newly formed Cardiff Wanderers, they eventually announced in September 1883 that they were pulling out permanently. A week later, because of the "dissention, strife and bad feeling" caused, the abandonment of the cup was debated at the WFU AGM. Although the motion was lost, from this time on, the competition began to lose momentum.[59]

A major area of contention which arose before the cup had barely got off the ground was the question of eligibility of players. There were accusations that some clubs were strengthening their teams by bringing in outsiders. It was a matter of particular importance to CP Lewis, the rugby master at Llandovery College, who wrote to the press with his concerns about the effect this might have on the school's prospects in the competition.[60] HW Davies responded to such complaints by confirming the eligibility rules of the cup in its first season. As in cricket, he wrote, a man could play for any club as long as he was a bona fide member. "In town matches too, it has always been understood that the same man may play for more than one club … [but] no player will be allowed to compete in the cup ties for more than one club".[61] In subsequent seasons, however, cup rules limited selection to those who lived within a radius of a club's ground. So, reflecting the increasingly competitive environment, from its very inception the cup became embroiled in argument and dispute.

South Wales Challenge Cup winner's medal, 1886-7. This was the last season the senior clubs participated. It belonged to the Swansea captain, Evan Richards, who played twice for Wales.   Swansea RFC

Despite these difficulties, from the outset it was a success in its primary objective of stimulating interest in the game. This matches similar events in Yorkshire where, following the introduction of their cup, new clubs sprang up everywhere and rugby quickly became embedded in the local culture. Tony Collins argues that attendance at Yorkshire cup matches also gave the working class one of the few opportunities, perhaps for the first

---

59   *SWDN* 5 Feb. 1883; *WM* 5 Feb., 3, 10, 17 Sept. 1883. See Appendix 4.
60   *WM* 24 Nov. 1877.
61   *SWDN* 16 Nov. 1877.

Newport were the first winners of the South Wales Challenge Cup in 1877-8. Will Phillips (with the ball) was captain. He and his brother W. Clifford Phillips (front row third from left) and Charles Newman (front row second from left) had set up the club only three years earlier. Richard Mullock (in an overcoat) later became the first secretary of the WFU.   *Newport RFC*

time, to express their local pride.[62] In its account of the first Welsh final, the *Western Mail* reported that the cup had "aroused the greatest interest throughout [south Wales] and the ties ... have been most eagerly awaited". The final was played in front of a crowd of perhaps 2,000, easily the largest to attend a match so far. The occasion even merited comment in a *Western Mail* editorial, which described the game as "perhaps the most exciting football match which has ever taken place in the district." The victorious Newport team received a wildly enthusiastic welcome by huge crowds on their return home, with the all the attendant rituals of brass bands and parades around the town, which were to became the customary response to cup success over the following decade. The celebrations later included a special banquet at which the local MP presided and during which the cup was filled with champagne and handed round to the tune of *Rule Britannia*.

---

62   Collins, *Rugby's Great Split*, pp. 21-2; Collins, *Social History*, pp. 25-6; David Russell,
      " 'Sporadic and Curious': The Emergence of Rugby and Soccer Zones in Yorkshire
      and Lancashire, c. 1860-1914", *IJHS*, 5, 2 (1988), p. 195.

The joy in Newport was matched by the disappointment in Swansea, where at least one player was verbally abused for his poor performance. His "fingers … were all thumbs … and … he shunned the ball at critical moments as though it were a red hot shot". Rugby was fast becoming ingrained in Welsh urban culture.[63]

The cup channelled competitiveness between towns into a relatively structured format with a clear winner. However, the increased levels of foul play and dispute, which it also encouraged, were regularly used as arguments against repeated calls for the introduction of an official Welsh league from the late 1880s onwards and they delayed its introduction for a hundred years. Nevertheless, at a lower level, the demand for competition was met by a proliferation of cups and leagues by the 1890s. The WFU, however, took no direct responsibility for these, so they were not co-ordinated in any structured way and were left to local unions to organise. Nevertheless, this still contrasted with the attitude of the RFU which regularly refused consent for county unions to run competitions.[64]

The appeal of the game continued to breach social barriers. New clubs at Aberavon, Blaenavon, Cwmavon and Maesteg probably relied substantially on working men for their teams. Boilermakers at the Uskside Works in Newport formed a club.[65] Youngsters outside schools were also being attracted to the game as evidenced by the matches arranged between Cardiff, Newport and Roath boys' teams during 1877-8.[66] Crowd trouble was increasing this season. In a Neath versus Cwmavon match and in the cup semi-final between Newport and Llandovery College, supporters spilled onto the field and disrupted play.[67] When Swansea WMC played Neath, "A great deal of noisy feeling was shown by the spectators and, as usual, the play was hampered by their crowding in over the touch-line and round the goal … the scrimmages at times [were] dangerously rough".[68]

---

63   *WM* 4 Mar., 25 Apr. 1878; Smith and Williams, *Fields of Praise*, pp. 1-2.
64   Collins, *Social History*, pp. 44-5.
65   *WM* 17, 25 Jan. 1878.
66   *WM* 24 Dec. 1877, 3 Jan. 1878.
67   *SWDN* 18 Mar. 1878 (Neath), 18 Feb. 1878 (Newport), 3 Oct. 1878 (cup draw). Eifion Morgan, *Llandovery RFC Centenary 1881-1981* (Llandovery, 1981), pp. 5-8 contends that it was the town which played Newport in the cup. The *SWDN* does refer just to "Llandovery" but describes them as boys. Earlier references to the College in the cup draw and in SWFC meetings confirm that it was not the town which played this fixture. There is other evidence to support this. Llandovery College competed every year in the cup until 1881.
68   *SWDN* 25 Mar. 1878.

A match at Rodney Parade, first used in September 1877, when Newport defeated the 10th Glamorgan Rifle Volunteers of Cardiff.

As the decade drew to a close, these trends continued. Attendances at matches rose substantially, with Newport, in particular, regularly attracting large crowds of several thousands. In 1879, for example, 2,000, 3,000 and anything between 5,000 and 8,000 spectators were reported to have watched them play Manchester Rangers, Neath and Blackheath respectively. For this last game, supporters lined the walls, fences and tops of houses.[69] Even local clubs sometimes found themselves playing in front of a hundred or so spectators. For example, during their inaugural season, when Pontymister played Newport Crusaders, over a hundred visiting supporters turned up.[70] Though press reports of crowd sizes must always be viewed with scepticism, such figures do nevertheless indicate a trend of increasing fascination amongst the wider south Wales public. The prospect of watching an exciting football match, however, was not the only attraction. Neil Tranter argues that gambling was one of several reasons for the growing interest in attending sporting events. Certainly, frequent references to betting were beginning to appear in reports of major Welsh matches, though there seems to have

---

69 *WM* 27 Oct. 1879 (Manchester); *SWDN* 17 Mar. 1879 (Neath); *WM* 21 Nov. 1879, *SWDN* 21 Nov. 1879 (Blackheath).

70 *Star of Gwent* 6 Feb. 1880.

been no concerted efforts to stop the practice. For instance, for the 1877-8 South Wales Challenge Cup final, 2 to 1 was offered on Swansea; while at the 1878-9 final at Sophia Gardens, "a number of sporting gentlemen were present on the field ... Betting ... was freely indulged in". Rugby, then, also provided new opportunities for gambling and this must have stimulated the fervour, aggression and occasional violence of some of the spectators.[71]

Though hard evidence of the process is difficult to locate, the growing enthusiasm for watching the game contributed to the increased level of participation. The most successful Welsh side of the 1870s were Newport, who remained undefeated in their first five seasons, during which time they won the first two Challenge Cup competitions. Townsend Collins explains that:

> the success of the team led to an outburst of enthusiasm for the Rugby game at Newport. It was taken up by schoolboys, it extended beyond the then somewhat exclusive circle of the Newport club, and new clubs were formed in the town ... *The little band of players had done more than found a club, they had established a game.*[72]

By 1880, many new clubs had appeared in the town and its neighbourhood, including Alexandra Rangers, Caerleon, Caerau Park Rovers, Clytha, Excelsiors, Gas Yard Rangers, Gold Top Rangers, Lliswerry, Maindee, Maindee Star, Newport Albion, Newport Crusaders, Newport Rovers, Newport Wanderers and Royal Oak.[73] A clear example of the diffusion from spectatorship to participation is demonstrated by the Pontymister club which was formed in November 1879 by local cricketers. Forty took part in the first practice and the majority "had never played before, but they have taken great interest in watching the movements of the Newport team and ... [they] did their best to emulate their powerful neighbours."[74]

Of particular significance for the future of the game in the town, local youngsters were

Rugby's first superstar, Joseph Arthur Gould of Newport.

---

71 Neil Tranter, *Sport, Economy and Society in Britain, 1750-1914* (Cambridge, 1998), pp. 52-4; *WM* 4 Mar. 1878; *SWDN* 10 Mar. 1879.

72 Townsend Collins, *Newport Athletic*, p 19 (italics added).

73 *WM, SWDN* and *Star of Gwent* 1879-1881 passim.

74 *Star of Gwent* 28 Nov., 5 Dec. 1879.

enthusiastically taking up rugby, either with junior teams, like Newport Rovers for whom rugby's first superstar, Arthur Gould, played, or for a variety of educational institutions, like Caerleon Industrial Schools, Newport Grammar School and Stow Hill Board School.[75] Following Newport's cup final victory in March 1879, it was claimed that every school in the town had its team.[76] Of course, such events were not restricted to Newport and similar developments were to be found throughout south Wales, in particular in the major towns, though it was probably in Newport that they first emerged.

This investigation into the origins of Welsh rugby supports David Smith and Gareth Williams's view that it was mainly public school old boys who were the founder players of the earliest clubs, with their "ranks ... stiffened by the ever-increasing self-confident class of solicitors, doctors, clerks, and engineers".[77] But now the game was reaching out beyond these groups to the lower middle class and to the fringes of the working class. Cardiff (as will be shown later), Newport and Swansea were still predominantly socially exclusive clubs at the end of the decade. A correspondent to the *SWDN* replied to an earlier press "accusation" that Newport had included "artisans" in their team which had defeated Cardiff in the 1878-9 cup final. The writer identified the occupations of all fifteen players and there were no artisans. The Newport team comprised four partners in local businesses, four clerks, two draughtsmen, two civil engineers, a mining engineer, an accountant and a student. David Dow's recent research has revealed that the Swansea team which won the 1879-80 cup was comprised of players with a broadly similar background, though interestingly, it did include one manual worker.[78] However, such exclusivity, in playing personnel at least, if not in administration, would soon change. Townsend Collins locates the arrival of working men in the Newport team shortly afterwards.

> There was no more striking feature in ... 1880-1 ... than the broadening of the bounds of selection. With the rise of new clubs it was recognised that the town club were duty bound to make the team as far as possible representative of the playing talent of the town.

---

75 *SWDN* 5 Nov. 1878 (Caerleon); *Star of Gwent* 5 Dec. 1879 (Grammar); *SWDN* 19 Mar. 1880 (Stow Hill).

76 *SWDN* 10 Mar. 1879. This is quoted in full in Chapter 4.

77 Smith and Williams, *Fields of Praise,* p. 24.

78 *SWDN* 14 Mar. 1879 (Newport); David Dow, *"White Gold": The Story of Swansea R.F.C. 1872-1914* (in preparation); *WM* 8 Mar. 1880.

He also claimed that Newport's subsequent success was accounted for by its lack of class distinction and by the acceptance that the club was a town institution and a symbol of civic unity.[79]

Elsewhere, working men were playing the game in greater numbers. Clubs were not only springing up in Newport but also in Cardiff, Swansea and elsewhere and these were not located exclusively in middle-class districts. Given their proliferation, neither could they have been exclusively middle class in membership. It is known that a club existed in Felinfoel by 1877. According to the Llanelli club history, it had been set up by their first secretary, William Nevill who "prevailed upon men who worked in his father's foundry … and colliers living in Felinfoel to turn out". Unfortunately no date for this is mentioned and this account is based on recollections published in 1934.[80] Llanelli may have begun to include working men earlier than many. Though it relates to the mid-1880s, the response of "Old Stager" to a suggestion that the club was composed entirely of colliers is revealing. "I fail to see that it matters two-pence-half-penny whether a team is made up of gentlemen or sweeps, provided they play an honest and fair game". He listed the occupations of the 1886 Llanelli cup winning team. There were no colliers, but ten were clearly working class. As well as two ironworkers and two tinplaters, the other occupations were painter, plasterer, plumber, blacksmith, saddler and stonecutter. Two schoolmasters, a chemical factor, a clerk and a (presumably idle) Cambridge graduate made up the rest of the side.[81]

Teams were also beginning to emerge in the overwhelmingly working-class coalfield valleys. In March 1879, there are press reports of the Mountain Ash club playing Mountain Ash Temperance. The latter were described as mainly "underground workmen" who had begun playing only three weeks earlier.[82] Whilst examples of exclusively working-class clubs at this time are difficult to identify with certainty, the existence of teams such as Neath Institute and Llandovery Working Men's Club, and pub sides like the Crown, Mountain Ash and the Star, Aberdare is evidence that rugby was beginning to infiltrate working-class culture across south Wales.[83]

---

79   Townsend Collins, *Newport Athletic*, pp. 20, 38.
80   Gareth Hughes, *The Scarlets: A History of Llanelli Rugby Football Club* (Llanelli, 1986), p. 9.
81   *SWDN* 12 July 1886.
82   *WM* 8 Mar. 1879; *SWDN* 10 Mar. 1879.
83   *WM* 16 Apr. 1879 (Neath), *SWDN* 5 Jan. 1880 (Llandovery), 25 Nov. 1879 (Crown and Star).

Players wait for the ball in a line-out in an early match.

The SWFC became less exclusive in composition in April 1879 when it changed its constitution so that clubs, rather than individuals, were to comprise its members. This was reflected in a change of name to the South Wales Football Union (SWFU). However, as Gareth Williams argues, it is important to recognise that the *control* of the game, particularly at the level of the SWFU/WFU and the senior clubs, remained very firmly in the hands of the middle class throughout the century and beyond.[84] For instance, Maurice Ivor Morris of Briton Ferry, the first secretary of the reconstituted SWFU, was an old boy of Cheltenham College. Besides playing rugby for Swansea, Morris was also a good cricketer and it may have been through his influential contacts, like JTD Llewellyn, CC Chambers, CP Lewis and Lewis Kempthorne, with whom he played in the South Wales Cricket Club, that he secured the appointment.[85] However, as will be shown later in relation to Cardiff, it was the lower middle and working classes who would soon begin to dominate in terms of playing numbers and even administration of neighbourhood clubs.

The widening of interest in rugby raised the level of competitiveness with which matches were fought and this led to increased disruption both on and off the field. Similar trends were noted by Stuart Barlow in his research into early rugby in Rochdale.[86] Evidence that Welsh rugby was diverging from any public school code (if it had ever adhered to it in the first place), is contained in a letter to the *Western Mail* in February 1880 from "An Old Cheltonian" who criticised the conduct of the Welsh game. He first complained about the frequency with which letters appeared in the press disputing match results. Then he attacked the players who continually argued with umpires and referees. "You never see this in matches in England", he claimed, because the transgressors would be dismissed from the field. The game in Wales, on the other hand, was "a series of disreputable squabbles". As Tony Collins has shown, English rugby was not quite so free of disputes as "Cheltonian" alleged, but his comments probably do record the Welsh rugby public's increasing divergence from the ethos of the game's gentlemen founders. There were no responses to his letter.[87]

"Cheltonian" was right about the growing level of disputes, however. There were, for instance, several major disagreements involving senior clubs, particularly in the cup, where increasing partisanship often led to disorderly crowd behaviour. When Newport suffered their first ever cup

---

84 Gareth Williams, *1905 and All That: Essays on Rugby Football, Sport and Welsh Society* (Llandysul, 1991), pp. 16-17.

85 *WM* 21 Apr. 1879 (Morris); A. A. Hunter (ed.), *Cheltenham College Register 1841-1889*, (London, 1890), p. 257; http://cricketarchive.com/Archive/Teams/2/2355/Players.html (SWCC) (accessed 6 Sept. 2014).

86 Stuart Barlow, "The Diffusion of 'Rugby' Football in the Industrialized Context of Rochdale, 1868-1890: A Conflict of Ethical Values", *IJHS*, 10, 1 (1993), p. 57.

87 *WM* 28 Feb. 1880; Tony Collins, *Social History*, pp. 32-3.

defeat in a contentious match against Swansea in 1879, they threatened to appeal to the RFU after the SWFU upheld the referee's decision over a disputed score. So disgruntled were they by this, they even held onto the cup at the end of the season until forced to hand it over. This event may have persuaded the Newport secretary, Richard Mullock, that a Welsh Union was needed. Much of the trouble in this game was caused by the crowd spilling onto the field and obstructing players and officials, one of whom was Mullock.[88] This also happened in a later match with Cardiff, when the Newport team walked off the field after a disputed try. Here the crowd frequently surrounded the players and "the scene became one of uproar and confusion".[89]

The theology students and their supporters at Lampeter College had a

fearsome reputation. In one cup tie, they were accused not only of hitting but also of biting a Cardiff player during a maul. This match ended in the inevitable dispute.[90] In the subsequent replay, up to fifteen minutes were wasted in arguments. Even though the "clerical element was well represented", there was much "avowed partisanship". Some of the College supporters viewed the game as a contest between "Welsh" Lampeter and "English" Cardiff, wrongly accusing the visiting team of having only two Welsh-born players.[91] When Swansea later defeated Lampeter College in the final, they too received the "same objectionable treatment ... as Cardiff [had]" from the Lampeter supporters.[92] During a match between Newport and Cardiff reserves, a supporter ran on the field and struck the Cardiff umpire. The perpetrator justified his actions by claiming his victim had kicked a Newport

The whereabouts of the South Wales Challenge Cup today is unknown. However, this shield, recording Swansea's victory in 1879-80, and which was once fixed to the trophy's base, still survives. Swansea RFC

88   *SWDN* 15 Dec. 1879; *WM* 15, 26 Dec. 1879; *SWDN* 27 Mar. 1880; *Star of Gwent* 30 Apr. 1880.
89   *WM* 10 Nov. 1879.
90   *SWDN* 25 Feb. 1880.
91   *SWDN* 1 Mar. 1880.
92   *WM* 3 Mar. 1880

player in a previous match.[93] Bridgend supporters were accused of "disgraceful", but unfortunately unspecified, behaviour after losing to Cowbridge Grammar School, while against the 10th GRV, Bridgend frequently interrupted play with "unruly conduct."[94] Cheating also went on. In a game against Bridgend, Neath Abbey players kept pushing the posts out of perpendicular every time their opponents attempted a goal kick, "anything but a gentlemanly act" according to one correspondent to the *SWDN*.[95]

The more enterprising administrators, like Newport's Richard Mullock, sought new ways of appealing to an ever growing audience. To attract more spectators, Newport became the first Welsh club to arrange fixtures with strong English clubs. Mullock promoted a "Football Week" in November 1879, which involved several important matches. These included Newport's victory over the South of Ireland; and their first ever defeat since they were founded in 1874, at the hands of Blackheath. In December 1878, Newport hosted the first recorded floodlit match in Wales, when they met Cardiff under electric lights.[96] This was only eight weeks after the earliest ever floodlit rugby match at Broughton on 22nd October. Here again is evidence of the willingness of Welsh rugby to experiment to widen the appeal of the game. Had Newport gone ahead with their initial proposal to use lights in their opening match on 19th October, they might have been able to claim to be the innovators of this form of rugby.[97]

For the 1878-9 cup, the SWFU introduced new regulations restricting teams to selecting players from within a ten mile radius. They also decided, in the absence of any specification in the RFU laws, to adopt a standard pitch size of 120 x 75 yards.[98] These were relatively small matters, but they do indicate that Welsh rugby was beginning to develop a degree of independence from the RFU. The SWFU continued with an ambitious programme of fixtures but turning out the strongest teams was still a problem, with away games being particularly difficult. There was an enormous variation in the composition of South Wales teams from match to match, with no apparent consistency in selection. A fixture with Cheltenham College could not be fulfilled because of a cup clash. However, a good win was achieved over the visiting South of Ireland team in November 1879, arguably the first

---

93   *Star of Gwent* 5 Dec. 1879.
94   *WM* 22 Oct., 7 Dec. 1878.
95   *SWDN* 20 Feb. 1880.
96   *SWDN* 19, 21 Nov. 1879 (Football Week); 17 Dec. 1878 (floodlights).
97   John Griffiths, *Rugby's Strangest Matches: Extraordinary but true stories from over a century of rugby* (London, 2000), pp. 9-10 (Broughton); *WM* 16 Sept. 1878.
98   *SWDN* 3 Oct. 1878.

real "representative" match played in Wales. The status of this touring side is in some doubt. The official Irish historian says that it was Munster and that they received a severe reprimand from the IRFU for travelling to Wales without permission. Strangely, he places the tour in 1881 but in describing the three fixtures played, it is clear that it was the 1879 tour to which he referred.[99] In the following two seasons, similar unofficial Irish teams returned to play against South Wales and leading Welsh clubs, including Cardiff, and undoubtedly this fuelled the appetite for greater international competition.

Welsh rugby had changed out of all recognition during the 1870s. A minority leisure pastime was becoming the passion of a wider public. This was well summed up by the *SWDN* at the very end of the decade, following Newport's defeat by Swansea in the 1879-80 cup:

> To the uninitiated it is quite a remarkable feature to notice the interest taken by the inhabitants generally in the result of these periodical contests, but the fact is that they have grown to look upon the matter as one where the credit of the town is at stake ... in South Wales ... the rivalry between the leading clubs has added much to the interest taken in [rugby] by the general public.[100]

Wales in Union

The 1880-1 season marked a major turning point in the development of Welsh rugby, for in that year the WFU was formed and Wales played her first international. Technically, the first Welsh XV was an unofficial one, since the Union was not brought into being until several weeks later, but the match has traditionally been accepted as a full international. Besides, Scotland played three officially recognised internationals against England before the Scottish Union was founded in 1873, so there is precedence for this. These events are well covered by David Smith and Gareth Williams in their unrivalled history of Welsh rugby, *Fields of Praise*.[101] Whilst their general argument is confirmed, on some points of detail, new evidence has emerged, especially about the role of Richard Mullock. The creation of the Welsh Football Union cannot be considered in isolation from the circumstances surrounding the 1881 international at Blackheath, so these will first be examined in some detail.

---

99 Van Esbeck, *Irish Rugby*, pp. 33-4.
100 *SWDN* 15 Dec. 1879.
101 Smith and Williams, *Fields of Praise*, pp. 34-45.

The season opened with a remarkable letter to the press which criticised the SWFU secretary, Maurice Ivor Morris, for not arranging a general meeting in accordance with the constitution.[102] This *was* remarkable because the author was Richard Mullock and it was just the kind of complaint that he would receive when he later became secretary of the WFU. The SWFU meeting was eventually held when Sam Clarke of Neath was appointed the new secretary. Mullock's growing irritation with the existing administration cannot have been improved when the SWFU organised an East v West trial in which, apart from one Newport Crusader and three Bridgend players, a geographically challenged fourteen-man "East" team included ten from Neath.[103] Players from the Cardiff and Newport clubs either appear to have been ignored or they deliberately made themselves unavailable for some reason. Either way, it suggests that all was not well within the South Wales Union and perhaps their absence is an

Richard Mullock, who – with some difficulty – arranged the first ever Welsh international.

indication that Mullock was already beginning to make his own plans for a match with England.

It is generally accepted that an informal meeting had been convened in March 1880 at the *Tenby Hotel* in Swansea when discussions were held about arranging an international with England. David Smith and Gareth Williams disprove the previously widely held view that it was here that the WFU was founded. They also establish beyond any reasonable doubt that the "clubs" which were believed to have attended were identified retrospectively, and therefore incorrectly, simply by listing the clubs (or in some cases merely the place of residence) of the players who represented Wales in the first international.[104] Though no written confirmation of the *Tenby Hotel* meeting has survived, there is new evidence which suggests that it may have happened. In the 1881 *Football Annual*, Mullock wrote as the new WFU secretary:

---

102 *WM* 5 Aug. 1880.
103 *SWDN* 5 Nov. 1880.
104 Smith and Williams, *Fields of Praise*, pp. 37-8. Despite this evidence, many sources still incorrectly give 1880 as the founding date of the WRU.

> Some time previous to the formation of this Union, *and after consultation with the leading clubs*, International matches were arranged with England and Ireland.

Of course, "consultation" does not necessarily mean that a meeting of clubs was actually held. Perhaps Mullock was simply trying to deflect criticism by claiming that his actions were based on a consensus of clubs. However, this is the nearest that we have at present to a corroboration of the *Tenby Hotel* meeting. Though writing only a few months after the event, when describing the actual foundation of the Welsh Union, Mullock places it in Swansea and not Neath where it was held in March 1881.

> At a meeting at *Swansea* in March last it was decided that such a Union should be formed. At the same time the South Wales FU was dissolved and its Challenge Cup handed over for competition by any club belonging to the Welsh Football Union.[105]

Was Mullock confusing his meetings?

Whether as a result of the *Tenby Hotel* meeting or of his "consultations", Mullock presumably felt he had a sufficient mandate to proceed. It is significant that Newport appeared for the first time amongst the forty-one clubs represented at the RFU AGM on 25th October 1880 and they were the only Welsh club to do so.[106] There can be little doubt that Mullock attended the meeting to sound out English officials and he must have made a favourable impression. Only four days later, the press announced, "The Rugby Union committee want to arrange an international match between England and Wales to be played at Newport in February next." Since this appeared in a newspaper report about Newport, it almost certainly came from the hands of Mullock, no doubt with an element of "spin", particularly regarding the venue for the fixture.[107] Nevertheless, only a few weeks afterwards on the 30th November, the RFU minutes record:

> A letter from Mr. R. Mullick [sic] of Newport Monmouthshire was read proposing a match with Wales – after considerable discussion it was proposed by L. Stokes [and] seconded by J. McLaren That the challenge be accepted – the match to be played in London on 8th Jan.[108]

---

105 *Football Annual* 1881, p. 169 (italics added).
106 RFU minutes 25 Oct. 1880.
107 *WM* 29 Oct. 1880; *Star of Gwent* 29 Oct. 1880.
108 RFU minutes 30 Nov. 1880.

Because the Welsh team performed so badly in the first match against England, a great deal of criticism has been levelled against Mullock, some of it justified, some of it not.[109] He arranged a trial at Swansea for 29th December 1880. Most accounts of the events leading up to the international say that the match did not take place and this is often presented as an example of Mullock's incompetence. Yet, as the *SWDN* reveals, the match *was* held. It was admittedly not a great success though, throughout the nineteenth century, Welsh trials rarely were. In this case, there was too much individual, selfish play with little passing of the ball. Nevertheless, at least five, perhaps six, of the eventual Welsh XV took part and a good spread of clubs was represented.[110]

Lennard Stokes (Blackheath) proposed that the RFU accept Mullock's offer of a fixture. He captained England and kicked six conversions in the match.

However, the RFU decided on the 30th December that the international match would have to be postponed until the 22nd January and a subsequent meeting reported that "the Wales committee" had accepted this. A severe frost resulted in further delays and at one point the RFU, brazenly revealing their priorities, warned Mullock that the game might have to be cancelled because they were looking for new dates to accommodate Scotland and Ireland.[111] However, it was eventually fixed for the 19th February. These delays caused problems for Mullock's selections, but it also meant that during the seven weeks between the trial and the match, there were plenty of opportunities to publicise the team. The frequently asserted view that some players were unaware that they had been selected is therefore hard to believe. On at least three occasions, the team was published in the local press. There *were* admittedly some variations in these teams and, given two postponements, injuries and unavailability this was perhaps inevitable. What is surprising is how *few* changes there were. The team published on 13th January contained thirteen of the eventual side plus one reserve who played; that of the 12th February (a squad of seventeen) also had thirteen; and that published on the 19th February had twelve of the team plus the three reserves who subsequently played.[112] Thus, the selection was not as

---

109 See, for example, Martin Johnson, *Rugby and All That* (London, 2001), pp. 41-4.
110 *SWDN* 30 Dec. 1880. "Lewis" may have been EJ Lewis.
111 RFU minutes 30 Dec. 1880, 10 and 25 Jan. 1881.
112 *WM* 13 Jan., 12 Feb. 1881; *Star of Gwent* 14 Jan. 1881; *SWDN* 10, 19 Feb. 1881.

The first Welsh XV in 1880-1. Back: WD Phillips, GF Harding, R Mullock, F Purdon, G Darbishire, E Treharne, RDG Williams; Middle: TA Rees, E Peake, JA Bevan (captain), BE Girling, BB Mann; Front: L Watkins, CH Newman, EJ Lewis, RHB Summers.

haphazard as usually claimed. What is invariably ignored, by those who criticise the apparent disarray in the Welsh match organisation, is that only twelve of the originally selected England XV played on the day.[113]

CP Lewis (Llandovery College), a gifted player who later captained Wales, is alleged to have refused to take part in the match.[114] This may be true, particularly as he may have been closely associated with the officials of the SWFU, which was effectively being by-passed by Mullock. His name does not appear in any of the published team lists, so he may have made Mullock aware of his opposition to the game from the outset.[115]

It is widely believed that some players had not even been notified of their selection and that, as a result, Wales were forced to include men from amongst the spectators on the touchline. Precisely *who* these men were, however, no-one has ever established. This version is based on the

---

113 *WM* 12 Jan. 1881 (original English team); John Griffiths, *The Book of English International Rugby 1871-1982* (London, 1982), p. 30 (England XV v Wales).

114 *WM* 1 July 1949.

115 As was customary for masters at the time, Lewis played regularly for the college team. See Harragan and Hignell, *C.P. Lewis* for an account of his life and sporting career.

recollections of Richard Summers. Speaking on the BBC some fifty years later, he recalled:

> When we got to the changing room, we discovered that we were two men short, their invitations apparently having gone astray. However, we picked up two 'Varsity men with Welsh qualifications, and they agreed to fill vacancies on condition that they were allowed to play three-quarter.[116]

This account does not fit entirely well with the contemporary evidence. The (two) three-quarters who played at Blackheath were the captain James Bevan of Cambridge, who had always been in the team, and Edward Peake of Oxford.[117] Peake was originally selected but was then dropped to reserve to accommodate a more experienced player, Robert Knight. On the morning of the international, the *SWDN* published the Welsh team, of whom three did not play. Those who came into the side as replacements were Edward Peake, Edward Treharne and Godfrey Darbishire. Since all three were *named reserves*, the idea that Wales had to rely on players from the touchline can be dismissed.[118] Indeed, it is to Mullock's credit that Wales arrived *with* reserves. Despite having far greater playing resources and administrative experience, England twice travelled to away matches without reserves around this time and on both occasions were forced to pick up players locally. This happened in Ireland in 1880 when one player suffered badly from the effects of sea-sickness and in Scotland in 1881 when Henry Taylor missed the train.[119]

Two of the men who dropped out of the Welsh team were talented Oxford Blues. Robert Knight was a half-back from Tythegston Court, near Porthcawl, and an old boy of Cowbridge Grammar School; whilst three-

---

116 Quoted in John Reason and Carwyn James, *The World of Rugby: A History of Rugby Union Football* (London, 1979), pp. 39-40.

117 Bevan was presumably selected as captain as, having played for Cambridge University since 1877, he had the most experience of playing against strong English teams. Peake was captain of Chepstow in 1880-1. *Bristol Mercury* 8 Oct. 1880. He also played briefly for Newport. His Welsh cap is held by the St. Fagans National History Museum.

118 *SWDN* 19 Feb. 1881 (selected Welsh team). The other named reserves were: T King (Newport), WF Evans (Newport) and R [WB] Roderick (Llanelli). See Huw Richards, *The Red and the White: The Story of England v Wales*, (London, 2009), pp. 12-20 for a recent account which adopts a revised view of the events of 1881. He reveals that the Welsh team was also published before the match in *The Sportsman*.

119 Griffiths, *English International Rugby*, p. 26 (Ireland), p. 31 (Scotland).

Arthur McDonnell Evanson turned down a Welsh cap but later played for England.

quarter Arthur Evanson came from Llansoy in rural Monmouthshire, where his father was the rector.[120] Arthur's older brother, Wyndham Evanson, had become – after Thomas Whittington and Foster Cunliffe – the third Welsh-born rugby international when he won the first of his five caps for England in 1875.[121] A Blue in 1879, Robert Knight missed the December 1880 Varsity Match because of injury. His selection was a logical one, as he would have renewed his Oxford half-back partnership in the Welsh team with his fellow Blue, Leonard Watkins. Only the week before the England international, the two had played together for Oxford against Blackheath. Marshall and Jordan's history of the Varsity Match claims that Knight turned down a Welsh cap in the hope of being selected for England, though he never was.

Arthur Evanson, on the other hand, *was* later capped four times by England between 1882 and 1884 and was regarded as an outstanding international three-quarter. It would appear then that Mullock was justifiably keen to select two Welsh-born Oxford Blues who were of, or very near, international standard for England. It is doubtful if there were any more experienced players available than these two Welshmen. It made good sense to invite them to play and their absence on the day no doubt seriously affected the Welsh team's performance and their on-field organisation. Unfortunately, it seems the promise of a possible English cap meant more than a guaranteed Welsh one.[122] However, these particular selections can hardly be taken as evidence of Mullock's maverick policy when it is remembered that, when the first ever *officially* selected Welsh team was picked to play the North of

---

120 *WM* 16 Apr. 1878 (Cowbridge GS); 1881 Census (Evanson's birthplace). Little is known about the third player who dropped out, JW [or JA/JL/HT] Lewis of Narberth. He may have played in Mullock's December trial match ("Lewis").

121 TP Whittington (Merchistonians, Scotland 1873) was from Neath; while FL Cunliffe (RMA Woolwich, England 1874) was born in Montgomeryshire.

122 *The Times* 14 Feb. 1881 (Knight and Watkins for Oxford); Howard Marshall and J.P. Jordan, *Oxford v Cambridge: The Story of the University Rugby Match* (London, 1951), p. 34 (Knight); Ross McWhirter and Andrew Noble, *Centenary History of Oxford University Rugby Football Club* (Oxford, 1969), Blues Biographical Section, pp. [20] (Evanson), [35] (Knight); Titley and McWhirter, *Centenary History Rugby Football Union* (London, 1970), Biographical Section, p. [33] (Evanson).

England a year later, both Knight and Evanson were again included, though they again withdrew.[123]

John Brooks of Pontypridd is often regarded as one of the unluckiest Welshmen of all time because, as he later claimed, despite being picked for Wales, he was never informed of his selection.[124] This, however, cannot be sustained by the evidence. He did not take part in the trial, he had never previously represented South Wales and, importantly, his name is not included in any of the Welsh team lists published before the match. Indeed, his name does not appear in any published *Pontypridd* team in the *SWDN* or *Western Mail* until well after the 1881 match. It is difficult, therefore, to see how he could have been considered for selection at this time.

Robert Lougher Knight missed the opportunity of becoming an international.

Where Mullock might justifiably be criticised is his decision to include some players who were not particularly well known in Wales – though, it has to be admitted, almost all of the Welsh XV *had* previously represented South Wales. It is evident that his primary concern was to select players who had experience of playing in England or against English teams. This perhaps was not such a foolish policy, for there cannot have been any realistic hope that Wales would defeat England, whichever side was picked. What was wrong with this approach was that some of the selected players were simply not good enough. Another criticism is that Mullock ignored the justifiable claims of players from other clubs, Swansea, Neath and Llanelli in particular, while Newport, with six players, and Cardiff, with four, were well represented. Despite the close rivalry that already existed between Cardiff and Newport, it is possible that there may have been some collusion between the east Wales clubs and Cardiff officials may have been involved in the team selection. Even before the match took place, complaints were made about Mullock's team.[125] That there was a cup semi-final on the day of the international does not exonerate him for failing to pick anyone from Llanelli and Swansea, as players from these

---

123 *WM* 7 Jan. 1882.

124 Gareth Harris and Alan Evans, *The Butchers Arms Boys: The Early Years* (Neath, 1997), pp. 23-4; Gareth Harris, *Taff Vale Park: Memories Lost in Time* (Pontypridd, 2000), pp. 177-180.

125 *WM* 14, 18 Jan. 1881; *SWDN* 12 Feb. 1881.

two clubs had also been omitted from the earlier team selections for the two earlier postponed dates.[126] There seems little doubt that Mullock could have found some players of a better standard from within the personnel playing regularly in Wales.

An examination of the social background of the first Welsh XV reveals few surprises. It would be three years yet before the first genuinely working man, Cardiff's William Stadden, would win a Welsh cap. Though the education of two of the team is unknown, eleven had been to public school, while one attended a grammar and another a private school in Bridgend. Half of the team were students. Peake and Watkins were at Oxford, while three, Bevan, Lewis and Newman, were at Cambridge. Lewis had played for Cambridge the week before the international; but Newman didn't win a Blue until 1882 and was really in the side as a Newport player. Treharne was a medical student and was a member of the St. Bart's team which won the Hospitals Cup a couple of weeks later. Summers was studying prior to joining the Army. Richard Garnons Williams, whose family were Breconshire landowning gentry, had left Cambridge six years earlier and was now a serving Army officer.[127] North Wales resident, Godfrey Darbishire, was a civil engineer and had previously played for his home-town club Manchester and probably for Lancashire.[128] Rees was a farmer and later became a solicitor, while Mann was articled to a land agent. The remainder, Girling, Harding, Phillips and Purdon were all clerks. The team, therefore, was representative only of the middle class and the gentry. There were no artisans. In addition, seven had been born outside Wales: Bevan in Australia; Purdon and Mann in Ireland; and Darbishire, Girling, Harding and Peake in England.[129] An investigation by Martin Johnes and Ian Garland into the social composition of the first Welsh international soccer team in 1876 provides an interesting comparison.

---

126 *WM* 13 Jan. 1881. However, GL Morris (Swansea) and WB Roderick (Llanelli) were selected as reserves for 22 January and 19 February respectively.

127 *The Times* 14 Feb. 1881 (Lewis), 16 Mar. 1881 (Treharne). For RDG Williams, see Gwyn Prescott, *"Call Them to Remembrance": The Welsh Rugby Internationals who Died in the Great War*, pp. 1-11 (Cardiff, 2014).

128 *Leeds Mercury* 19 Jan. 1875 (Manchester; and Lancashire v Yorkshire), *Liverpool Mercury* 15 Feb. 1875 (Manchester), (G. "Darbyshire"). However, in its England v Wales match report, the *Leeds Mercury* 22 Feb. 1881 claims that Wales's G. Darbishire had previously played for Leeds. The *York Herald* 7 Nov. 1879 has Leeds and Hull; while the *Huddersfield Daily Chronicle* 18 Nov. 1879 has Hull, and Yorkshire v Durham.

129 1881 Census; Smith and Williams, *Fields of Praise*, pp. 39-41; John M. Jenkins, Duncan Pierce and Timothy Auty, *Who's Who of Welsh International Rugby Players* (Wrexham, 1991).

Table 2: The Welsh Team of 1881 (See team photograph on page 84)

Name	Position	Club	Born	School	Occupation
Charles Newman	Back	Newport	Newport	Monmouth School	Student
Richard Summers	Back	Haverfordwest	Haverfordwest	Cowbridge Grammar School and Cheltenham College	Student
James Bevan	Three-quarter	Cambridge University and Newport	St. Kilda, Victoria, Australia	Hereford Cathedral School	Student
Edward Peake	Three-quarter	Chepstow and Newport	Tidenham, Gloucestershire	Marlborough College	Student
Leonard Watkins	Half-back	Cardiff and Oxford University	Abergavenny	Sherborne School	Student
Edward J Lewis	Half-back	Cambridge University	Llandovery	Llandovery College	Student
Edward Treharne	Forward	Pontypridd and St. Bart's Hospital	Rhondda	Cowbridge Grammar School	Student
Richard Garnons Williams	Forward	Newport	Llowes, Radnorshire	Magdalen College School	Army Officer
Frank Purdon	Forward	Newport	County Westmeath, Ireland	Not Known	Clerk
George Harding	Forward	Newport	Rusholme, Lancashire	Monmouth School	Clerk
Barry Girling	Forward	Cardiff	Clifton, Gloucestershire	Not Known	Clerk
Bathurst Mann	Forward	Cardiff	The Curragh, Ireland	Uppingham School	Articled Land Agent
William D. Phillips	Forward	Cardiff	Cardiff	Bridgend School	Clerk
T. Aneurin Rees	Forward	ex-Llandovery College	Llandovery	Llandovery College and Sherbourne	Farmer
Godfrey Darbishire	Forward	ex-Manchester	Cholton, Lancashire	Rugby School	Civil Engineer

England overwhelmed Wales in 1881, scoring thirteen tries in the process.

They found that it was mainly middle class in character but, unlike the first rugby team, there was *some* working-class representation in the Welsh XI, which included a miner, a stonemason and a chimney-top maker. Nevertheless, they conclude that the "social networks of the middle-class FAW" would have determined the broadly middle-class make-up of the team. Similar networks in the administration of Welsh rugby guaranteed the social character of the 1881 XV, especially given the apparent selection policy with regard to experience in England.[130]

The Welsh performance at Blackheath was dire. England trounced them by thirteen tries, seven conversions and one drop-goal to nil. Even Mullock later admitted they received a "fearful thrashing".[131] Only five of the team wore the Welsh jersey again. It was a poor start, but it *was* a start and, within twenty years, there would be something to really cheer about.

Even though the match against England was an embarrassing disaster, it nevertheless had a long-term beneficial outcome. One immediate response was an understandably irate letter to the press asking if it was "a private team, got up by Mr. Mullock".[132] Sam Clarke replied that the SWFU had had nothing to do with it and that "Mr. Mullock was one of the committee who selected the Welsh team".[133] However, even *before* these letters were published, as *Fields of Praise* reveals, the *Athletic World* of 24th February was reporting that "The Welsh are, I understand, about to form a Union". Coming so soon after the 19th of February, this resolution can only have been made by interested parties at the *Princess of Wales* public house in Blackheath, where the Welsh and English teams assembled. The next time they would all get together again would be on the 12th March for the Cardiff v Llanelli cup

---

130 Johnes and Garland, 'The New Craze', pp. 287-8.
131 *Evening Express* 13 Feb. 1897.
132 *WM* 28 Feb. 1881.
133 *WM* 3 Mar. 1881.

final held at Neath, so it was decided to convene the meeting then and there.[134]

At that meeting, "after considerable discussion", it was unanimously resolved to form the Union and Mullock was elected secretary also by a unanimous vote. In addition, the meeting charged Mullock with arranging the selection of a team to play Ireland before the end of the season. The clubs reported as being represented at the Neath meeting included Bangor, Brecon, Cardiff, Llandeilo, Llanelli, Merthyr, Newport, Pontypool and Swansea. Two others were "Lampeter" and "Llandovery". A careful scrutiny of the reported club matches before and during 1880-1 and of Mullock's list of "principal" clubs, referred to below, reveals that it must have been the college teams rather than the town clubs who were present at the foundation of the WRU. Indeed, Lampeter College had been runners-up in the South Wales Challenge Cup final only a year earlier, while Llandovery College had been semi-finalists in 1878. Both had been members of the SWFU since its inception and both had competed in the cup only weeks before the meeting at Neath. Indeed, it was the

FOOTBALL.

WELSH RUGBY UNION.

A meeting was held at the Castle Hotel, Neath, on Saturday last, the following clubs being represented :—Swansea, Lampeter, Llandilo, Cardiff, Newport, Llanelly, Merthyr, Llandovery, Brecon, Pontypool, and Bangor, to consider the question of establishing a Welsh Rugby Union. The chair was taken by Mr Richardson, captain of the Swansea Club, and, after considerable discussion, it was proposed by the Chairman, and seconded by Mr F. Meager (Swansea), that a Welsh Rugby Football Club be formed. This resolution was carried unanimously.—It was proposed by Mr Mullock (Newport), and seconded by Mr Margrave (Llanelly), that Mr C. C. Chambers, president of the Swansea Football Club, be elected president of the Welsh Rugby Football Union for season 1881-2.—The next proposition by the Chairman, and seconded by Mr Mullock, was that Mr E. C. Fry (Cardiff) and Mr C. P. Lewis be elected vice-presidents of the Welsh Rugby Union for the season 1881-2. Carried unanimously. The election of a committee (which will in all probability consist of a member of each club in the union) was left until the next meeting, which will be held during this month.—Mr Forester, Merthyr, proposed, and Mr Knill, Swansea, seconded, that Mr R. Mullock be elected hon. sec. of the Welsh R.F. Union. Carried unanimously. The hon. sec. was instructed to prepare for the next meeting a draft copy of the proposed bye-laws to govern the Union. The annual subscription to the Union was fixed at one guinea, with an entrance fee of one guinea. It was decided that in the International Match with Ireland on the 9th April at Dublin the selection of players be left to the same committee that selected the players for the English match. A vote of thanks to the chairman brought the meeting to a close.

The formation of the Welsh Football Union in March 1881.

college (and not the town) teams who participated in the *following* season's cup, now organised by the WRU in 1881-2.[135] Nevertheless, though neither of the town clubs had ever played in the cup, they were accorded "founder member" status by the WRU and, as such, took part in the centenary celebrations. So too did Bangor, though the club history acknowledges

---

134 Smith and Williams, *Fields of Praise*, pp. 41-6; *WM* 15 Mar. 1881.
135 *WM* 26 Sept. 1881. Cup draw: Aberdare v Bridgend, Pontypool v Blaenavon, Newport v Pontypridd, Cardiff v Newport Crusaders, Llandeilo v Llanelli, Lampeter College v Carmarthen, Llandovery College v Neath, Swansea v Aberavon, Carmarthen College bye.

Edward Fry captained Cardiff in 1877-8 and was appointed a vice-president of the WFU in 1881.

that there was no rugby club in the city at the time. Bangor's inclusion was probably an attempt to demonstrate that the new Union embraced the whole of Wales. It is possible that Godfrey Darbishire attended the meeting as a representative from north Wales, as he was appointed one of three vice-presidents of the Union for 1881-2. One of the other first vice-presidents was Edward Fry, a former captain of Cardiff, perhaps confirming that his club was closely involved in the various negotiations which took place during the previous year.[136]

A few months later, writing on behalf of the WFU in the 1881 edition of the *Football Annual*, Mullock recorded the "Principal Rugby Clubs" in Wales. The town clubs of Lampeter and Llandovery were not included though the college teams were, confirming their standing at the time. The clubs listed by Mullock were Abergavenny, Aberdare, Bangor, Bridgend, Cardiff, Carmarthen, Carmarthen College, Chepstow, Denbigh, Lampeter College, Llandeilo, Llandovery College, Llanelli, Neath, Newport, Pontypridd, Pontypool and Swansea. A rugby club had been formed in Denbigh in 1880-1 and played several matches but it does not appear to have survived very long.[137] The following year, the 1882 *Football Annual* again lists all these clubs, as well as eleven additional ones, but not Llandovery or Lampeter town.[138]

In his 1881 article, Mullock argues that, during the previous two years, the game had made rapid progress in south Wales and had become very popular, "but unfortunately the style of play has not improved". Whilst this was perhaps an attempt to divert attention from his team selection, it was evidently Mullock's expectation that the new Union would lead to improvements in playing standards. The WFU had also been formed, he wrote, "to promote a greater amount of sociability and good fellowship between

136 Smith and Williams, *Fields of Praise*, p. 43. *WM* 15 Mar. 1881.

137 *North Wales Express* 7 Jan. 1881 (v Rhyl); *North Wales Chronicle* 26 Mar. 1881 (v Chester), 8 Oct. 1881 (v Chester).

138 *Football Annual* 1881, p. 171-2; 1882, pp.181-184: the eleven additional clubs were: Afan (Aberavon), Blaenavon, Cowbridge Grammar School, Ebbw Vale, Maindee, Merthyr, Monmouth, Monmouth School, Newport Crusaders, Penarth and Usk.

the clubs." Mullock had already been involved in several major rows, so he may have been less confident about this aspiration. He went on to explain that a match with Ireland had been arranged for the 9th April 1881 and a team was selected, but the IRFU then cancelled the fixture because "no ground could be obtained".[139] This seems a feeble excuse by the Irish and it was the first in a series of problems which Wales were to experience in international match arrangements with Ireland in the early years.

George Rowland Hill was the secretary of the RFU in 1880-1 and later became its president.

To sum up, then, Mullock was a key figure in the development of the game in Wales. He was secretary of Newport when they became for several seasons the most dominant club in Wales. He generated increasing interest in the game there with a number of initiatives, particularly by promoting a series of attractive matches with teams from outside Wales. During his stewardship at Newport, rugby spread like wildfire in the town, both in terms of spectators and new clubs and it can be justifiably argued that Newport became the first community in Wales to develop a deep obsession with the game. It was his ambition and dogged persistence which led to Wales becoming accepted as international opponents. This was no easy task, especially given the somewhat condescending manner with which Wales was treated at the time, not merely in sporting circles. Sixteen years later, clearly still smarting from the reception he had received, Mullock wrote of the difficulties he had encountered in trying to arrange that first international.

> I had to go to London to attend meetings at the Westminster Hotel, as well as a private conference at Somerset House, chiefly with Mr. [George Rowland] Hill. When I advocated the claims of Wales … I was met by the question by some members of the English Union as to where Wales really was. Some of them, apparently had never heard of Cardiff or Newport, but, fortunately, others had received a little geographical education, and they managed to clear the matter up. For a long time, however, some of the members, and more especially Mr. [Henry] Vassall, were staggered at the idea of a young Union like Wales presuming to challenge England … and I received many letters from Mr. Vassall in the most motherly style. I remember one particularly, in which he told

---

139 *Football Annual* 1881, pp. 169-172. Mullock's account of the unplayed fixture with Ireland is confirmed by Van Esbeck, *Irish Rugby*, pp. 33-4.

Henry Vassall (Blackheath), despite his scepticism about the match, still played against Wales in 1881 and scored three tries.

me we were simply children, and had no right to talk to the parent nation in the manner I had ...[140]

That Mullock was able to arrange the match almost single-handedly raises the question as to why the SWFU had not previously attempted to have done so. Did they lack sufficient ambition, confidence or even ability to do this themselves? Mullock also recognised that, if Wales were to achieve anything beyond mere county standard, it was necessary to establish a national ruling body responsible for all aspects of the game. Huw Richards neatly sums up the man. "Mullock's entrepreneurial skills were not matched by has administrative efficiency."[141] He certainly had his faults, which included a tendency to go his own way, slack financial management and, at times, poor administration and record keeping. It is probably no coincidence that the earliest WFU minutes begin in 1892, the year in which he resigned as secretary. However, his failings were surely outweighed by the crucial contribution he made to the establishment of Welsh rugby on firm foundations. This was acknowledged by his contemporaries, who after all were in a better position to judge him than we are, when they unanimously elected him as the Union's first secretary. He deserves a more balanced assessment than the excessively critical judgements which are sometimes made about him.

The 1880-1 domestic season was characterised by continuing growth in the numbers playing and watching rugby and, as a consequence of this, by increasing press coverage of the game at all levels. Competition was getting keener and, especially for cup matches, players were taking the game more seriously by practising and training. However, disputes on the field were becoming more common and there were more crowd disturbances involving pitch invasions and even violence against visiting teams.

Welsh rugby had travelled a long way in a decade. Evidence of the game's expansion can be easily found in the columns of the Welsh press. During the 1880-1 season, the *Western Mail* and *SWDN* alone referred to over a hundred teams. As these two newspapers were published in Cardiff,

---

140 *Evening Express* 13 Feb. 1897. The RFU AGM was held in October 1880 at the Westminster Hotel.

141 Huw Richards, *The Red and the White*, p.16.

they probably under-reported teams elsewhere in Wales particularly in the west, so the actual total may have been much higher.[142] Four thousand spectators attended the cup tie between Newport and Cardiff and large crowds watched that between Swansea and Llanelli. At the 1881 cup final in Neath, "thousands … surrounded the ropes … [while] as many were stationed outside", seated on railway trucks or in the upper windows of surrounding houses. In a preview of this match, an editorial in the *SWDN* spoke of "the growing popularity of this favourite game".[143]

Neil Tranter believes that, given the number of football matches played in Britain, incidents of crowd misconduct were atypical.[144] Most rugby games in Wales, too, probably passed off without any serious trouble. Nevertheless, there does appear to have been an increase in the number of unpleasant incidents. In the Neath-Bridgend cup tie in December 1880, the visitors were pelted with turf, though whether this was because Bridgend played like "semi-savages", as the *Neath Gazette* claimed, is not clear.[145] One of the worst incidents of the season occurred in the cup semi-final at Newport, when Cardiff recorded their first ever win over their arch rivals. The pre-match anticipation for the meeting between "the two best clubs in Wales" was intense. "The two towns had been well placarded" and the teams widely publicised. Fighting broke out between players but it was Cardiff's disputed winning try which caused the crowd to erupt. After the match, the "mob surrounded the pavilion", where they verbally abused the Cardiff team. As the players left the ground, some were kicked and beaten and one was pulled off a cab. The angry supporters even attempted to throw the try scorer into the river. The Cardiff press was outraged, of course. For the *Western Mail*, "the disturbance was a disgrace to the town and to the noble game of football." The *Star of Gwent*, on the other hand, ignored these incidents but thought, "It was most unbecoming … of the visitors to claim a try". Evidently, partisanship was no longer merely confined to club supporters: after all, the reputation of the whole town was now dependent on success in these encounters.[146]

For example, when the *Llanelly Guardian* previewed the cup match against Bridgend in February 1881, it announced, "We notice that several

---

142 See Appendix 1 for a list of rugby teams in Wales in 1880-1.

143 *SWDN* 12, 14 Mar. 1881.

144 Tranter, *Sport, Economy and Society*, pp. 47-8.

145 W.A.D. Lawrie, *Bridgend Rugby Football Club: The First Hundred Years* (Bridgend, 1979), pp. 18-20.

146 *WM* 20 Dec. 1880; *SWDN* 20 Dec. 1880; *WM* 25 Oct. 1897; *Star of Gwent* 24 Dec. 1880.

The Cardiff team which won the 1880-1 South Wales Challenge Cup. Back: JA Jones, JS Smith, H Shewbrooks (umpire), BB Mann, T Williams, WH Treatt; Middle: WB Norton, PK Heard, WD Phillips (captain), HFD Sewell, JV Davies, A Hybart; Front: ED Thomas, R Trotter, AJ Evans; Absent: BE Girling.   Cardiff RFC

of the players are in offices and shops, and we appeal to their employers to permit special facilities for this important match, *as the honour of the town is at stake.*"[147] Although Llanelli's later victory over Swansea was only a semi-final match, the team was, nevertheless, given a huge welcome on returning home, including a torchlight procession headed by the local band.[148]

Pitch invasions were another way in which supporters were beginning to display their displeasure and even to influence the outcome of matches. The Llanelli-Bridgend tie was frequently disrupted by disputes during which spectators rushed onto the field to participate in the arguments. The game came to an abrupt end with the field full of spectators.[149] The cup final at Neath ended when Cardiff scored a try against Llanelli well into extra time. Hundreds ran on to the field: Cardiff supporters to celebrate and Llanelli

147 *Llanelly and County Guardian* 6 Jan., 24 Feb. 1881 quoted in: Gareth Hughes (ed.), *One Hundred Years of Scarlet* (Llanelli, 1983), pp. 25-7 (italics added).
148 *WM* 21 Feb. 1881.
149 *SWDN* 14 Feb. 1881.

supporters to protest. A number of fights broke out and the Cardiff umpire, schoolmaster Henry Shewbrooks, had to be escorted off the field by the police. The match ended in chaos with Cardiff unable to take the conversion and Llanelli unable to use the final couple of minutes to attempt to equalise.[150] The *Western Mail* commented:

> owing to the animosity which is excited by the contests for the challenge cup several of the leading clubs in the South Wales Football Union contemplate withdrawing from the competition; and it is probable that the "rowdyism" displayed at Neath on Saturday last will precipitate their decision.[151]

It was hoped that the new Union would prevent such incidents in the future, but following more violent matches, Cardiff permanently withdrew from the competition in 1883 and this decision began the process of the South Wales Challenge Cup's decline. Four years later the tournament was suspended.[152] The Welsh game was in desperate need of greater control, both to develop its enormous potential and to deal with the wilder excesses of its growing number of adherents on and off the field. From 1881 onwards, though it was not always successful in doing so, Wales now had a Union which could, at least, attempt to achieve these objectives.

In summary, rugby became the clear choice of footballers in south Wales by the mid-1870s. The number of clubs, players and spectators was increasing substantially and the game's organisation was evolving. Formed in 1875, the SWFC changed from a members club to a more democratic union of clubs in 1879. This body was responsible for introducing both representative and cup rugby to Wales. While it was largely, if not entirely, dominated by the middle and upper classes, its membership nevertheless displayed a keen interest in competitive rugby. Although it involved the senior clubs for only ten seasons, the South Wales Challenge Cup had an immediate and dramatic impact on the development of Welsh rugby as a cross-class sport. In particular, it appealed to the competitive nature of working-class culture and it stimulated strong and lasting club loyalties and partisanship. Associated with this, clubs evolved from private institutions run for the enjoyment of a few young gentlemen into standard bearers of the town's honour. In an increasingly competitive environment, civic pride now mattered, but there was also a downside. By the end of the decade,

---

150 *SWDN* 14 Mar. 1881.
151 *WM* 14 Mar. 1881.
152 See Appendix 4.

A woodcut of the Swansea team in 1886-7, the last senior club to win the South Wales Challenge Cup. Evan Richards the captain is seated third from left.   *Swansea RFC*

match disputes, foul play and crowd disturbances were becoming more commonplace.

By the later 1870s, rugby had expanded from the coastal and market towns into the industrial hinterland; the first working-class clubs began to emerge; and working-class players began to appear in previously socially exclusive teams. Youths and schoolboys were also taking up the game, particularly in Newport where the success of the town team resulted in an explosion of interest and participation in the game. Major club matches were now attracting crowds of several thousand, one consequence of which was the gradual monetisation of the game in Wales, as admission charges became standard practice.

Though his role has often been criticised, there is no doubt that Richard Mullock was primarily responsible both for introducing international rugby to Wales and for establishing the Welsh Football Union in 1881. These were very powerful symbols of the immense changes experienced in the Welsh game during the previous decade. As early as 1882, it was possible for the press to proclaim, "it is now a recognised fact that [rugby] football is the national outdoor game of the Welsh".[153]

---

153 *SWDN* 6 Mar. 1882.

Very soon, following their adoption of the four three-quarter system, Welsh clubs would become acknowledged as amongst the strongest, most entertaining and most innovative teams in the land. Admittedly, at the international level, it would take a little longer. Scotland would not be defeated until 1888, enabling "Freelance" of the *Western Mail* to declare, "We are coming on, and no mistake".[154] Even so, Wales would have to wait a further two years for their first victory over England in 1890. During the WRU's first nineteen years of existence, only one Triple Crown would be achieved, in 1893. However, Wales's international fortunes would soon change very much for the better.

Following the stunning 26-3 Welsh victory over England in January 1899, "Welsh Athlete" of the *Western Mail* could hardly contain himself:

The beginning of the first Golden Era: the Welsh team which defeated England 13-0 in January 1900. Back: WH Williams (Pontymister), J Blake (Cardiff), G Boots (Newport), W Millar (Mountain Ash), J Hodges (Newport), A Brice (Aberavon); Second Row: R Hellings (Llwynypia), D Rees (Swansea), G Davies (Swansea), W Trew (Swansea), AJ Davies (WRU); Third Row: W Rees (WRU), W Llewellyn (Llwynypia), W Bancroft (Swansea) (captain); Front: R Thomas (Swansea), GL Lloyd (Newport), LA Phillips (Newport).
Courtesy of Gloucester RFC and Gloucestershire Archives

---

154 *WM* 6 Feb. 1888.

[From 1881] England has assumed a patronizing manner towards us, treating our chances ... in a very cavalier fashion ... [but] we proved conclusively on Saturday that, not only in club football, but in representative matches, our football is stronger, more scientific, and of a better all round class ...

Wales, where Rugby football is general amongst all classes, is in a better position to continue her strength as an expounder of the Rugby game than either England, Ireland or Scotland and is ... in a better position to assert her superiority both in club and international football than has ever been before.[155]

His confidence was well placed. After 1900, even the Henry Vassalls of the world would have to accept that Welsh rugby had come of age. With six Triple Crowns and the unofficial world championship, the first "Golden Era" of 1900-1911 was to be a period of astonishing success for Wales.[156] But even so, it was in the preceding decades of the 1870s, 1880s and 1890s that a distinctive Welsh domestic and international game was created and a firm foundation for what was to come was laid down. Within this wider context, then, rugby came to dominate the sporting culture of late Victorian Cardiff. This is the subject of the following chapters.

The ball used in the historic Wales v New Zealand match, 1905. Swansea RFC

---

155 *WM* 9 Jan. 1899.

156 Between 1899-1900 and 1910-11, Wales played forty-seven matches and lost only seven. Of the six Triple Crowns, after France joined the Championship in 1908, the last three were converted into Grand Slams. There were victories over New Zealand and Australia and in thirteen meetings with England between 1899 and 1911, Wales lost only once.

4

THE CLUBS:
'In Cardiff and District surely their name is legion'

Rugby in nineteenth-century Wales is often portrayed as a cohesive and socially inclusive sport, which enjoyed mass support across the classes and which therefore became a cornerstone of Welsh popular culture. The following chapters will consider the validity of this view by examining in detail the impact which rugby football had in the largest town in Wales.

At the beginning of the century, Cardiff was a small, insignificant market town with a purely local trade and a population of just 1,870. Within a hundred years, however, it had become not only the regional capital of south Wales but also one of Britain's largest ports and a trading centre of global importance.[1] This extraordinary transformation was acknowledged by a Board of Trade report in 1908.

> There is no more interesting study in town growth and development than Cardiff. At the Census of 1851 it was a place of some 20,000 inhabitants with no influence in commerce and no reputation. Now, it is one of the most thriving cities in the country, a centre of trade and commerce and a great port. In every respect the development has been remarkable.[2]

Though Cardiff began exporting iron from Merthyr following the opening of the Glamorganshire canal in 1798, its rise as a major port and regional centre was based on the expansion of the coal trade. From around 1850, coal began to overtake iron as the main staple of the south Wales economy and Cardiff became its main place of export. It also began to replace Bristol as the commercial centre for south Wales. By 1871, Cardiff had overtaken Merthyr to become the largest town in Wales.[3]

1   M.J. Daunton, *Coal Metropolis: Cardiff 1870-1914* (Leicester, 1977), p. 11.
2   *Report of an Enquiry by the Board of Trade into Working Class Rents, Housing and Retail Prices*, 1908, p. 132 quoted in Daunton, *Coal Metropolis*, p. [1].
3   Daunton, *Coal Metropolis*, pp. 2-8; William Rees, *A History of Cardiff* (Cardiff, 1969 edn.), pp. 231-241.

By the 1880s, south Wales dominated British coal exports and Cardiff dominated the south Wales trade. In 1870, three million tons were shipped from Cardiff; by 1900 the figure had risen to nearly eight million.[4] However, though Cardiff developed a range of commercial and recreational services as it evolved into the regional capital, it never became a centre of manufacturing. Nevertheless, at the end of the century, it was being described as both the "metropolis of Wales" and the "coal metropolis of the world".[5] Indeed, the town's rugby players were often referred to as the "Welsh Metropolitans" at this time.

Between 1851 and 1911, Cardiff's population grew from 20,000 to 182,000, an astonishing rate of increase, which was not matched by any other major town in Britain, apart from Middlesbrough.[6] Following the construction of new docks, the populations of neighbouring Penarth and Barry also expanded, as shown in Table 4. Barry, in particular, grew phenomenally and, by 1913, it had even overtaken Cardiff in tonnage of coal exports.[7]

These events led to immense changes in the way of life of the town and its surrounding area, including an unprecedented enthusiasm for organised sport and overwhelmingly for rugby football. Commenting on the "lovers of the popular winter pastime" in 1890 the *SWDN* said of them "in Cardiff and district surely their name is legion."[8] Strangely, then, histories of Victorian Cardiff largely or, in some cases, completely ignore the impact that rugby had on the social, cultural, economic and civic life of the town.[9]

This chapter therefore aims to assess the importance of the game in Cardiff by examining the extent and nature of the participation. This will be done by establishing, for the first time, the number of teams in the Cardiff area up to 1900 and by attempting to trace their origins and background. The organisation of the game and the social class of its participants; and the social and economic impact of rugby on the life of the town will be explored in later chapters. Finally, an attempt will be made to assess the importance of rugby in the popular culture of Cardiff in the late nineteenth century.

---

4   Rees, *A History of Cardiff*, p. 271.

5   Daunton, *Coal Metropolis*, p. [1].

6   Daunton, *Coal Metropolis*, p. 11.

7   Daunton, *Coal Metropolis*, p. 7; Rees, *A History of Cardiff*, pp. 296-8.

8   *South Wales Daily News* 22 July 1890.

9   For example, see Rees, *A History of Cardiff*; Daunton, *Coal Metropolis*; Dennis Morgan, *The Cardiff Story: A History of the City from its Earliest Times to the Present* (Cowbridge, 1991); Nick Shepley, *The Cardiff Story* (Stroud, 2014).

The "lovers of the popular winter pastime" at the Arms Park included many women.

In order to provide a measure of the growth of the game in the nineteenth century, every local team mentioned in the *South Wales Daily News* and *Western Mail* was recorded for each season between 1870 and 1900. This research was carried out using hardcopy or micro-filmed editions rather than digitised versions. The results of this exercise are shown in Table 3 and Figure 1.[10] Demonstrating the huge range of teams involved, Appendix 2 lists the 236 traced for 1895-6, the season with the highest number. These figures include clubs from Penarth and Barry, as well as those from within the administrative boundaries of the modern city and its surrounding villages. This was done because clubs and players from these neighbouring port towns have always been an integral part of "Cardiff and District" rugby, where they have regularly contested both friendly and competitive matches. For instance, as will be seen, Penarth were winners of the Cardiff District Challenge Cup for three seasons, while Barry were founder members of

---

10   Owing to the unavailability at the time of the research of the *Western Mail* for January to June 1891, the *Evening Express* was used as a replacement. This had broadly the same level of coverage of local rugby as its sister paper. In addition, the figures for the first three seasons up to 1872-3 include the references to Tredegarville in the *Football Annual,* as discussed in Chapter 2. The number of teams recorded for 1899-1900 may have been affected by the greatly reduced press coverage of sport during the South African War. The figures do not include the nine a-side teams referred to in Chapter 5.

A faded image of Penarth, with the 1889-90 Cardiff District Challenge Cup, which they won outright after three successive victories. The captain was Dickie Garrett.   Penarth RFC

the Cardiff and District Football Union. From the earliest days, players from Penarth and Barry have represented Cardiff teams, while Cardiff men have often played for Penarth and Barry sides.[11]

Attempting to record the number of clubs in this way over such a long period is not without difficulties. Apart from simple human error, negative micro-films and missing and defaced pages and editions, the reliability of the collected data has to be questioned. Some clubs may have changed their name during the season while others may have had their names reported incorrectly, both of which would inflate totals. Unfortunately, there is often no way of reliably dealing with this, though where such incidents were clear, the results were adjusted. However, a surprisingly large number of clubs ran second XVs and though these were noted (see Appendix 2), they have not been included in the overall totals in Table 3, partly to avoid double-counting where some club reserve teams played under a separate name. In 1895-6, for instance, 38 reserve teams were recorded; but these were not included in the 236 total for that season. Therefore, any such inflation of the figures might be roughly offset by the exclusion of these reserve teams. There is no doubt that many of the teams recorded were transitory and did not play regular fixtures throughout the season. However,

11   Appendix 3 (1) (Penarth cup); *WM* 15 Nov. 1892 (Barry).

distinguishing established teams from transient ones is not easy since some regular clubs rarely featured in the press. In addition, such teams were still an important part of the local rugby culture, even though they were short-lived. It should also be pointed out, of course, that the activities of some, possibly many, teams never reached the columns of the local newspapers at all.

Both Alan Metcalfe and Mike Huggins, in their respective studies of early association football, noted a very high annual turnover rate of clubs.[12] This was also very true for the rugby clubs of Cardiff. As a result, except for a very limited number of major clubs, it proved impossible to trace the season-by-season progress of individual teams over the period. Newspapers were surprisingly uninformative about the bewildering frequency with which clubs changed their names, merged, split, disbanded and re-formed.[13] Despite this, the research has confirmed that many of today's clubs can trace their (sometimes severed) roots to the nineteenth century, or at least share their name with a forerunner from that period. Though some may have been formed earlier, the seasons in which existing clubs were first mentioned in the local press were: Llandaff (1875-6); Canton (1878-9); Cardiff Harlequins (1879-80); Penarth (1880-1); Cathays (1880-1); Cardiff University (1883-4); Taffs Well (1884-5); Tongwynlais (1885-6); Whitchurch (1885-6); Pentyrch (1886-7); Llandaff North (Llandaff Yard) (1886-7); Barry (Cadoxton) (1887-8); St. Peter's (1888-9); Dinas Powys (1888-9); St. Alban's (1890-1); Glamorgan Wanderers (Old Monktonians) (1894-5); Rumney (1894-5); Llanishen (1896-7); and Cardiff Medicals (1896-7).

No other comparable detailed study of Welsh club rugby has been undertaken before and it is believed that, despite the limitations of the data, they are sufficiently reliable to confidently draw conclusions not only about the extent but also, as will also be shown, about the nature of club rugby in Cardiff and Wales in the late Victorian period.

An examination of the results shown in Table 3 and Figure 1 suggest there were five phases of the development of the game in the Cardiff area during the last three decades of the nineteenth century.

---

12   Alan Metcalfe, "Football in the Mining Communities of East Northumberland 1882-1914", *International Journal of the History of Sport*, 5, 3 (1988), p. 274; M. Huggins, "The Spread of Association Football in North-East England, 1876-90: The Pattern of Diffusion", *IJHS*, 6, 3 (1989), p. 303.

13   See Michael G. Bassett, *Games of Interchanging Praise: A Centenary History of Rugby Football in Barry* (Barry, 1988), pp. 10-30 for a well-researched account which reveals just how complex the turnover of clubs could be.

Tongwynlais 1899-1900. Rugby had already been played in the village for at least fifteen years when this photograph was taken.
Courtesy of Tongwynlais RFC and Tongwynlais Community Council

1870-1 to 1876-7. In this phase, the game was initially established in the town. The number of clubs never reached double figures and rugby was played only by an elite minority.

1877-8 to 1883-4. This was a period of slow but gradual growth, as the game began to gain some popularity and reach out to the lower middle and working classes.

1884-5 to 1889-0. During these five years, the game took off. This was a period of rapid growth with the number of teams increasing five times in as many years to well over 200. Both the success and the style of play of Hancock's Cardiff team in 1885-6 had a strong impact, particularly on the numbers of school and street teams in following seasons. Working men were now playing in large numbers.

1890-1 to 1896-7. This was the high summer for Cardiff (and Welsh) rugby teams in terms of their complete domination of the local sporting scene. Wales secured their first victory over England in 1890; and in 1893 they

Table 3: Cardiff and District Rugby Teams Recorded in the Local Press[14]

Phase	Year	School	Church	Work	Public House	Street	Neighbour-hood	Misc.	Total
Initial Establishment	1870-1						2		**2**
	1871-2	2					1		**3**
	1872-3	1					1		**2**
	1873-4						1		**1**
	1874-5	1					2		**3**
	1875-6	3					4		**7**
	1876-7						3		**3**
Slow Growth	1877-8	2					7	1	**10**
	1878-9	3	1	1			7	1	**13**
	1879-0	2					7	2	**11**
	1880-1	2					13		**15**
	1881-2	3					16		**19**
	1882-3	2	1	1		1	18	1	**24**
	1883-4	2		2	2	2	14	1	**23**
Rapid Growth	1884-5	3		5	4	4	21	4	**41**
	1885-6	4	2	9	2	8	34	3	**62**
	1886-7	12	4	3	1	8	52	2	**82**
	1887-8	13	6	7	2	11	60	6	**105**
	1888-9	10	16	19	4	19	97	5	**170**
	1889-0	19	10	25	7	40	115	12	**228**
Consolida-tion	1890-1	16	15	26	8	41	105	9	**220**
	1891-2	6	11	25	7	33	115	7	**204**
	1892-3	7	11	28	1	38	100	6	**191**
	1893-4	3	22	29	5	31	100	7	**197**
	1894-5	6	17	35	6	25	136	10	**235**
	1895-6	2	25	43	7	23	125	11	**236**
	1896-7	7	22	24	4	27	129	7	**220**
Contrac-tion	1897-8	4	19	21	2	18	104	6	**174**
	1898-9	3	14	13	1	8	86	11	**136**
	1899-0	4	12	4		7	79	8	**114**

14 Compiled from the *South Wales Daily News* and *Western Mail*. See footnote 10.

won their first Triple Crown. Cardiff were playing attractive and successful rugby against the best sides in the country. The number of teams in the Cardiff area consolidated at an average of over 200 each season. Working-class players dominated in terms of playing numbers.

1897-8 to 1899-1900. In the previous phase, participation in the game had probably reached a level of saturation which could not be sustained, so the final years of the century saw a process of rationalisation and contraction, though the number of clubs was still substantial. For the first time, rugby faced serious competition from association football, which was at last beginning to attract adherents in substantial numbers.

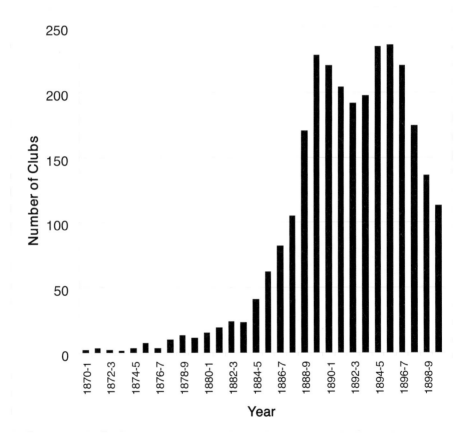

Figure 1: Annual Numbers of Cardiff and District Rugby Teams[15]

---

15   Compiled from the *South Wales Daily News* and *Western Mail*. See footnote 10.

Perhaps the most important causal factor accounting for this astonishing growth in participation in the game was the dramatic demographic change which occurred in the area over the period, in particular during the 1880s and 1890s when Cardiff's population doubled.

Table 4: Population of Cardiff and District 1871-1901[16]

Census Year	Cardiff	Penarth and Barry	Total
1871	57,400	3,600	61,000
1881	82,800	6,700	89,500
1891	128,900	25,700	154,600
1901	164,300	41,200	205,500

By themselves, the figures in Table 4 do not adequately explain the growth in the number of clubs – why would Cardiff's many new citizens necessarily take up rugby? Indeed, the eventual establishment of association football in Cardiff was at least partly the result of the efforts of migrants from soccer playing areas in England and Scotland. Nevertheless, with rugby firmly entrenched as the preferred sport of both the working and the middle classes in the town by the 1880s, it provided recently arrived citizens with a simple way of quickly identifying with their new community and integrating into its social life. As David Smith and Gareth Williams have shown, rugby helped in-migrants to develop a sense of their Welsh identity[17]. At the same time and at the urban level, it also provided newcomers – through their allegiance to their town team – with a sense of *local* pride and of belonging to their adopted place. Richard Holt argues that the supreme appeal of (association) football lay in its expression of civic pride and identity. The massive expansion of Britain's towns created new problems of identity for their inhabitants. He suggests that, as far as *playing* football was concerned, the neighbourhood was all important. But the inhabitants of streets were also the citizens of new cities and they also needed a cultural expression of their urbanism which went beyond the immediate ties of family and locality.[18] What was true of the English centres of professional soccer was

16   Extracted from John Williams, *Digest of Welsh Historical Statistics*, Volume 1 (Cardiff, 1985), pp. 62-4 (figures rounded off).
17   David Smith and Gareth Williams, *Fields of Praise: The Official History of the Welsh Rugby Union* 1881-1981 (Cardiff, 1980), pp. 103-4.
18   Richard Holt, *Sport and the British: A Modern History* (Oxford, 1989), pp. 166-7.

A typical period advertisement from 1896-7 depicting a soccer match.

just as true of the rugby playing towns of south Wales, in particular Cardiff, which now had one of the best teams in Britain.

Before examining the findings of the research, it might be useful here to consider the position of association football in the town. In contrast to many other parts of Britain, there was very little organised soccer in south Wales before the mid-1890s.[19] With only a tiny handful of association teams in Cardiff during the 1880s, rugby was able to take off with very little competition.

It is a widely held view, even in some rugby reference books, that Cardiff began life as a soccer club but press reports of 1876 make it quite clear that the new club was formed to play rugby.[20] It is also indisputable that both Cardiff's forerunners, Glamorgan FC and Cardiff Wanderers were rugby clubs and there is no hint of their ever having been founded to play association football. It is difficult to establish where this myth originated as there is absolutely no contemporary evidence for it.[21] Newspaper articles published in 1892 on the origins of the leading Welsh clubs referred to Swansea and Newport briefly having soccer roots but no such suggestion was made about Cardiff. Nor does either of the club's two official histories,

---

19   See Brian Lile and David Farmer, "The Early Development of Association Football in South Wales, 1890-1906", *Transactions of the Honourable Society of Cymmrodorion*, (1984), pp. 193-215.

20   See, for example, Lile and Farmer, "Early Development", p. 195, who incorrectly claim Cardiff RFC initially played soccer; *WM* 8-23 Sept. 1876 (club merger).

21   J.R. Jones, *The Encyclopaedia of Rugby Football* (London, 1960), p. 24 claims Cardiff was founded as an association football club and then turned to rugby in 1876. Since this was one of the earliest rugby reference books, used by many later rugby writers, it may be the source of the widely reported but entirely incorrect account of Cardiff's origins.

the first of which was published in 1908, make any reference at all to this clearly erroneous claim.[22]

Founded in 1881-2 and initially based around the clergy at Roath church, St. Margaret's was the first association club in Cardiff. For a number of years, St. Margaret's was Cardiff's *only* soccer club and so they often had difficulty in finding opponents, even having to rely in January 1882 on the members of the Cardiff club to give them a game, which the rugby players won 4-2. "There was not a large attendance."[23] Such was the lack of interest in soccer locally that in 1883 one supporter informed the press that it was "useless to form a club in Cardiff" unless other clubs were set up in the neighbourhood.[24] A new arrival from Birmingham complained shortly afterwards that "since coming to Cardiff I have not found one club playing the Association game."[25] The limited impact of soccer in the region meant that when North Wales played the South in 1884, the most southerly players came from as far north as Welshpool and Oswestry.[26] Following the one-all draw in the 1885 international with England, "Old Stager" remarked that in south Wales, "Association football is almost, if not entirely, at a discount."[27] In 1887, he was able to report *some* growth, but while he noted "no fewer than four clubs" in Cardiff, there were then over eighty rugby teams in the town.[28] The four clubs were Cardiff Scottish, Cardiff Villa, White Star and St. Margaret's. Some months later, the first three of these amalgamated to form the first Cardiff AFC but this club had little success and it soon folded.[29]

Two years later in 1889, the town still had only four soccer clubs.[30] However, on one Monday during the same season, the local press recorded forty-two rugby matches involving seventy-seven Cardiff district teams.[31]

---

22 *Cardiff Times* 1 Oct. 1892 (Swansea); *SWDN* 31 Oct. 1892 (Newport); *Cardiff Times* 3 Sept. 1892 (Cardiff); C.S. Arthur, *The Cardiff Rugby Football Club: History and Statistics, 1876-1906* (Cardiff, 1908); D.E. Davies, *Cardiff Rugby Club: History and Statistics, 1876-1975: "The Greatest"* (Cardiff, 1975).
23 *SWDN* 16 Jan. 1882, *WM* 17 Jan. 1882. In later seasons, they also played soccer matches against both Penarth and Cardiff Harlequins rugby clubs.
24 *WM* 9 Nov. 1883.
25 *WM* 15 Nov. 1883.
26 Martin Johnes and Ian Garland, " 'The New Craze': football and society in north-east Wales, c.1870-90", *Welsh History Review*, 22, 2 (2004), pp 302-3.
27 *SWDN* 16 Mar. 1885.
28 *SWDN* 25 Mar. 1887. See Table 3 figures for 1886-7.
29 *SWDN* 28 Nov. 1887; *WM* 5 Dec. 1887.
30 *WM* 16 Dec. 1889. They were St. Margaret's, St. Saviour's (Splott), Western Mail and Cardiff Scottish.
31 *SWDN* 25 Nov. 1889; *WM* 25 Nov. 1889.

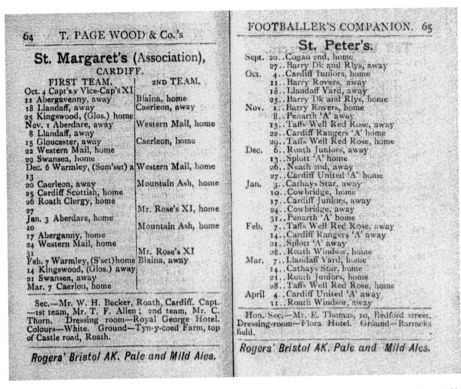

64   T. PAGE WOOD & Co.'s

St. Margaret's (Association),
CARDIFF.

FIRST TEAM.   2ND TEAM.
Oct. 4 Capt's v Vice-Cap's XI
11 Abergavenny, away   Blaina, home
18 Llandaff, away   Caerleon, away
25 Kingswood, (Glos.) home
Nov. 1 Aberdare, away   Western Mail, home
8 Llandaff, away
15 Gloucester, away   Caerleon, home
22 Western Mail, home
29 Swansea, home
Dec. 6 Warmley, (Som'set) a Western Mail, home
13
20 Caerleon, away   Mountain Ash, home
25 Cardiff Scottish, home
26 Roath Clergy, home
27   Mr. Rose's XI, home
Jan. 3 Aberdare, home
10   Mountain Ash, home
17 Abergavenny, home
24 Western Mail, home
31   Mr. Rose's XI
Feb. 7 Warmley, (S'set) home Blaina, away
14 Kingswood, (Glos.) away
21 Swansea, away
Mar. 7 Caerleon, home

Sec.—Mr. W. H. Becker, Roath, Cardiff. Capt.
—1st team, Mr. T. F. Allen ; 2nd team, Mr. C.
Thorn.   Dressing room—Royal George Hotel.
Colours—White. Ground—Tyn-y-coed Farm, top
of Castle road, Roath.

Rogers' Bristol AK. Pale and Mild Ales.

FOOTBALLER'S COMPANION. 65

St. Peter's.

Sept. 20..Cogan 2nd, home
27..Barry Dk and Rlys, away
Oct. 4..Cardiff Juniors, home
11..Barry Rovers, away
18..Llandaff Yard, away
25..Barry Dk and Rlys, home
Nov. 1..Barry Rovers, home
8..Penarth 'A' away
15..Taffs Well Red Rose, away
22..Cardiff Rangers 'A' home
29..Taffs Well Red Rose, home
Dec. 6..Roath Juniors, away
13..Splott 'A' home
26..Neath 2nd, away
27..Cardiff United 'A' home
Jan. 3..Cathays Star, away
10..Cowbridge, home
17..Cardiff Juniors, away
24..Cowbridge, away
31..Penarth 'A' home
Feb. 7..Taffs Well Red Rose, away
14..Cardiff Rangers 'A' away
21..Splott 'A' away
28..Roath Windsor, home
Mar. 7..Llandaff Yard, home
14..Cathays Star, home
21..Roath Juniors, home
28..Taffs Well Red Rose, home
April 4..Cardiff United 'A' away
11..Roath Windsor, away

Hon. Sec.—Mr. E. Thomas, 10, Bedford street.
Dressing-room—Flora Hotel. Ground—Barracks
field.

Rogers' Bristol AK. Pale and Mild Ales.

St. Margaret's AFC 1890-1 fixture list. Note the need to refer to "Association". "Llandaff" probably refers to the Cathedral School. The adjoining page reveals St Peter's were not yet the power they were to become in local rugby.

A local football handbook for 1890-1 published fixture lists for some seventy Welsh rugby teams, thirty-seven of which were based in Cardiff, but the only soccer teams whose fixture lists were included were those of St. Margaret's First and Second XIs.[32] In 1891, the *Evening Express* tellingly referred to St. Margaret's playing "Association, which is popular in the North and Midlands". It seems that, at a time when association football was flourishing elsewhere, it was just being kept alive in Cardiff by a small handful of enthusiasts.[33] Looking back in 1901, by which time the game was beginning to grow in popularity in Cardiff, one soccer official recalled the difficulty he had had ten years earlier in 1891 in finding shopkeepers who could even supply balls for his new club.

32 *Cardiff and South Wales Footballer's Companion: 1890-91* (Cardiff, 1890), pp. 3-67.

33 *Evening Express* 5 Mar. 1891; Tony Mason, *Association Football and English Society 1863-1915* (Brighton, 1981), p. 31.

To find a salesman who could at once supply a few 'soccer' balls was no easy task. To carry one of those funny round balls through the streets meant running the gauntlet of curious onlookers ... [my club] used a pitch at Sophia Gardens and very often our only 'crowd' would at first consist of our linesmen and perhaps one or two reserves. It was amusing to hear the comments of the followers and supporters of the Rugby clubs playing on a pitch a few yards away ... "What the something game do they call this?" was a mild example of the remarks.[34]

The local organisation of soccer remained poor in the early 1890s. The *SWDN* reported in October 1890 that the "isolated effort [in Cardiff] ... to awaken interest in the association game, has not so far been attended with any large measure of success." "Socker Player" from London complained to the same paper in January 1891 that he could never find any information on league matches in south Wales whilst "Association Enthusiast" responded, "The game has not yet attained to great popularity in Wales ... It is only recently that any interest has been taken".[35] The South Wales League was established in 1890-1, but it was not well organised at first. Of the thirteen teams which entered, only seven remained by the end of the season. The sole Cardiff representatives, St. Margaret's, played only one league match, prompting one correspondent to comment, perhaps with some justification, "they might as well not be in it". He added that neither Newport nor Swansea possessed a club of any significance.[36] Cardiff AFC then re-formed

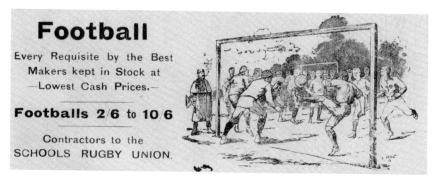

By 1908, when this advertisement was published by a local retailer, it had evidently become much easier to obtain soccer balls in Cardiff.

34 *Evening Express* 29 Apr. 1901.
35 *SWDN* 27 Oct. 1890 (isolated effort), 29 Jan. (Socker Player), 31 Jan. 1891 (Enthusiast).
36 Peter Corrigan, *100 Years of Welsh Soccer: The Official History of the Football Association of Wales* (Cardiff, [1976]), p. 10 (league); *SWDN* 8 Apr. 1891 (St. Margaret's).

in August 1891. However, they received virtually no gate money and in 1895 they dropped out of both the Welsh Cup and the South Wales and Monmouthshire Cup. The club then collapsed again after being expelled from the Western League for failing to complete their fixtures. The pioneers of soccer in Cardiff, St. Margaret's, eventually disbanded in 1899, just when the game there was taking off.[37]

Therefore, against this background of initial public indifference to soccer and its poor organisation, rugby in Cardiff, and in south Wales generally, had virtually a free run for over twenty years. But interest did at last begin to stir during the later 1890s. Even though there was not a great deal of local soccer to report initially, the *SWDN* began to give greater coverage to the game in England, particularly after the formation of the Football League in 1888. As a result of the influence of teachers who had been educated at soccer playing training colleges, Cardiff's elementary and higher grade schools started taking up the game from around 1895.[38] In addition, the continual flow of migrants into Cardiff during the 1890s now included many newcomers who had already acquired a love of association football *before* they arrived. Almost all of the St. Margaret's team in 1890, for instance, had learned the game outside Wales.[39] In 1893, the *SWDN* observed, "Geordies and Caledonians, "Sockers" to a man, who hold aloof from the [Arms] Park nowadays will suffice to keep the other game going." [40] The number of association teams in Cardiff began to grow steadily from around 1893-4 but, nevertheless, the game still lagged behind in popularity. By the turn of the century, there were probably as many soccer as rugby teams in Cardiff, although many of these were junior clubs and at this time there were no "first class" soccer outfits equivalent to Cardiff rugby club. In mid-September 1899, Riverside AFC – the forerunner of Cardiff City FC – was formed, some twenty-five years after the parent clubs of Cardiff RFC. It was necessary for the new club to include "Association" in their title, since "Riverside Football Club" had already been adopted by a long-established rugby club, then playing in the Cardiff and District Leagues.[41] Attendances at club rugby matches in Cardiff at the end of the century still far outstripped

---

37 *WM* 7 Aug. 1891 (CAFC), 5 Mar. 1894 and *SWDN* 5 Mar. 1894 (gate money), 4 Nov. 1895 (cups), 17 Jan. 1896 (expulsion); *SWDN* 2 May 1899 (St. Margaret's).

38 *WM* 8 Oct. 1894.

39 *SWDN* 27 Oct. 1890.

40 *SWDN* 4 Dec. 1893; see also Martin Johnes, "That Other Game: A Social History of Soccer in South Wales c.1906-39" (Ph.D. thesis, University of Wales, Cardiff, 1998), pp. 17-18.

41 *SWDN* 28 Aug. 1899, 22 Sept. 1899.

Riverside's fixtures in 1890-1. There had been a rugby team in Riverside from 1886-7, thirteen years before Riverside AFC was formed.

those at soccer. As Martin Johnes puts it, association football was not "able to claim such a pivotal role in working-class culture" as rugby. However, as he also shows, it was during the following decade that soccer quickly began to rival rugby's pre-eminence.[42]

Though soccer was a potential competitor for the hearts and minds of local sportsmen, rugby enjoyed a different relationship with cricket. Many of the first football clubs were founded by cricketers wanting to keep active during the winter months. As we have seen, cricketers were responsible for bringing an early version of football to Cardiff in the late 1860s. It is also evident from a comparison of club team and membership lists that many local sportsmen during the 1870s and 1880s played for Cardiff (and, for that matter, it was a similar story in Newport and Swansea) at both cricket and rugby.[43] Whether cricket had any *major* influence in the formation of

---

42 Johnes, *Soccer and Society*, p. 3, passim; Johnes, 'Other Game' passim.

43 *Bridgend Chronicle* 20 Mar. 1868; W. Alan Thomas, *Cardiff Cricket Club: 1867-1967* (Cardiff, 1967), p. 20; Cardiff Cricket Club Members Lists 1883 and 1884.

rugby teams in Cardiff in the boom years of the 1880s and 1890s, however, is open to question. In his account of early cricket in south Wales, Andrew Hignell provides a chronological list of the founding dates of cricket clubs from 1785 to 1890.[44] This reveals that over thirty Cardiff cricket clubs were in existence before similarly named rugby clubs. However, merely sharing a name does not necessarily prove any relationship. Moreover, a mere thirty out of the many hundreds of rugby teams which were formed at this time represents only a very small proportion. This suggests that cricket's influence on club formation may not have been especially strong, in Cardiff at least. On the other hand, of course, some rugby clubs could have been formed by cricketers who chose to adopt a different name, but finding much evidence for this may now be virtually impossible. It is conceivable that from the 1880s, given rugby's popularity by then, the process was occasionally reversed. For instance, the Blue Anchor, Hayes, Radyr, Rookwood Rangers and Star cricket clubs all appeared the season *after* similarly named rugby clubs. Of course, there were always strong informal individual links between the two sports and a review of cricket match press reports will identify many names of prominent and less prominent rugby footballers from the area.

Analysis of Cardiff's Clubs

If it is difficult to estimate the number of teams accurately, then any attempt to categorise them reliably is even more problematic. Previous research on nineteenth-century English soccer, cricket and rugby has identified the existence of teams with a variety of origins, including schools, churches and chapels, workplaces, public houses, streets and local communities and these groupings were adopted in this analysis.[45] But, as Dave Russell reminds us, such categories are inevitably loose and overlapping, while Martin Johnes advises caution when assuming that a link with an institution is necessarily suggested by a club name.[46] Even with a good knowledge of the social history and geography of the town, categorising Cardiff's rugby clubs based on their names alone is not straightforward. "St. Peter's", for instance, at different

---

44 Andrew K. Hignell, *A 'Favourit' Game: Cricket in south Wales before 1914* (Cardiff, 1992), pp. 217-220.

45 See Mason, *Association Football and English Society*, pp. 21, 24-31; Holt, *Sport and the British*, pp. 150-1; Huggins, "Spread of Association Football", pp. 311-112; Stuart Barlow, "The Diffusion of 'Rugby' Football in the Industrialized Context of Rochdale, 1868-1890: A Conflict of Ethical Values", *IJHS*, 10, 1 (1993), pp. 61-5.

46 Dave Russell, *Football and the English: A Social History of Association Football in England, 1863-1995* (Preston, 1997), pp. 14-15; Johnes, 'Other Game', p. 88.

times could be a school, street or parish team. "Cambrian" was probably a pub side, but a workplace or neighbourhood club is also a possibility. There might be some uncertainty, therefore, about the precise numbers shown in each classification but, despite the inherent difficulties in this approach, it is believed that the findings are sufficiently robust to make comparisons with earlier studies and to draw generalised conclusions.

Drawing partly on DD Molyneux's unpublished research on late nineteenth-century cricket and soccer in Birmingham, Tony Mason refers to three particular pre-existing institutions which played an important part in the origin of soccer clubs. These were churches and chapels; workplaces; and public houses[47]. However, none of these categories seems to have been quite so relevant in the formation of rugby teams in Cardiff, where the evidence appears to support

A favourite with supporters, the Cambrian (renamed the Cambrian Tap) in St. Mary Street was also the probable home of the Cambrian team of the 1890s.   Courtesy of SA Brain and Co.

Holt who emphasises the importance of locally organised "neighbourhood" clubs.[48]

---

47   Mason, *Association Football and English Society,* pp. 24-31.

48   Holt, *Sport and the British,* pp. 150-1 also draws on Molyneux's research (Birmingham), as well as that by Tranter (Stirling), Crump (Leicester) and Rees (Liverpool).

The detailed research still has to be carried out for other rugby areas of Wales but it is likely that Cardiff was not noticeably different from the rest of the country in this respect.[49]

However, before investigating the categories in Cardiff in detail, it is first necessary to comment on the issue of "junior" teams. The term was used throughout the period in a loose and sometimes confusing way. As a consequence, no attempt has been made to classify them as a separate group. Many clubs described themselves as such, for instance, Canton Juniors and Roath Juniors. Whilst these were probably examples of boys or youths teams, they were not all necessarily so. Sometimes the term was used merely to distinguish a club from a more senior one in the locality. Adult sides are often described as "junior" clubs in the contemporary press. For example when the Cardiff and District Football Union introduced leagues in the 1890s, the first and second divisions were described as "senior" and "junior" respectively.[50] Until recently, the Welsh Junior RU, (which was formed in 1904 as the "Union of Welsh Junior Leagues"), was the name of the body which represented adult clubs not in membership of the WRU.[51] Sometimes "junior" was used to describe a club's second XV, but the existence of a junior club in a locality did not necessarily mean that such a team was attached to a senior one. Usually they were separately run organisations (e.g. Cardiff Juniors were not part of Cardiff FC). The issue is further complicated by those many juvenile teams which did *not* incorporate junior into their title, such as Melingriffith Stars.

During the 1889-90 and 1891-2 seasons, rugby reports in the *South Wales Daily News* and the *Western Mail* revealed the age profiles of fourteen local clubs (only three of which, incidentally, described themselves as "junior"). These were: Bute Engineers Second XV (15-16); Cardiff Juniors (16); Canton Rovers (11-13); Clyde Rovers (15); Criterion (14-16); Grangetown Red Stars (15-17); Llandaff Yard Stars (14); Longcross Juniors (13-14); Melingriffith Stars (12-16); Railway Street Crusaders (12); Rennie Stars (10-12); Saltmede Rangers (14); Star Juniors (13-14); and Tongwynlais White Stars (14-15).[52] The ages range from ten to seventeen years, so there appears to have been

---

49   For research in west Wales, see Jack S. Rickus," 'A Fair Field of Spectators' The Development of Rugby Football in the Swansea, Neath and Llanelli Region, 1864-1900" (M.A. thesis, Swansea University, 2011).

50   *SWDN* 10 Nov. 1894. See Appendix 3.

51   Renamed the Welsh Districts Rugby Union, it was dissolved in 2009 and all "district" clubs were affiliated to the WRU.

52   At least six of these were named after streets: Clyde, Longcross, Railway, Rennie, Saltmede, and (probably) Star.

Penarth United, a youth team, with the 1898-9 Cardiff FC Junior Cup. The captain (with the ball) was Edward Best. A Penarth United boys team existed as early as 1888.

Howard Evans

no special attempt to standardise formal age groups at that time. Presumably clubs arranged fixtures as best as they could with those of a similar profile. However, matches between boys or youths teams and adult clubs were not uncommon. In 1892, for instance, the youngsters of the Penarth United club created a surprise when they defeated the Cardiff Police team.[53]

It might be assumed that, by their very nature, such teams were ephemeral but some, at least, were as well organised as their adult counterparts. Despite having an average playing age of only fifteen, Clyde Rovers (a street team) still published their twenty-six fixture programme for 1890-1 in a local football handbook. Only some of these matches appear to have been against other junior teams.[54] Canton Rovers (11-13) were reported to have won all of their twenty-two fixtures in 1889-90, and they were also undefeated during the following season. Their secretary was then only

---

53   Gordon Westcott, *A Century on the Beat: A History of Police Rugby Football in the South Wales Constabulary Area* (Bridgend, 1992), p. 91.

54   *Cardiff and South Wales Footballer's Companion: 1890-91*, p. 46.

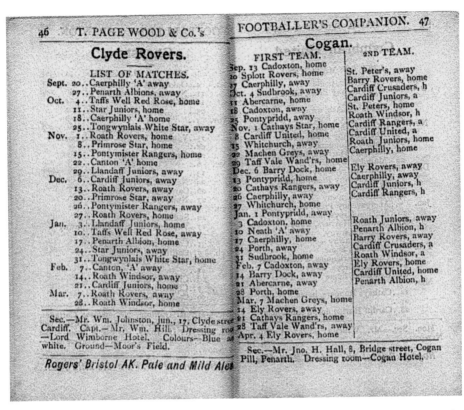

Clyde Rovers, a street team for fifteen year-olds, had a full fixture list in 1890-1. The Cogan club, whose fixtures are alongside, joined the WFU two years later.

fourteen years old.[55] In 1889-90, Railway Street Crusaders (12) not only appointed a captain and vice-captain but also had a secretary and treasurer.[56] The apparent independence of these sometimes very young Victorian rugby footballers contrasts with the modern practice of close supervision of junior players.

As early as 1877-8, there are references to under-fifteen matches being played by Cardiff against Newport and Roath.[57] Evidence of the organisation of junior matches is very hard to locate but an early example from Newport in March 1879, when the captain of the winning team was only twelve years old, reveals a surprising degree of sophistication.

---

55 *SWDN* 19 Jan., 13 Apr. 1891.

56 *SWDN* 1 Nov. 1889.

57 *WM* 24 Dec. 1877 (Newport), 3 Jan. 1878 (Roath).

To such a height has the rage for football grown that in most of the schools of the town clubs have been formed, and these juveniles draft regulations, send out challenges ... to play a match on a given date with all the formalities attendant upon clubs whose members embrace those of riper years. Only on Saturday two school clubs ... styled Green versus Chandler [played each other]. A field had been engaged ... the ground properly marked out, goal posts erected, a systematic plan of battle arranged with captains, backs, quarter backs, half backs, three quarter backs and forwards regularly drawn out ... some of the combatants underwent an enforced training in anticipation of the event.[58]

There is no reason to suppose that such arrangements were at all unusual elsewhere in south Wales. Richard Holt reminds us that Victorian Britain was a very young society with about a third of the population aged under fourteen, so it is no surprise, therefore, that many of the teams catered for young players.[59] From 1896-7, the Cardiff club successfully instituted an age restricted junior cup competition, which regularly attracted entries from around sixteen teams, with the final being played at Cardiff Arms Park.[60] In addition, an under-nineteen league was organised by the Cardiff and District Football Union in 1899 and another for under-seventeens followed soon afterwards. Such age restricted competitions, however, were frequently plagued by disputes about the use of over-age players.

Undoubtedly, the personnel of junior clubs must have overlapped with those of the first category adopted in this analysis: *school teams*. Although schools made up only a small percentage of the total number of teams in the period, their impact on the game in Cardiff, through the development of players, was far greater, of course, than is suggested by the figures in Table 3. As demonstrated earlier, the role of schools in the early development of rugby in Wales was crucial. Private schools in the locality were heavily involved throughout the period and they made a significant contribution to the game. Monkton House, in particular, under the guidance of Henry Shewbrooks, was a highly regarded rugby nursery for Cardiff.[61] Several Welsh internationals began playing at such institutions, for example, Frank Hill, George Young and William Cope (Monkton House); Albert Hybart and Norman Biggs (Cardiff Collegiate); and Percy Bush (St. Mary's Hall and Penarth Collegiate). The Wesleyan School also produced several prominent

---

58   *SWDN* 10 Mar. 1879.
59   Holt, *Sport and the British*, p. 141.
60   *SWDN* 22 Oct. 1896.
61   *WM* 30 June 1894.

Cornish-born Percy Bennett was one of two men capped by Wales directly from the Cardiff Harlequins club.

Cardiff players, including at least two internationals, Percy Bennett (Cardiff Harlequins) and Syd Nicholls, whilst his more famous brother, Gwyn Nicholls, almost certainly began his illustrious rugby career there.[62]

However, it was not until 1885-6 that the elementary schools, which educated children up to the age of fourteen, began to have any noticeable influence on Cardiff rugby. That they had any at all during the nineteenth century appears to have been largely unrecognised. Carl French's study of the Welsh Schools RU, which was formed in 1903, suggests that there was little rugby organised by the elementary schools at this time because of the lack of school playing fields and because of the emphasis placed on physical drill rather than organised games.[63] However, discussing the forthcoming 1888-9 rugby season, the *Cardiff Argus* reported that "Every school in the neighbourhood has now its football club among its students and those belonging to different schools often have matches arranged between them".[64]

Whilst this might be an exaggeration, at least twenty-three elementary school rugby teams in the Cardiff area were identified in the press from the mid-1880s onwards.[65] It may be no co-incidence that the number of school teams playing the game increased markedly in 1886-7, the season which followed "Hancock's year," Cardiff's most successful season.[66] It is evident, therefore, that rugby *was* played by elementary school teams in Cardiff in the nineteenth century. In the light of French's observations, the likelihood is that, as in the earlier example from Newport, these teams were largely

---

62   *SWDN* 28 Nov. 1884 (Hill); *Evening Express* 15 Sept. 1888 (Young); *WM* 19 Mar. 1892 (Cope); *SWDN* 20 Nov. 1882 (Hybart), 17 Oct. 1884 (Biggs); *Evening Express* 6 Apr. 1901 (Bush), 5 Jan. 1891 (Wesleyan).

63   Carl French, "The History of the Welsh Schools Rugby Union 1903-1939" (M.Ed. thesis, University of Wales, Cardiff, 1991), pp. 1-52.

64   *Cardiff Argus* 26 Sept. 1888.

65   The elementary schools whose matches were reported in the *WM* and *SWDN* between 1885-6 and 1896-7 included: Adamsdown, Albany Road, Canton, Cathays, Court Road, Cogan, Crwys Road, Eleanor Street, Grange, Llandough, Radnor Road, St. David's RC, St. John's, St. Mary's, St. Paul's RC, Severn Road, South Church Street, Splottlands, Stacey Road, Taffs Well, Whitchurch Board, Whitchurch National and Wood Street.

66   See Table 3.

run by the boys themselves outside school hours. Certainly, their opponents were not always restricted to other school sides and this may suggest that the teams were generally not supervised by schoolmasters, until around the time the Cardiff Schools Rugby Union was established a few years later.

Cardiff's first secondary school, which catered for pupils aged twelve to seventeen, also played rugby. David Parry-Jones's biography of Gwyn Nicholls suggests that, while he *may* have attended Cardiff Higher Grade School at Howard Gardens, he could not have learned his rugby there, since it was a soccer school.[67] This conclusion is understandable since the voluminous school history claims that football was first played there only in 1896 and that the code adopted then was association.[68] However, newspaper reports confirm that, within weeks of the school opening in 1885, the Higher Grade was turning out rugby teams, though no doubt these were organised by the boys themselves. This continued throughout the nineteenth century and there is no evidence in the press that soccer was being played at the school before 1896. Whether or not Gwyn Nicholls was an old boy, the Higher Grade produced a Welsh international before him in Frank Mills (Swansea and Cardiff), a distinction which is unrecorded in the school history.[69] From 1896-7, Penarth County School was another local secondary school which began to appear in press rugby reports.

The Cardiff Teachers AFC was one of a small number of soccer clubs to emerge in Cardiff in the early 1890s. Their existence should have acted as a warning to the rugby authorities that soccer might eventually be taken up in local schools. In 1895-6, for the first time in over ten years, there were no elementary school rugby matches mentioned in the press and it cannot be a co-incidence that the first reported schoolboy soccer matches took place that season. Shortly afterwards, members of the Cardiff Teachers club initiated the establishment of a Cardiff Schools Association League. By 1899-1900, eleven schools were taking part, while there was also a seven team schools league covering Barry and Penarth. Rugby had clearly failed to take advantage of the lead it had built up in Cardiff's schools and it allowed the initiative to pass to the rival code, at least for the time being. This represented a major capture by soccer in Cardiff and it contributed significantly to the subsequent growth of the game there.

---

67 David Parry-Jones, *Prince Gwyn: Gwyn Nicholls and the First Golden Era of Welsh Rugby* (Bridgend, 1999), p. 20. There is no evidence that Nicholls did attend Howard Gardens.

68 T.J. Foster, *Floreat Howardia: The Story of Howard Gardens Schools Cardiff 1885-1990* (Cardiff, 1990), pp. 27, 50-1.

69 *SWDN* 5 Jan. 1896.

In 1900, it was being claimed that the league had done much to promote soccer in Cardiff.[70] It may be significant that when Barry Grammar School and Cardiff High School opened in 1896 and 1898 respectively, they were both *initially* soccer schools.[71] In response to the growing interest in soccer amongst local youngsters, the Cardiff club donated a cup for competition for boys under seventeen in 1896, "a step in the right direction and one that should be followed in other districts in South Wales" in the opinion of the *SWDN*.[72] However, not until December 1902 was the Cardiff Schools Rugby Union formed and, whilst it was a very healthy offspring with twenty-three schools playing in three divisions, rugby's initial overwhelming advantage had undoubtedly been surrendered.[73] Local rugby administrators had clearly failed to take heed of the *Western Mail*'s warning as early as 1894 that "Association legislators are a bit energetic and only need half a chance to find their way to the front".[74]

Tony Mason suggests that almost a quarter of soccer clubs in England may have owed their origin to religious organisations.[75] A rather different picture emerges in Cardiff rugby, however, where throughout the 1890s, the category of *church teams* comprised only around 10% of the total. It should also be remembered that, as Richard Holt suggests, "parish" teams may often have been in reality neighbourhood clubs run without any particular church involvement.[76] Throughout south Wales, the number of clubs with religious affiliation or foundation was relatively small. Unlike English soccer and rugby league, there are no examples in Wales of major rugby clubs with church or chapel origins. St. John's Canton is the first church name to appear in the Cardiff press in 1878-9. Such early references were rare, though by the 1890s church based teams were more frequently mentioned. From the mid-1890s, the numbers were boosted by Boys Brigade, Church Lads Brigade and YMCA teams.

Of course, there may have been some clubs whose connection with a church was not evident in their name and who are not, therefore, included in the category totals, but this would also apply to the data collected in

---

70   Lile and Farmer, "Early Development", pp. 204-5; *SWDN* 5 May 1900 (Cardiff league), 19 Dec. 1899 (Barry and Penarth).

71   Bassett, *Rugby Football in Barry*, p. [130]; Gwyn Prescott, *The Best and Happiest Team: A History of Cardiff High School Old Boys Rugby Football Club 1929-1978* (Cardiff, 1979), p. 1.

72   *SWDN* 22 Oct. 1896, 10 Feb. 1897.

73   *Cardiff Schools Rugby Union Handbook Season 1987-88* (Cardiff, 1987), p. [4].

74   *WM* 24 Jan. 1894.

75   Mason, *Association Football and English Society*, p. 26.

76   Holt, *Sport and the British*, pp. 150-1.

St. Teilo's, an Anglican parish team from Cathays, won the District Union shield in 1903-4. The captain, wearing a cap, was S. Dimond. This photograph was taken at the Arms Park at the rear of the Cardiff and County Club on Westgate Street.

Cardiff and District RU

other comparable research. The figures suggest, therefore, that "muscular Christians" – who believed in the moralising influence of vigorous sports – did not have a particularly prominent role in organising rugby in Cardiff. Some historians like Dunning and Sheard, and also Adair, have argued that church groups may have regarded soccer as more "civilised" and so this might explain their reluctance to reach out to the working class by establishing rugby clubs.[77] Gareth Williams suggests that far from curbing disorderly behaviour and violence, rugby could incite it. It could also encourage drinking. In his study of rugby in Rochdale, Stuart Barlow points to the game's intrinsic violence as a deterrent to missionary zeal. For these reasons then, Gareth Morgan contends, some nonconformists in particular

---

77   Eric Dunning and Kenneth Sheard, *Barbarians, Gentlemen and Players: A Sociological Study of the Development of Rugby Football* (London, 2005 edn.), pp. 120-3; Daryl Adair, "Competing or Complementary Forces: The 'Civilising' Process and the Commitment to Winning in Nineteenth Century English Rugby and Association Football", *Canadian Journal of History of Sport*, XXIV, 2 (1993), p. 54.

were sceptical about the moralising influence of rugby. Barlow's research also reveals a remarkable similarity to Cardiff when he concludes that churches provided "a significant, though *relatively minor* input into the diffusion of the sport" in Rochdale.[78] However, Daryl Adair's argument that "the class based nature" of rugby alienated working-class parishioners, causing "muscular Christians" to abandon rugby, cannot explain the church's relatively low level of involvement in the socially democratic game played in Cardiff and south Wales.

The majority of the religious institution teams in Cardiff were associated with the Anglican Church, for example, St. Agnes, St. Andrew's, St. German's, St. Mary's and St. Vincent's; but increasingly the period saw the emergence of Roman Catholic parish teams, which were to have, and indeed still do have, a strong and distinctive influence on the strength and character of Cardiff rugby. Cardiff's large Irish community was overwhelmingly working class and its origin lay in the flood of immigrants who arrived during and immediately after the Famine in the 1840s and 1850s. Their lives were largely ones of squalor and poverty but by the late 1880s, living conditions had improved sufficiently for their descendants to be able to take up sport in their spare time.[79] The first Catholic club, St. David's, appeared in 1887-8 and, within a couple of years, it had become one of the strongest in Cardiff and had joined the WFU. Amongst its playing membership were many with Irish surnames, though these would have been mostly Welsh born, since large scale Irish immigration had ceased by this time.[80] Dai Fitzgerald was the most prominent product of this club and he was twice capped by Wales from Cardiff in 1894 before turning professional. Although born in Cardiff, he was often referred to in the press as an Irishman and it was rumoured – perhaps unreliably given his working-class background – that the Irish selectors were interested in him. He was not the only St. David's man to join Cardiff, as by 1891-2 there were five former players in the senior club and it appears that these and other defections led to the club disbanding.[81] St. David's re-formed a few years later but, in the meantime, they were

---

78   Gareth Williams, *1905 and All That: Essays on Rugby Football, Sport and Welsh Society* (Llandysul, 1991), pp. 73-4; Barlow, "The Diffusion of 'Rugby' Football", pp. 54, 63 (italics added); Gareth Morgan, "Rugby and Revivalism: Sport and Religion in Edwardian Wales", *IJHS*, 22, 3 (2005), p. 435.

79   J.V. Hickey, "The Origin and Growth of the Irish Community in Cardiff", (M.A. thesis, University of Wales, Cardiff, 1959), p. 113.

80   Paul O'Leary, *Immigration and Integration: The Irish in Wales, 1798-1922* (Cardiff, 2002), p. 105.

81   *SWDN* 30 Nov. 1891.

Cardiff's first Catholic club, the re-formed St. David's with the District Union shield in 1901-2.
Cardiff and District RU

replaced by other strong Catholic parish teams like St. Paul's and St. Peter's, who would attract hundreds of supporters to their matches. Both became leading clubs in Cardiff during the 1890s.[82] St. Paul's were based in Newtown, one of Cardiff's early Irish communities, and were sometimes referred to as "the Irishmen" in match reports, while their teams and officers were dominated by men with Irish surnames.[83] Located in Roath, a place of later Catholic Irish settlement, St. Peter's ("The Rocks") were first mentioned in the press in 1888.[84]

There does not appear to have been any obvious religious segregation in fixtures and, in any case, the establishment of Cardiff and District leagues in 1894-5 ensured this could not happen. For example, in 1896-7, St. Peter's completed their twenty-four match season without defeat and almost all of

---

82   See Appendix 3 (2) for the competition successes of St. Paul's and St. Peter's at this time.

83   *WM* 21 Aug. 1897; *SWDN* 1 Aug. 1896, 5 Apr. 1899.

84   See D.F. Childs, *One Hundred Years of the "Rocks": the History of St. Peter's R.F.C. 1886/1986* (Cardiff, 1986).

their fixtures were against clubs with no obvious Catholic or Irish affiliation.[85] From the 1890s, "Cardiff Irishmen" were not only representing their town, but also Wales, and consequently they were becoming heroes of the wider community. After Dai Fitzgerald, the son of Irish parents, scored all Wales's points in the 7-0 victory over Scotland in 1894, in a public display of pride, he was chaired by supporters through the streets of Cardiff. Shortly afterwards, he was presented with a gold watch for his performance by his "local admirers".[86] Rugby allowed Cardiff's Irish, perhaps for the first time, to visibly display their commitment to their home town and to Wales.[87] An in-depth study has not been undertaken here, but it appears that, although there may have still been antipathy and even occasional hostility to this community in general, rugby playing Catholics of Irish descent experienced nothing like the level of prejudice encountered by their soccer counterparts in Scotland.[88] The experience in Cardiff, however, was mirrored in Liverpool, where research on Irish soccer clubs there has shown that they suffered from no discernible hostility and, indeed, the sport acted as a bridgehead with the local community.[89] Though ignored by JV Hickey in his study of the Irish in Cardiff, Paul O'Leary briefly comments on rugby's role as a means of assisting the social integration and assimilation of the Irish into the wider community of both Cardiff and Wales.[90] The contribution of rugby to this process in Cardiff warrants further study.

---

85   *SWDN* 3 May 1897.

86   *WM* 5 Feb. 1894; *SWDN* 21 Feb. 1894. Fitzgerald won only two caps but in 1895 joined Leigh just before the Northern Union was established. He then joined Batley with whom he won three Challenge Cups. John M. Jenkins, Duncan Pierce and Timothy Auty, *Who's Who of Welsh International Rugby Players* (Wrexham, 1991), p. 59.

87   Anon.,"Some Famous Footballers: Cardiff Rugby Football Club", *St. Peter's Magazine*, V. 2 (1925), pp. 43-5.

88   See G.P.T. Finn, "Racism, Religion and Social Prejudice: Irish Catholic Clubs, Soccer and Scottish Society – I The Historical Roots of Prejudice", *IJHS*, 8, 1 (1991), pp. 370-397; G.P.T. Finn, "Racism, Religion and Social Prejudice: Irish Catholic Clubs, Soccer and Scottish Society – II Social Identities and Conspiracy Theories", *IJHS*, 8, 3 (1991), pp. 374-397; Daniel Burdsey and Robert Chappell, " 'And If You know Your History ...' An Examination of the Formation of Football Clubs in Scotland and their Role in the Construction of Social Identity", *Sports Historian*, 20, 1 (2001), pp. 94-106.

89   David Kennedy and Peter Kennedy, "Ambiguity, Complexity and Convergence: The Evolution of Liverpool's Irish Football Clubs", *IJHS*, 25, 7 (2007), pp. 895, 909.

90   Hickey, *The Irish Community*, passim; O'Leary, *Immigration and Integration*, pp. 304-5.

It perhaps comes as a surprise to discover that there were also several teams with a nonconformist background in Victorian Cardiff. The conventional view is that Welsh chapels were vehemently hostile to football and there is plenty of evidence to support this.[91] However, the existence of several apparently chapel-based teams indicates that, in Cardiff at least, opposition from nonconformists may not always have been total. Perhaps disapproval of rugby was less strong in the larger urban centres, where a more tolerant attitude to sport may have prevailed, as Tony Mason noted was the case in England.[92] This appears to be supported by Gareth Morgan's study of the Welsh religious "Revival" of 1904-5 which reveals that it had little impact on rugby in Cardiff.[93] The existence during the 1880s and 1890s of teams such as Bethany, Loudoun Wesleyans, Merthyr Street Mission, Presbyterians, Wesleyan Rovers, Wesleyans and Zion Harlequins may therefore suggest a greater level of tolerance than is often supposed.[94] However, these were almost certainly junior sides.

Of Irish parentage, Dai Fitzgerald played twice for Wales before enjoying a successful career in the Northern Union.

The extent of direct involvement of church officials in local rugby is difficult to assess. The St. Peter's club history records that its first secretary in 1888-9 was also secretary of the Catholic Young Men's Society, while the earliest team photograph of 1896-7 includes the St. Peter's rector who was the club president. This may indicate that the rugby club had at least the approval of the parish church, though the extent of its support and involvement can only be guessed at.[95] However, though Hickey makes no specific reference to sport in his study of Cardiff's Irish community, he shows that local Catholic clergy took the lead in developing a range of parochial

---

91   Gareth Williams, "From Popular Culture to Public Cliché: Image and Identity in Wales, 1890-1914" in J.A. Mangan, *Pleasure, Profit, Proselytism: British Culture and Sport at Home and Abroad 1700-1914* (London, 1988), pp. 132-3; Morgan, "Rugby and Revivalism", pp. 435-6; John Lowerson, *Sport and the English middle classes, 1870-1914* (Manchester, 1993), p. 85 refers to a suggestion that rugby may have been unpopular with evangelicals because of their phobia of bodily contact.

92   Mason, *Association Football and English Society*, p. 25.

93   Morgan, "Rugby and Revivalism", pp. 449, 434-456.

94   Hignell, *A 'Favourit' Game*, pp. 217-220 identifies one Congregationalist and six Wesleyan cricket clubs in Cardiff between 1875 and 1890.

95   Childs, *History of St. Peter's R.F.C.*, pp. 8-9.

St. Peter's were winners of the District Union shield in 1896-7. The captain (with the ball) was J. Ryan, while the club president was the rector of St. Peter's, Reverend John Hayde.
St. Peter's RFC

social activities and institutions in Cardiff.[96] So their participation in rugby may have involved more than merely giving their approval. He also argues that such activities and institutions helped to unite the Irish community as they spread out into the districts and suburbs of the town. If parish rugby matches contributed to this, then presumably the clergy supported them. The pronounced attachment to rugby of Cardiff's Catholic schools and parishes, therefore, may originate in the clergy's conviction that the sport could contribute significantly to the wider acceptance of the Irish Catholic community.

Hard evidence of the influence of Anglican clergy in Cardiff is also difficult to establish. In 1896, the local vicar was a vice-president of St. Andrew's, but then so was the landlord of the *Flora* public house.[97] Pentyrch, not a "church-based" team as such and, in the nineteenth century at least, very much a rural village club, was founded in 1883 by the local schoolmaster and rector, Morgan Thomas. A "muscular Christian", Reverend Thomas took his pupils to watch games at Pontypridd and was also keen on

---

96   Hickey, *The Irish Community*, pp. 130-8.
97   *SWDN* 15 July 1896.

cricket.[98] Llandaff began using the Bishop's Field, which adjoins the Cathedral, in 1876 and, since this land is owned by the Church, the club presumably played there with its blessing.[99] However, apart from Boys Brigade and Church Lads Brigade teams, it is quite likely that many church clubs were largely organised by their members for their own recreation, rather than by the clergy as an instrument of social control. As Tony Collins appositely puts it, many such teams operated "under little more than a flag of convenience".[100]

The number of *workplace teams* in Cardiff was never very substantial and they did not enjoy a high position in the rugby hierarchy. From the mid-1880s, in most years, works teams comprised around 10 to 15% of the total, peaking at 18% in 1895-6. However, many of these were not regular sides, playing perhaps a few fixtures or even only one. It was common for groups of employees to play together for charity and examples include bakers, butchers, cabmen, clothiers, coal-trimmers, hairdressers, printers, publicans, sail-makers, shoemakers and theatre staff. Since Cardiff is not situated on the coalfield, it is no surprise that there were no teams of colliers. Coal-trimmers, of course, were dock workers. Though such teams were essentially ephemeral, their sheer range and number does give support to the argument that rugby was integral to the day-to-day life of the Victorian town. These games were not restricted to working men, and occasionally employees in banks and in the offices of merchants and shipowners would hold matches. Andrew Croll demonstrates that a wide range of social classes were similarly involved in Merthyr.[101]

The extent and character of Victorian workplace teams depended, of course, on the structure of the town's economy. Cardiff's prosperity then was almost entirely based on its strategic position in the coal trade, on which many in the workforce, including those in the commercial sector, were highly dependent. Remarkably, there was little manufacturing in the town and most industrial activities were relatively small scale. There was no equivalent, for example, of the Lancashire cotton mill. Most of the waterside labour force was casual and the dock company did not employ

---

98   Arthur Llewellyn and Don Llewellyn, *Pentyrch R.F.C.: A Club For All Seasons 1883-1983* (Pentyrch, 1983), pp. 8-12. Reverend Thomas was the father of the Welsh international HW Thomas. For an account of his life, see Gwyn Prescott, *"Call Them to Remembrance": The Welsh Rugby Internationals who Died in the Great War*, pp. 109-120 (Cardiff, 2014).

99   Anon., *Llandaff Rugby Football Club American Tour Souvenir* (Cardiff, 1968), p. 1.

100 Holt, *Sport and the British*, p. 138; Tony Collins, *Rugby's Great Split: Class, Culture and the Origins of Rugby League Football* (London, 2006 edn.), p. 26.

101 Andrew J. Croll, *Civilizing the Urban: Popular Culture, Public Space and Urban Meaning, Merthyr c1870-1914* (PhD thesis, University of Wales Cardiff, 1997), p. 248.

men directly.[102] This was not a good environment, therefore, for the creation of work-related clubs.

Cardiff's few industrial activities, however, were reflected in some of the teams of the time. These included the Dowlais Iron Company (Dowlais Magpies, Dowlais Iron Works); railway rolling stock manufacturers (Western Wagon Works, Gloucester Wagon Works); timber importers and suppliers (Bland's Deal Carriers, Roath Saw Mills, Cardiff Steam Joinery); grain millers and brewers (Spillers, Anglo-Bavarian Brewery Rovers); paper manufacturers (Ely Paper Mill); engineering companies (Hill's Dry Dock, Tubal Cain Foundry); and tinplate manufacturers (Melingriffith).[103] Not one of these, however, had any significant impact on local rugby at the time. Nevertheless, reflecting Cardiff's changing economic and social circumstances, workplace teams became much more prominent after the First World War. In the twenty Cardiff and District Mallett Cup finals held between 1920 and 1939, works teams (Cardiff Gas, Spillers, Currans and Melingriffith) were successful on nine occasions[104].

Of those Victorian workplace teams which enjoyed some longevity, the main occupational groups were shop assistants and uniformed employees like railway and post office staff and, to a lesser extent, the police. Railwaymen often used their place of work around which to organise their soccer in England and they seem to have been active in Cardiff rugby too.[105] Both the Taff Vale Railway and the Great Western Railway had regular teams and there were also many instances of occasional matches involving various branches of these and other companies, including Barry Railway. Unlike most dock workers, who were hired by a large number of employers for short periods, railwaymen tended to be employed permanently by one company.[106] This may explain why railway teams were better organised, played to a higher standard and survived longer than most other works teams.

In the mid-nineteenth century, Cardiff replaced Bristol as the commercial centre for south Wales.[107] This too was reflected in the town's rugby provision. As Cardiff's service economy expanded to meet the demands of its growing

---

102 M.J. Daunton, '"Coal to Capital: Cardiff since 1839" in Prys Morgan (ed.), *Glamorgan County History, Volume VI, Glamorgan Society: 1780-1980* (Cardiff, 1988), pp. 216, 220.

103 See Daunton, *Coal Metropolis*, pp. 37-49 and Rees, *History of Cardiff*, pp. 285-298 for details of Cardiff's main industries in this period.

104 See Appendix 3 (2).

105 Mason, *Association Football and English Society*, p. 30.

106 Daunton, *Coal to Capital*, p. 220.

107 Daunton, *Coal Metropolis*, pp. 53-4.

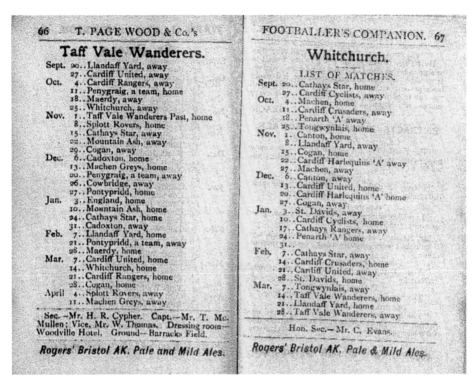

<table>
<tr><td colspan="2">66   T. PAGE WOOD & Co.'s</td><td colspan="2">FOOTBALLER'S COMPANION. 67</td></tr>
</table>

Taff Vale Wanderers.		**Whitchurch.**	
Sept.	20..Llandaff Yard, away		
	27..Cardiff United, away		LIST OF MATCHES.
Oct.	4..Cardiff Rangers, away	Sept.	20..Cathays Star, home
	11..Penygraig, a team, home		27..Cardiff Cyclists, away
	18..Maerdy, away	Oct.	4..Machen, home
	25..Whitchurch, away		11..Cardiff Crusaders, away
Nov.	1..Taff Vale Wanderers Past, home		18..Penarth 'A' away
	8..Splott Rovers, home		25..Tongwynlais, home
	15..Cathays Star, away	Nov.	1..Canton, home
	22..Mountain Ash, away		8..Llandaff Yard, away
	29..Cogan, away		15..Cogan, home
Dec.	6..Cadoxton, home		22..Cardiff Harlequins 'A' away
	13..Machen Greys, home		27..Machen, away
	20..Penygraig, a team, away	Dec.	6..Canton, away
	26..Cowbridge, away		13..Cardiff United, home
	27..Pontypridd, home		20..Cardiff Harlequins 'A' home
Jan.	3..England, home		27..Cogan, away
	10..Mountain Ash, home	Jan.	3..St. Davids, away
	24..Cathays Star, home		10..Cardiff Cyclists, home
	31..Cadoxton, away		17..Cathays Rangers, away
Feb.	7..Llandaff Yard, home		24..Penarth 'A' home
	21..Pontypridd, a team, away		31..
	28..Maerdy, home	Feb.	7..Cathays Star, away
Mar.	7..Cardiff United, home		14..Cardiff Crusaders, home
	14..Whitchurch, home		21..Cardiff United, away
	21..Cardiff Rangers, home		28..St. Davids, away
	28..Cogan, home	Mar.	7..Tongwynlais, away
April	4..Splott Rovers, away		14..Taff Vale Wanderers, home
	11..Machen Greys, away		21..Llandaff Yard, home
			28..Taff Vale Wanderers, away

Sec.—Mr. H. R. Cypher. Capt.—Mr. T. McMullen; Vice, Mr. W. Thomas. Dressing room—Woodville Hotel. Ground—Barracks Field.

Hon. Sec.—Mr. C. Evans.

Rogers' Bristol AK. Pale and Mild Ales.   *Rogers' Bristol AK. Pale & Mild Ales.*

The 1890-1 fixture lists of Taff Vale Wanderers, a railway workers club; and Whitchurch, who joined the WFU in 1895.

hinterland, so too did the number of teams coming from this sector. The impact of the Saturday half-day on the growth of football has been well documented, but nevertheless many of those who were employed in service industries, of course, still had to work on Saturday afternoons. However, they were not all denied the opportunity of playing rugby as there was a thriving Wednesday rugby scene in Cardiff. Some teams drew on groups of employees, for instance, one long established mid-week club, Cardiff Rovers, originated as Cardiff Drapers, whilst Cardiff Assistants and Cardiff Commercials accommodated shop workers and office workers generally. Others were restricted to one employer like the department store teams Hayes (David Morgan) and Wharton Wanderers (James Howells), the grocers Liptons Rovers and the Post Office. These players sometimes took their game seriously. Three of the twelve teams which competed in the 1888-9 Cardiff Junior Cup were Wednesday clubs.[108] Mid-week rugby, however, was

108 *SWDN* 17 Oct. 1889. The clubs were Cardiff Rovers, Wharton Wanderers and Post Office.

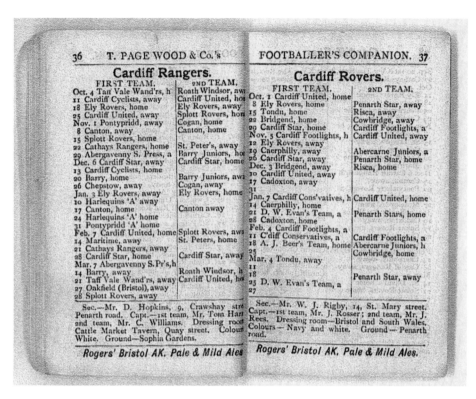

Cardiff Rovers were a long-standing Wednesday club for shop workers. A local handbook for 1890-1 reveals that they ran two sides.

not always restricted to specially organised works teams and a number of clubs, like Cardiff Harlequins, also ran a regular Wednesday XV. Mid-week rugby was common throughout south Wales, whilst in the mining districts, "Mabon's Day", a holiday for miners on the first Monday in the month, was also a very popular football day. Occasionally, Cardiff teams would travel north to provide the opposition, when no doubt the receipt of a healthy match guarantee softened the blow of losing an afternoon's work.

The distinctive nature of Cardiff's narrow economic base was, therefore, an influential factor in determining the rather low incidence of regular workplace teams in the nineteenth century. They had little overall impact, with perhaps only the railway clubs providing any decent standard of regular rugby. It seems that the majority of workers preferred to play their rugby elsewhere. Significantly, there is no evidence of any employers providing pitches and accommodation.

There were very few *public house teams* in Cardiff and their numbers never reached double figures in any year. Of course, these must be distinguished from those clubs which used public houses as their headquarters and of which there were very many, as will be shown in the following chapter. It is likely that pub teams such as Blue Anchor, Cambrian, Cottage Rovers, Globe Revellers, Rising Sun, Royal Oak and Rose and Crown were working class in composition, since the pub was essentially a working-class institution. These particular teams were based on town centre pubs, but the Duke of Edinburgh and Green Fields of Erin were situated in the strongly working-class district of Newtown. However, public house sides were not necessarily adult teams, as revealed by the existence of Tredegar Arms Juniors in 1893-4. No doubt the establishment of pub teams often arose on the initiative of the landlord. For instance, Tom Cooke, the licensee of the *Blue Anchor* was a former player, who in 1891 claimed to be the oldest member of Cardiff FC.[109]

In contrast to pub teams, *street teams* in Cardiff were very common. It is highly likely that the majority of these were junior sides, as only a few of them lasted for more than one season. Arabella Rangers, Broadway Quins, Ethel Street, Glossop Road Rangers, Gold Street Rangers, Holton Crusaders (Barry), Louisa Street Stars, Ludlow Street, Merthyr Street Bruisers, Prince Leopold Street Juniors, Maughan Rovers (Penarth), System Blue Stars, Tin

The Cottage in St. Mary Street was not only a popular meeting place for rugby followers, it also hosted its own team, Cottage Rovers, for a while.
Courtesy of SA Brain and Co.

---

109 *Welsh Athlete* 19 Oct., 2 Nov. 1891.

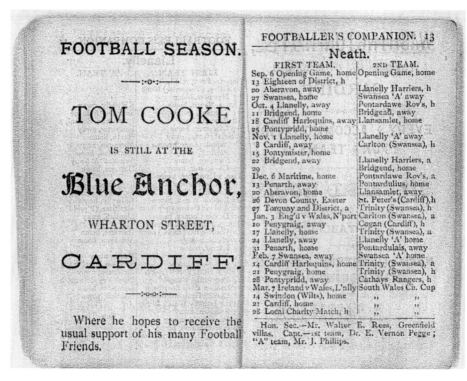

An advertisement from the 1890-1 handbook for the Blue Anchor, another pub which had its own team. The licensee Tom Cooke was obviously well known in rugby circles.

Street Rovers and many others enjoyed only a brief existence. It would have been natural for youngsters to form such highly localised teams and then, when they began to grow more financially and socially independent, merge with or move to clubs further away from their homes. Alternatively, as suggested by Richard Holt, informal street teams may have developed into organised junior clubs, as was certainly the case with Clyde Juniors and Richmond Road Juniors who survived for several years, and Charles Street Rangers and Tresillian Quins who appear to have evolved into adult clubs.[110] Nevertheless, from the late 1880s, street teams became a thriving, if constantly shifting, feature of local rugby. There was no particular geographical concentration – they arose in all the working-class residential districts of the town – though there was only a handful recorded in the outlying and less densely populated areas, such as Philog Rovers and College Rovers in Whitchurch and Paradise Rovers in Rumney.

---

110 Richard Holt, "Working-Class Football and the City: The Problem of Continuity", *British Journal of Sports History*, 3, 1 (1986), p. 7.

St. Fagans 1900-1. The captain (with the ball) was V Davies. There had been a team in the village from at least 1891.　　*Courtesy of St. Fagans National History Museum*

Almost all of the remaining clubs fall into the category of *neighbourhood teams*.[111] Holt stresses the significance of neighbourhood (and street) teams in two particularly important respects, both of which are applicable to Cardiff. Firstly, place-names, he argues, "underline the sustaining role of the neighbourhood in sport: despite vast changes in the city itself, loyalty to a street or parish was deeply held". Local teams could provide an uprooted population with a new sense of belonging and pride. Secondly, the establishment of such a range of clubs was "not the achievement of well-intentioned middle-class reformers; it was the work of the members, of the people themselves".[112]

111　"Town" clubs Cardiff, Penarth and Cardiff Harlequins have been included in this category in Table 3. The Harlequins evolved into a town team over time. Barry did not really become a town club as such for reasons explained in Bassett, *Rugby Football in Barry*, passim.

112　Holt, *Sport and the British*, pp. 150-4.

This was easily the largest category in the Cardiff area and Stuart Barlow found similar results in his study of Rochdale rugby.[113] Every residential district eventually had its representatives: Roath, Canton, Butetown, Adamsdown, Splott, Cathays, Grangetown, Riverside, Blackweir, Ely, Llandaff, Llandaff North, Penylan, Rumney and Whitchurch. The game had also spread throughout the immediate surrounding district to the neighbouring towns and villages of Barry, Cadoxton, Cogan, Dinas Powys, Penarth, Pentyrch, St. Fagans, Tongwynlais and Taffs Well. Indeed, the outward spread of Cardiff in the last three decades of the nineteenth century can be traced in the emergence of its rugby clubs. With the proliferation of teams, it was inevitable that many would share a neighbourhood name in their title, so they were forced to find ways of distinguishing themselves. For example, between 1885 and 1900, there were at least thirty teams which included the residential district of "Roath" in their name.[114]

In adopting names, the Victorians were more far inventive than their modern counterparts: they had to be, as there were so many clubs. Examples of popular name constructions of the time include Adamsdown Crusaders, Canton Wanderers, Cathays Excelsiors, Ely Rangers, Grangetown Stars, Heath Rovers, Moors United, Penarth Harlequins, Roath Windsors and Splott Raglans. Less common suffix names were chosen by Barry Victoria, Canton Lilywhites, Cathays Albions, Penarth Dreadnoughts, Riverside Warriors and Tongwynlais Ramblers. Some clubs dispensed with a local name altogether, for example, Bowry [sic] Boys, Harbour Lights and Maggie Murphy's Pups. There were always some who didn't take themselves too seriously, of course, such as North Central Buffoons, Salmon Tin Rovers and Waistcoat Tearers. The naming of Alpine Rangers was clearly a joke as the club played at East Moors, the lowest and flattest part of the town. Even black humour occasionally had its place. During the Whitechapel Murders, the Jersey Rippers took part in a local nine a-side tournament.

Borrowing a tradition which originated at Rugby School, many neighbourhood teams were simply named after the emblem worn on their jerseys.[115]

---

113 Barlow, "The Diffusion of 'Rugby' Football", pp. 54, 64.

114 They were Roath: Albion, Albion Juniors, Court, Crescents, Crusaders, Elm, Excelsiors, Harlequins, Hornets, Institute, Juniors, Marlborough, Park Juniors, Park Wanderers, Park United, Pouncers [sic], Ramblers, Raglans, Rangers, Star Juniors, Stars, Road, Rovers, Shamrocks, Wanderers, Waterloo, Wednesday, Wednesday Juniors, Windsors and United.

115 Jennifer Macrory, *Running with the Ball: The Birth of Rugby Football* (London, 1991), pp. 78-84. See Parry-Jones, *Prince Gwyn*, p. 96 for a photograph of Cardiff Stars c.1890 which shows a very large star sewn on the jerseys.

The Roath club, Mackintosh were known as "The Gravediggers". They are shown here with their medals for the 1900-1 Mallett Cup, after defeating Cardiff Romilly ("The Laughing Philosophers") 11-9 in the final. E. Rumbelow, standing second row fourth from left, later played at forward for Cardiff over six seasons.   Cardiff and District RU

These included Blackweir Diamonds, Canton Red Anchor, Cathays Crescent, Grange Thistles, Harp of Erin Juniors and Roath Shamrocks. A surprisingly common practice was for some teams to be named after flowers, for instance, Cogan White Rose, Grangetown Red Rose, Taffs Well Red Rose, Lily of the Valley, Wild Rose and White Lily. It has to be wondered, though, whether Llandaff Blossoms, Penarth Tulips and Tongwynlais Flowers were short-lived because of recruiting difficulties. The existence of teams like Harp of Erin, Canton Shamrocks, Roath Shamrocks, M'Ginty's Pups and Maggie Murphy's Pups not only provide further evidence of the strong participation of Cardiff's Irish community but also suggests that not all of them necessarily played for parish teams.

There were many clubs, of course, which included "Cardiff" in their title, such as those which adopted Alexandra, Crusaders, Hornets, Mohawks, Northern, Rangers, Star and United as a suffix. Whether these were based in a particular locality or were clubs which drew on a wider catchment area and social background is impossible to establish with certainty, though,

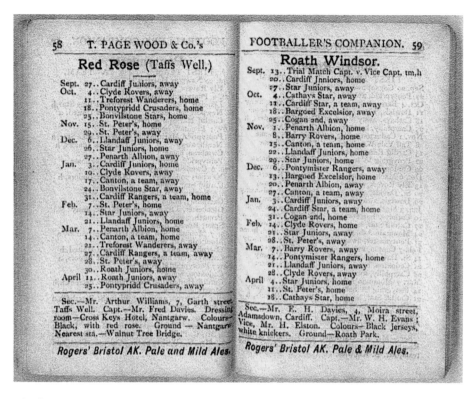

58 T. PAGE WOOD & Co.'s	FOOTBALLER'S COMPANION. 59
Red Rose (Taffs Well,)	**Roath Windsor.**

Red Rose (Taffs Well,)

Sept. 27..Cardiff Juniors, away
Oct. 4..Clyde Rovers, away
    11..Treforest Wanderers, home
    18..Pontypridd Crusaders, home
    25..Bonvilstone Stars, home
Nov. 15..St. Peter's, home
    29..St. Peter's, away
Dec. 6..Llandaff Juniors, away
    26..Star Juniors, home
    27..Penarth Albion, away
Jan. 3..Cardiff Juniors, home
    10..Clyde Rovers, away
    17..Canton, a team, away
    24..Bonvilstone Star, away
    31..Cardiff Rangers, a team, home
Feb. 7..St. Peter's, home
    14..Star Juniors, away
    21..Llandaff Juniors, home
Mar. 7..Penarth Albion, home
    14..Canton, a team, home
    21..Treforest Wanderers, away
    27..Cardiff Rangers, a team, away
    28..St. Peter's, away
    30..Roath Juniors, home
April 11..Roath Juniors, away
    25..Pontypridd Crusaders, away

Sec.—Mr. Arthur Williams, 7, Garth street,
Taffs Well. Capt.—Mr. Fred Davies. Dressing
room—Cross Keys Hotel, Nantgarw. Colours—
Black, with red rose. Ground — Nantgarw.
Nearest sta.—Walnut Tree Bridge.

Rogers' Bristol AK. Pale and Mild Ales.

Roath Windsor.

Sept. 13..Trial Match Capt. v. Vice Capt, tm,h
    20..Cardiff Jnniors, home
    27..Star Juniors, away
Oct. 4..Cathays Star, away
    11..Cardiff Star, a team, away
    18..Bargoed Excelsior, away
    25..Cogan 2nd, away
Nov. 1..Penarth Albion, home
    8..Barry Rovers, home
    15..Canton, a team, home
    22..Llandaff Juniors, home
    29..Star Juniors, home
Dec. 6..Pontymister Rangers, away
    13..Bargoed Excelsior, home
    20..Penarth Albion, away
    27..Canton, a team, away
Jan. 3..Cardiff Juniors, away
    24..Cardiff Star, a team, home
Feb. 14..Cogan 2nd, away
    14..Clyde Rovers, home
    21..Star Juniors, away
    28..St. Peter's, away
Mar. 7..Barry Rovers, away
    14..Pontymister Rangers, home
    21..Llandaff Juniors, away
    28..Clyde Rovers, away
April 4..Star Juniors, home
    11..St. Peter's, home
    18..Cathays Star, home

Sec.—Mr. E. H. Davies, 4, Moira street,
Adamsdown, Cardiff. Capt.—Mr. W. H. Evans ;
Vice, Mr. H. Elston. Colours—Black Jerseys,
white knickers. Ground—Roath Park.

Rogers' Bristol AK. Pale & Mild Ales.

The fixture list in 1890-1 for Taffs Well Red Rose, probably a junior team.

given their fixture lists, the likelihood is that the majority were essentially neighbourhood clubs.

There is one further, very small, group of *miscellaneous clubs* with institutional backgrounds which cannot be easily classified in the categories so far discussed. It includes military teams, in particular, the Welsh Regiment Depot and the Volunteers such as 2nd Glamorgan Artillery. Higher education was represented by University College Cardiff and Cardiff Medicals. The University rugby club began playing in 1883-4, the year of the college's foundation, and thereafter became a permanent feature of the local rugby scene, often using the Arms Park for important matches. The Medics, however, only played occasional matches, as did various Liberal and Conservative Working Men's Clubs and benevolent organisations like the Barry Dock Buffalo Institute. A few clubs were established by special interest groups, Cardiff Cyclists being the most prominent. Old Monktonians were the *only* example of a regular Old Boys club and this is further evidence of the predominantly working-class nature of the game in Cardiff. Founded in the 1890s, they were elected to the WFU in 1910. They gave up any formal ties

Cardiff Northern had some attractive fixtures in 1894-5, the season in which they won the Mallett Cup. Their secretary AM Ricketts later played for Cardiff.

Penylan in the early 1900s. Though they were members of Cardiff and District, with a strong fixture list, they did not participate in competitions. Founded in 1892, Penylan folded in the 1920s because of the lack of a ground.

Cardiff Roxburgh 1908-9. The captain (with the ball) was SR Jackson. They were another middle-class club, affiliated to Cardiff and District but not interested in local competitions. However, around this time, they made several successful tours in France.

with Monkton House in 1913-14 when they became Glamorgan Wanderers, though they remained a somewhat socially exclusive club until after the Second World War. However, the connection with Monkton House means that the roots of the modern Glamorgan Wanderers club can be traced right back to the very origins of the game in Wales. There were other clubs with a predominantly middle-class membership and neighbourhood teams Penylan and Kymin (Penarth) were examples. However, it is virtually impossible to identify many others with any great certainty. Such clubs tended to eschew competition but they appear to have made no obvious attempt to create exclusive fixture lists.

To summarise, then, the analysis of Cardiff's Victorian rugby teams reveals a rather different picture from that which has emerged in some studies of soccer in England.[116] Churches, workplaces and pubs were important institutions in the origin of many English soccer clubs. Mason suggests that a considerable proportion of soccer clubs owed their origins to organisations which were previously in existence for another purpose. However, the evidence is that their influence was rather weaker in Cardiff rugby, where the proportion of church, workplace and pub teams never rose above 32% (in 1895-6), and was typically at around 25% or less. This may be explained, at least in part, by religious hostility to rugby and by Cardiff's distinct economic structure.

---

116 Mason, *Association Football and English Society*, pp. 24-31.

This difference is further illustrated by a comparison with research findings on the "place of association" of 193 soccer clubs in Teesside in 1888-9. As shown in Table 5, Mike Huggins reveals that 57% of the Teesside clubs could be categorised as church, workplace or pub teams.[117] This was well over double the percentage of rugby clubs in the same categories in Cardiff, where the equivalent figure that season was only 23%. It would appear that in Cardiff, location was of far greater significance in the establishment of teams.

Table 5: Comparison of Clubs in Teesside and Cardiff in 1888-9

Place of Association	Teesside Soccer		Cardiff Rugby	
	Number	%	Number	%
Workplace	53	27.5	19	11.2
Church/Chapel	46	23.8	16	9.4
Public Houses	12	6.2	4	2.3
Schools	20	10.4	10	5.9
Other	62	32.1	121	71.2
Total	193	100.0	170	100.0

Stuart Barlow argues that in Rochdale, loyalty to the street, neighbourhood or parish was strongly held and that it was the working class, rather than religious or philanthropic members of the middle class, who were responsible for organising many of these local rugby teams.[118] The experience in Cardiff appears to have been similar. From 1880 onwards, neighbourhood and street teams comprised between approximately two-thirds and three-quarters of the total every season. This supports Richard Holt's view that the impact of churches and employers was limited only to a minority and hence there was no effective middle-class imposition in the name of social control.[119] Most clubs were based on the street or neighbourhood and were therefore probably established and organised by and for working people. Neil Tranter also points out that the profusion of local clubs confirms that the spread of football came about as much from efforts from below as from middle-class

---

117 Huggins, "The Spread of Association Football", p. 311. I am grateful to Professor Mike Huggins for giving his permission to use the results of his research published in this article in the compilation of Table 5.

118 Barlow, 'The Diffusion of 'Rugby' Football', pp. 61-5.

119 Holt, *Sport and the British*, pp. 352-3.

example and initiative.[120] As Gareth Williams puts it, local teams in Wales "block-built identity upwards".[121] In Cardiff, there is no doubt that strong local allegiances were attracted to neighbourhood teams and these were largely working class in origin and composition. Their emergence also began to influence the wider game, as will be shown in the next chapter.

---

120 Neil Tranter, *Sport, Economy and Society in Britain, 1750-1914* (Cambridge, 1998), p. 29.
121 Williams, *1905 and All That*, p. 74.

5

ORGANISATION AND PARTICIPATION:
'Administered by the few, played by the many'

While local newspaper coverage of rugby expanded greatly during the Victorian period, the reports concentrated heavily on match details. As far as these go, they do confirm that, as Gareth Williams puts it, the game was administered by a few officials but played and watched by many.[1] However,

Penarth in 1893-4, when they recorded doubles over Gloucester and Bristol. The captain and Welsh trialist, Herbie Morgan, is seated third row centre; Welsh international Dickie Garrett is seated fifth from left; between them is Hubert Alexander, a reserve wing for Wales; and John Hayes, the secretary, is standing on the far right.   Penarth RFC

---

1   Gareth Williams, "Community, Class and Rugby in Wales 1880-1914", *Society for the Study of Labour History Bulletin*, 50, Spring, (1985), p. 11.

The Cardiff Challenge Cup was presented to the short-lived Cardiff District FU in 1886-7 by T Page Wood. Contested only four times, it was won outright by Penarth in 1888-9.   *Penarth RFC*

surprisingly little detail is revealed about the day-to-day administration of the game and how matches were organised, especially at the local level, so we have to piece together what few clues are available.

Most of the teams identified here were never affiliated to any union. However, as rugby became increasingly popular and competitive, there was an evident need for stronger control over its administration, particularly at a local level. Issues such as match disputes, foul play, crowd control, player transfer, referee appointments and demands for competitive structures all took on increasing importance during the 1890s. Only a very small number of the leading local sides joined the Welsh Football Union. Cardiff, of course, were founder members in 1881, while Penarth and Cardiff Harlequins both joined in 1886. They were followed by Cardiff Star (1891), Llandaff (1891), St. David's (1891), Cathays (1892), Cogan (1892), Grangetown (1893), Barry (1895), Whitchurch (1895 and 1898) and Taffs Well (1900). The WFU abandoned the South Wales Challenge Cup for two seasons, but re-introduced it for clubs outside the top level in 1889-90. This enabled several of these Cardiff clubs to participate in the cup, which Llandaff won in 1891-2.[2] All nine, however, dropped out of the WFU at some point shortly afterwards and most disbanded, at least temporarily, at around the same time. Of all the many rugby clubs in the locality, only Cardiff and Penarth can claim continuous membership of the WRU from the nineteenth century.[3]

---

2   See Appendix 4.

3   For WFU membership see *South Wales Daily News* and *Western Mail*, 1886-1895 and WFU minutes 1892-1902 passim; *SWDN* 28 Mar. 1892 (Llandaff win Welsh Challenge Cup).

In order to administer a new competition, known as the Cardiff Challenge Cup, a Cardiff District Football Union was set up in 1886[4]. It was a requirement that clubs wishing to compete had to join this new Union, whose sole function was to organise the competition. A junior cup was added in 1889 but the Cardiff District Football Union was wound up shortly afterwards when, after three successive victories in the Challenge Cup, Penarth won the trophy outright under the competition rules in 1890.[5] The cup is still in the possession of the Penarth club.

However, there was clearly a desperate need for an organisation which could both supervise the burgeoning game at a local level and support the growing status of the town club. Unfortunately, it was a responsibility which the WFU was not prepared to accept. On the contrary, there was growing alarm in the WFU that

This Cardiff District Challenge Cup medal was awarded to an unknown Penarth player after his team defeated Llandaff 39-1 in the 1887-8 final.   Lindsay Jenkins

it might become swamped by "junior" clubs from Cardiff and elsewhere. So at the AGM in September 1892, the WFU resolved that, in future, strict criteria would be applied to all applications for membership; and it was also agreed to undertake a review of all existing member clubs. Moreover, when two Cardiff clubs were then proposed, their nomination was greeted with laughter from some of the delegates. In response to these rebuffs to the grassroots game in the town, HW Wells ("Welsh Athlete" of the *Western Mail*) suggested that the time had come for district clubs to take matters into their own hands and form their own union.[6] The catalyst for action seems to have been a match held at Sophia Gardens between Cardiff Rangers and Grangetown. According to a letter received by Wells, "the game was

---

4   *SWDN* 8 Sept. 1886.

5   *SWDN* 17 Oct. 1889. (Junior Cup); *Cardiff District Football Union Handbook 1886-87* (Cardiff, 1886), pp. 3-14; Chris Thau, *The Spirit of Penarth: One Hundred and Thirty-One Years of Seaside Rugby 1880-2011* (Penarth, 2012) pp.12-20; John Musselwhite, *The Butcher Boys of Donkey Island: An Historical Profile of Penarth R.F.C.* (Penarth, 1980), pp. 9, 20; see Appendix 3 (1) for cup wins.

6   *WM* 12, 14 Sept. 1892; *SWDN* 12 Sept. 1892.

a perfect farce all through, and was more noticeable for 'free fights' than an exposition of Rugby football." Cardiff Rangers' winning try was allowed even though the scorer ran off the pitch into the crowds of spectators and emerged up field to touch down. Wells was advised, "The sooner your suggestion of a local union is carried out the better it will be for the junior clubs in the district."[7]

This seems to have concentrated minds as a meeting of clubs was immediately called to consider the matter. Shortly afterwards on 14 November 1892, a new Cardiff and District Football Union (C&DFU) came into being at the *New Market Hotel*. Amongst the clubs represented that evening were: Barry, Canton, Dinas Powys and Llandaff. Also present were a further twelve clubs which no longer exist: Cardiff Rangers and Grangetown (who appear to have settled their differences), Bowry [sic] Boys, Canton Quins, Cardiff Alexandra, Cardiff Northern, Cathays, Cogan, Grange Stars, Roath, Post Office and St. David's. The new union had very much wider terms of reference than its predecessor and membership was initially available to "all junior teams within a radius of nine miles of Cardiff", but later extended to twelve miles.[8] Its objectives were to: foster rugby; support the Cardiff club; recognise club and individual merit; and settle disputes.[9]

Now renamed the Cardiff and District Rugby Union, it has successfully fostered the local game ever since; and over the years many hundreds of teams have benefitted from affiliation. With regard to supporting the senior club, Cardiff were given the right under the District's constitution to ask any player of a member club to play for them; and many went on to have successful careers for the Blue and Blacks.[10] To reward individual merit, a representative District XV was established which played occasional games with senior clubs including Neath, Bristol and Gloucester. The District's annual fixture with Cardiff began in 1893-4 and was held until 1966-7. It was revived in 2012-13. As for club merit, the Mallett Cup was introduced also in 1893-4, when it was won by Cardiff Reserves, from an entry of fifteen teams. The oldest surviving cup competition in Wales, it is one of the oldest for open clubs in Britain. By 2014-15, it had been contested on 110 occasions. Apart from Cardiff, other clubs still in existence which participated in the first ever Mallett Cup in 1894 were Barry, Canton, Llandaff, Pentyrch and Whitchurch. The other – long defunct – pioneering entrants

---

7   *WM* 31 Oct. 1892.

8   *WM* 15 Nov. 1892.

9   *WM* 4 Feb. 1897.

10   *The Handy Football Guide (Mortimer's) For South Wales and Monmouthshire: 1896-97* (Cardiff, 1896), p.21 (District constitution).

The New Market Hotel (renamed Old Market Tavern) where the Cardiff and District RU was formed on 14 November 1892. The Union held a celebration dinner here exactly 120 years later in 2012.
Siân Prescott

were: Blackweir, Cardiff Hornets, Cardiff Northern, Cardiff Star, Cathays, Garth, Grangetown, Grange Stars and Splott Crusaders.[11] The following year saw a two division league established.[12] The Union Shield (reputedly made by a committeeman for eight shillings) was also introduced in 1894-5 and was initially presented to the second division champions for two seasons. Thereafter it was adopted as the trophy awarded to the winners of the knock-out competition for clubs below Mallett Cup standard. It was replaced in 1910-11, by the Ninian Stuart Cup (presented by the son of the Marquess of Bute), which is still competed for annually.

By 1896-7, founder members Barry had moved on to the increasingly competitive Glamorgan League, which was virtually the second division of Welsh rugby.[13] At the end of the century, there were thirty-six local

---

11   *SWDN* 4 Jan. 1894.
12   *SWDN* 10 Nov. 1894. The clubs in the first Senior League were Barry, Canton, Grangetown, Cardiff Northern and Whitchurch; and in the Junior League (i.e. Second Division) they were Blackweir, Cathays United, Grange Star, Pentyrch, Roath and St. Mary's.
13   *SWDN* 14 Aug. 1896.

The Mallett Cup was donated to the Cardiff and District FU by Thomas H Mallett in 1893-4, when he was the landlord of the Blue Bell. Apart from the war years, it has been competed for every season since. Cardiff and District RU

clubs taking part in three leagues and three knock out cups.[14] However, Alan Metcalfe has shown that, as late as 1913, half of all soccer teams in East Northumberland were neither affiliated to the county FA nor involved in any leagues. This was very similar to Victorian Cardiff, where the majority of rugby teams never belonged to any union, nor played in any organised competitions.[15]

Nevertheless, some local clubs found an outlet for their craving for competition in a shortened version of the game. Just four years after sevens had been conceived in Scotland, a six a-side tournament was held in Cardiff in 1887. Only five of the expected ten teams turned up, which was probably just as well for Frank Hancock, as he was the sole referee. However, subsequent versions of the game involving nine a-side teams proved to be much more popular and throughout the late 1880s and 1890s knock-out tournaments were held in Cardiff at the beginning or the end of the season. The playing area was reduced to 80 x 45 yards, matches were limited to ten minutes each way and a handicap system was adopted. Teams normally participated under assumed, sometimes apparently humorous, names. Prizes were awarded to the winners: the players in the Nine of Diamonds team in 1888-9, for instance, each received items to the value of a pound, equivalent to perhaps £100 today. These nine a-side competitions were initially arranged by Cardiff Harlequins officials, though Cardiff and District took over the organisation in 1894-5. A number of promising local players were "spotted" this way.[16]

---

14   *SWDN* 24, 28 Feb. 1900; Gwyn Prescott, "Competitive Rugby in Cardiff Before the First World War", *Touchlines*, 46, April, (2010), pp.5-9.

15   Alan Metcalfe, "Football in the Mining Communities of East Northumberland 1882-1914", *International Journal of the History of Sport*, 5, 3 (1988), p. 270.

16   *SWDN* 13 May, 12 Sept. 1887; *WM* 9 Sept. 1889; *WM* 7, 10, 11 Sept. 1894. In 2015, C&DRU revived the tradition with a sevens tournament; won by Cardiff.

Before long, both Cardiff's First and Second XVs contained many former District players. In 1897, the Cardiff chairman declared that most of the club's players came from "the ranks of her own junior clubs".[17] A good number of these went on to play for Wales around this time, most notably Percy Bush (St. Vincent's and Cardiff Romilly), Gwyn Nicholls (Cardiff Star), and Bert Winfield (St. Andrew's), all of whom were key members of the 1905 team which defeated the All Blacks. Others who won Welsh caps in the 1890s and early 1900s and who began their careers with C&DFU affiliated clubs included Jere Blake (Blackweir and Whitchurch), John Brown (St. Peter's), Fred Cornish (Grangetown), Dickie David (Cathays United and Mackintosh), Tom Dobson (Llandaff Yard and Blackweir), Jack Elliott (Llandaff), Dai Fitzgerald (St. David's and Grangetown), Viv Huzzey (Canton),

64				
EMPIRE PALACES—Cardiff, Newport & Swansea.				
Barry.				POINTS. FOR. AGST.
Sept.	19	Pontypridd Chain Workers	home	
„	26	Treherbert L	away	
Oct.	3	Canton	home	
„	10	Ferndale L	„	
„	17	Treorky L		
„	24	Mountain Ash L	away	
„	31	Merthyr L	home	
Nov.	7	Risca	away	
„	14	Penygraig L	home	
„	21	Pontypridd L	„	
„	28	Bridgend	„	
Dec.	5	Ferndale L	away	
„	12	Mountain Ash L	home	
„	19	Penygraig L	away	
„	26	Bridgend	„	
Jan.	2	Risca	home	
„	9	Treorky L	away	
„	16	Treherbert L	home	
„	23	Canton	„	
„	30	Pontypridd L	away	
Feb.	6	Merthyr L	„	
„	13	Vacant	home	
„	20	Pontnewydd	away	
„	27	Cardiff Harlequins	„	
Mar.	6	Llwynypia L	home	
„	13	Newport Extras	„	
„	20	Roath	away	
„	27	Tondu	„	
April	3	Llwynypia L	„	
„	10	Pontnewydd	home	
„	17	Roath	„	
„	19	Tondu	„	
Or to their Liverpool Offices—8s, Queen Insurance Buildings, Dale St.				

Barry fixtures in 1896-7, when they played in the Glamorgan League (shown as "L").

Billy O'Neill (St. Peter's), Joe Pugsley (Grange Stars), Dai Westacott (Grange Stars) and Johnny Williams (Whitchurch).[18]

The importance of the fledgling C&DFU to rugby in Wales soon became evident in 1896, when the WFU suggested that it join the Union. This arose because the WFU had no jurisdiction over the transfer of the many District

---

17   *SWDN* 3 May 1897.

18   *WM* 4 Feb. 1897 (District players); John M. Jenkins, Duncan Pierce and Timothy Auty, *Who's Who of Welsh International Rugby Players* (Wrexham, 1991) passim; *Evening Express* 6 Apr. 1901 (Bush); *SWDN* 18 Jan. 1897 (Winfield), 14 Nov. 1898 (O'Neill); *SWDN* and *WM* match reports 1890-1910 passim. For an account of the lives of David Westacott and John L Williams, see Gwyn Prescott, *"Call Them to Remembrance": The Welsh Rugby Internationals who Died in the Great War*, pp. 47-59, 73-85 (Cardiff, 2014).

The "Nine of Diamonds" (Roath) team with their prizes for winning the 1888-9 nine a-side tournament. Percy Bennett, who later played for Wales, is standing third from left.
Courtesy of St. Fagans National History Museum

The 1905 Wales XV v New Zealand, which included three former players with Cardiff and District clubs: Gwyn Nicholls (ex-Cardiff Star) is seated with the ball; Bert Winfield (ex-St. Andrew's) is seated next to him fifth from left; and Percy Bush (ex-Cardiff Romilly) is front row third from left.

players who were joining WFU clubs, particularly those in the Glamorgan League. In September 1898, the Cardiff and District Football Union became full members of the Welsh Football Union, the first organisation of its kind to do so, three years before any similar district union. Two months later, the District reported both Penygraig and Pontypridd for using members of C&DFU clubs without transfers. The WFU decided that transfers *were* required but, if refused by the District, clubs could then apply directly to them. Clearly, they were not prepared to delegate too much power to the "junior" union and accepting C&DFU into affiliation was a subtle way of bringing many clubs under the WFU's jurisdiction without massively extending membership. Restricting entry to the Welsh Union was one way in which the control of the game at the top level was retained in the hands of the professional and business middle classes, even though the majority of clubs catered for working men.[19]

Despite the immediate success of the C&DFU, local clubs still rose and fell with remarkable regularity. With little or no gate money, most suffered from financial insecurity; while the loss of a pitch was another threat to viability for some. Many functioned with only a bare number of members and the departure of a few key players or officials could easily precipitate the club's demise. So, just as Alan Metcalfe recognised in soccer in Northumberland, there was a "chronic instability" of clubs and a "constantly shifting configuration" of the game at the time.[20] Leading clubs were just as vulnerable as the less successful teams. St. David's, for instance, who had fixtures with Bridgend, Bristol and Pontypridd went out of existence when many of their players joined Cardiff.[21] Another challenge facing the sustainability of local clubs was the advent of the professional game in the north of England. As soon as the Northern Union (NU) was established in 1895, District clubs immediately began to lose players, a surprisingly large number of whom became professional during the late 1890s. Grangetown, for instance, lost two players only a month after the NU was founded.[22] In 1899, it was reported that District clubs were affected "acutely" by the number of players "going North".[23] Even some "amateur" English clubs attempted to poach players. Torquay Athletic, for instance, were suspended by the RFU in 1898 for offering terms to St. Peter's players.[24]

---

19   WFU minutes 30 Dec. 1896, 21 Sept. 1898, 22 Aug. 1901, 7 Nov. 1898.
20   Metcalfe, "Football in East Northumberland", pp. 274, 278-9.
21   *WM* 8 Oct. 1894.
22   *SWDN* 8 Oct. 1895.
23   *SWDN* 18 Sept. 1899.
24   WFU minutes 8 Dec. 1898.

"Tinker's Favourites" (Roath), who won the 1894-5 Cardiff and District nine a-side competition. Roath also won the Union Shield that year and the Mallett Cup the following season. In 1896-7, C Smart (with the ball), PJ Brady (seated on his left) and a third Roath player all joined the Northern Union. Brady (Huddersfield) played in the first ever Rugby League international for Other Nationalities (effectively Wales) v England in 1904, winning 9-3.
Gaynor Jones

The increasingly ambitious valley clubs, especially those in the Glamorgan League, also enticed players. Undoubtedly, financial inducements or offers of employment were often involved. It is a widely held view in Wales that the Cardiff club's strength has traditionally depended on players from the valleys. Yet, in the 1880s and 1890s, there is no great evidence for this. On the contrary, many of the leading valley clubs relied on players from Cardiff. For example, Cardiff-born Percy Bush was spotted playing for Cardiff University by a Penygraig scout in 1896 and was invited to join the valley club. He captained them for two seasons before joining his home-town club in 1899. Another Welsh international, the Cardiff dock worker, Tom Dobson, first played for Llandaff Yard but later captained Llwynypia in the Rhondda before returning to become a stalwart of the Cardiff pack.[25] In 1899, there were calls to investigate the amateur status of some thirty

---

25   *Evening Express* 6 April 1901 (Bush); *SWDN* 24 Oct. 1892 (Dobson).

Cardiff men who were travelling to play for valley teams in the Glamorgan League.[26] Neighbourhood clubs in Cardiff, on the other hand, had virtually no gates and little income and, with many local rivals making claims on their players, they could rarely sustain the playing standard of the best valley clubs, who enjoyed clearly demarcated boundaries of community support and substantially greater revenues.

The organisation of leagues and cups by the District Union helped to create a more rational structure to the season, though the participants in the competitions varied considerably with the rise and fall of clubs. A highly efficient postal service meant that fixtures could be arranged easily and swiftly. Local newspapers helped by publishing details of clubs with free Saturdays. Annual football handbooks provided another means for advertising open dates, as well as for confirming previously made arrangements. They also reveal that most established clubs finalised their fixture list well before the opening of the season. For C&DFU competitions, it was initially customary for secretaries to arrange mutually acceptable dates. This was the general practice in other competitions, including the Glamorgan and Monmouthshire Leagues and it sometimes led to confusion, dispute and uncompleted league tables.

The mercurial Percy Frank Bush, who was dubbed "Will O' the Wisp" by the Australian press during the 1904 Great Britain tour.

A necessary condition for the expansion of the game in Cardiff was sufficient space in which to play. In Merthyr and in Bristol, as Croll and Meller respectively have shown, the lack of available land could restrict the development of sports.[27] In this regard, Cardiff was fortunate. Four main types of playing field were used: land occupied by a single club on a permanent or semi-permanent basis; land within the built-up area waiting for development; edge of town land; and public parks. But every conceivable piece of ground was used. There are even several reports of matches, presumably between juniors, taking place in residential areas on the open spaces in the middle of Adamsdown Square and Loudoun Square. The more established clubs like Cardiff, Cardiff Harlequins and Penarth

---

26   *SWDN* 28 Apr. 1899.

27   Andrew J. Croll, *Civilizing the Urban: Popular Culture, Public Space and Urban Meaning, Merthyr c1870-1914* (PhD thesis, University of Wales Cardiff, 1997), pp. 208, 224-6; 142-3; H.E. Meller, *Leisure and the Changing City, 1870-1914* (London, 1976), p. 236.

were able to lease and enclose their grounds and charge for entrance. The majority, however, would have occupied under licence, with the possibility of eviction at short notice. The loss of playing fields was a constant threat to many clubs and no doubt contributed to the high turnover. No independent clubs at this time owned the freehold of their ground. Only three city-based clubs, Cardiff, Cardiff Harlequins (formerly Cardiff High School Old Boys), and Glamorgan Wanderers, do so today.

From the very beginning of the game, the central location and convenience of the Arms Park guaranteed that it would be the main focus of any sporting activity. It was here that the pioneers of Glamorgan FC and Cardiff Wanderers played in the early 1870s. However, in April 1875 the Bute Estate announced that because of "repeated acts of mischief and injury done to trees and fences in the Cardiff Arms Park, no person will be allowed to enter it without special permission."[28] This decision was to have an effect on the early rugby players of Cardiff. At the start of the next season, one concerned member of the Glamorgan Football Club wrote to the press.

Last year, after several ineffectual attempts, the young men of Cardiff succeeded in forming a football club. The want of an institution of this kind had long been felt in Cardiff, as was shown by the speedy enrolment of upwards of 150 members, who testified their just appreciation of the benefit of their regular attendances on Wednesday and Saturday afternoons in the Cardiff Arms Park to take part in the old English game. Such was the proficiency attained that ... in no single instance did they sustain defeat, thus well upholding the honour of the town ... the prospects of the club [for the forthcoming season] seemed brighter than ever. Unfortunately, however, on applying for the use of the Cardiff Arms Park it was refused, notwithstanding the expressed intention of the club to maintain a man to look after the ground. Mr Corbett [the Bute Estate solicitor] kindly offered ... to find a suitable field elsewhere, but without success. Thus, for the want of a convenient ground, this club – a real boon to the town – must collapse. Although we have no doubt that Mr. Corbett had his reasons for refusing the Cardiff Arms Park, still we firmly believe that if the Marquess of Bute fully understood, not only the disappointment, but the great injury that this refusal will cause to so many young men in Cardiff, he would, with his usual generosity and desire to further the interests of the town, immediately give the required permission.[29]

---

28   *WM* 17 Apr. 1875.

29   *WM* 15 Oct. 1875.

Perhaps because JA Corbett had attended Cheltenham College, this appeal seems to have been considered sympathetically as the Glamorgan club were allowed to continue their use of the Park for most of their matches that season. However, the vandalism may have persisted because, the following year, the newly formed Cardiff club were able to play only their opening home fixture against Swansea at the Arms Park. Thereafter they spent their first three seasons at Sophia Gardens, though the club's official histories do not refer to this.[30] However, the Arms Park was still used occasionally for training at this time. Demonstrating how players were kept informed of the arrangements, this revealing notice appeared in the *Western Mail* at the beginning of the 1877-8 season:

> On and after Saturday, 29th September, there will be Practice Games every Saturday right through the Season, except when Matches are being played. Notices as to whether the Games will take place in the Sophia Gardens Field or the Cardiff Arms Park will be displayed every Wednesday in the respective windows of Mr. Banning's Fancy Shop in Duke Street, and Mrs. Williams's Stationery Depot in the Bute Docks.[31]

So it was Sophia Gardens, rather than the Arms Park, which hosted the final of the South Wales Challenge Cup in 1878-9 between Cardiff and Newport. Even in later years, Cardiff continued to use the Gardens occasionally when the playing conditions at the Arms Park were bad, as happened in their fixtures with Llanelli in 1884 and Castleford in 1886. However, since 1879, Cardiff RFC have enjoyed permanent and exclusive use of the Arms Park, though they constantly had to be wary of not upsetting the landlord's interest. The ground was shared with the cricket club, who had been using the Park since 1848 though, as the rugby club's use and development of the site grew, there were increasing conflicts between the two. In 1887, for instance, a dispute arose over responsibility for the cost of protecting the cricket pitch from the crowds attending the rugby matches.[32] In 1922, the freehold of the land was eventually acquired from the Bute Estate for

---

30   A. A. Hunter (ed.), *Cheltenham College Register 1841-1889*, (London, 1890), p. 175 (Corbett); C.S. Arthur, *The Cardiff Rugby Football Club: History and Statistics, 1876-1906* (Cardiff, 1908); D.E. Davies, *Cardiff Rugby Club: History and Statistics, 1876-1975: "The Greatest"* (Cardiff, 1975).

31   *WM* 26 Sept. 1877.

32   *WM* 4 Feb. 1884, 30 Mar. 1886, 11 Apr. 1887.

A packed 1890s Arms Park grandstand with supporters swarming over the roof and in surrounding trees, presumably unable to stroll out for a pint whenever they felt like it.

£30,000 by the Cardiff Athletic (i.e. sports) Club, of which the rugby and cricket clubs were the principal sections.[33]

The significance of the strategic location of the Arms Park to Cardiff rugby in the nineteenth century was recognised at the time. In 1896, "Ariel" of the *Western Mail* declared:

> the dear old park ... just as muddy and clammy, but just as convenient and get-at-able for everybody as it was when Cardiff was merely aping a large town. The value of this piece of ground to the Cardiff Football Club is really untold, and they will never rightly value it till they have to shift![34]

One hundred and thirteen years later, the club's twenty-first century professional descendants, Cardiff Blues, disregarded the concerns of modern-day Ariels, and decided to "shift" and become tenants at the new edge of town Cardiff City soccer stadium at Leckwith. However, after the commercial failure of this controversial move, Cardiff Blues returned to the "convenient and get-at-able ... dear old park" in 2012-13. A year later, the old problem of the "muddy and clammy" playing surface was finally dealt with, when a new artificial pitch was laid down.

---

33   See Andrew Hignell and Gwyn Prescott, *Cardiff Sporting Greats*, pp. 33-5, 115-16 for brief histories of the Arms Park and the Cardiff Athletic Club.

34   *WM* 27 Jan. 1896.

Some of the faithful at the "dear old park" for a match with Neath.

Most local match reports, especially in early years, give little indication of the exact location of many of the grounds used. There are occasional glimpses of games played in Roath, Cathays or Canton on sites subsequently taken for housing. For instance, Windsor, a strong early club, used land in Cathays before it was developed as Senghenydd Road, now largely occupied by the university. Ambitious clubs like Cardiff Harlequins sought their own enclosed facilities and occupied various grounds at Penarth Road, North Road and Newport Road.[35] The major landowners in Cardiff generally gave their support to the game, as long as it did not conflict with their wider estate management interests. When Penarth's new ground was opened in 1891, it was initially provided free of charge by Lord Windsor, whose agent referred to the similar generosity of the Marquess of Bute and Lord Tredegar who were "doing all they can to encourage the game of football". The Arms Park, of course, was Bute land, whilst Cardiff Harlequins leased their Newport Road ground from the Tredegar Estate.[36] It is interesting to note that the three senior clubs in the Cardiff area all played on land owned by the three principal landowners in the locality.

---

35   *SWDN* 10 Oct. 1892.
36   *WM* 5 Oct. 1891.

Tongwynlais, one of Cardiff's outlying village clubs in 1907-8.
Courtesy of SA Brain and Co.

Clubs on the urban fringe managed to find places to play more easily than those in the urban core. East Moors was a popular venue for Splott and Newtown teams, whilst those in the west used Canton Common (later Jubilee Park) and Ely Common (later Victoria Park). For a brief period, Canton and other clubs in the area were able to use Alexandra Park, situated about a mile from the town centre and just off Cowbridge Road, the main route west from Cardiff. Opened in 1880, this ambitious project was a purpose-built sports ground, which catered for cricket, horse-racing, athletics and cycling. It was also a venue for rugby and it hosted a number of senior matches. It was the home ground of the re-formed, but short-lived, Cardiff Wanderers, who met Penarth, Bridgend, Neath and Cardiff there in 1882-3. In the same season, when the Arms Park was unplayable, even Cardiff used Alexandra Park a couple of times, playing both Clifton and a District XV there; whilst it was also the venue for a representative match between South Wales and Old Leysians. Unfortunately, the proprietors of this venture soon found themselves in serious financial difficulties, and the ground was closed in 1885 and developed for housing soon after.[37]

Teams in outlying villages, like Llandaff, Tongwynlais and Whitchurch, with little competition from other clubs or from housing developers, were able to use their grounds more or less exclusively and permanently. The opportunity to take a twelve year lease allowed Whitchurch to erect a stand and enclose their ground at the rear of the *Fox and Hounds* and this enabled them to apply successfully for membership of the WFU in 1895.[38]

Most clubs, however, used public playing fields and hence were generally unable to rely on gate money. By far the most important such facility in nineteenth-century Cardiff was Sophia Gardens, the oldest public park in Wales.[39] The Gardens were opened to the public by the Marquess of Bute in 1858 and shortly afterwards, they were extended to include "Sophia Gardens Field" which became a much-used venue for rugby. Following the move from the Arms Park by Glamorgan County Cricket Club in 1967, the site was eventually absorbed into what is now the SWALEC cricket stadium and Test Match venue. Centrally located, close to public houses and transport terminals, it was the home of many rugby clubs, including junior and school teams, from all over the town.[40] Such was its popularity, Daryl Leeworthy reveals, that club officials were forced to turn up at the park gates at dawn on match day to lay claim to a pitch.[41] The contribution of Sophia Gardens to rugby was immense. Not only did it play host to Cardiff for three seasons and to the South Wales Challenge Cup final, more importantly, it was the place where an overwhelming number of Cardiff's Victorian citizens learned and developed their game from the earliest days. Without this large and accessible facility, it is questionable whether rugby would have expanded quite as it did. Contemporary reports show that, on many Saturdays, in the late 1880s and early 1890s, hundreds of young men played rugby there throughout the day.

---

37   Daryl Leeworthy, *Fields of Play: The Sporting Heritage of Wales*, (Aberystwyth 2012), p. 108; Andrew Hignell, "Alexandra Park – Cardiff's First-Ever Purpose-Built Sports Ground", *Morgannwg*, 57 (2013), pp. 103-119; *SWDN* 27 Nov. 1882 (Wanderers v Cardiff); *SWDN* 30 Oct. 1882 (Clifton); *SWDN* 27 Dec. 1882 (South Wales).

38   *WM* 17 Sept. 1894. This ground was often used for Cardiff and District cup matches.

39   For a detailed history of Sophia Gardens, see Andrew Hignell, *From Sophia to SWALEC: A History of Cricket in Cardiff*, (Stroud, 2009). Hignell's account of early rugby in Cardiff draws on the research for this book in places.

40   R.H. Morgan, "The Development of an Urban Transport System: The Case of Cardiff", *Welsh History Review*, 13, 2 (1986), pp. 178-181.

41   Leeworthy, *Fields of Play*, pp. 22-3.

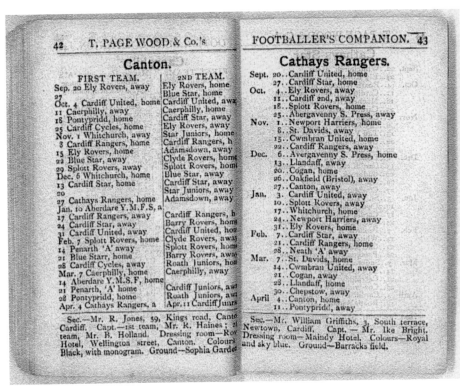

In 1890-1, Canton played their home matches at Sophia Gardens while Cardiff Rangers used Maindy Barracks.

Sophia Gardens, however, was not the only public space available. During much of the period, some local clubs used the Cathays recreation ground, which was then part of the site acquired by the Corporation for a burial ground. Inevitably, however, as the cemetery grew, the area available for recreation was gradually reduced. Eventually, in 1892, the Burial Board decided to prohibit rugby there because of the "unseemly conduct" of spectators which caused "great annoyance" to those attending funerals.[42] Nevertheless, there were other facilities available nearby, such as the new public recreation ground at Roath Park, and Maindy Barracks, which was a particular favourite of railway clubs like Taff Vale Wanderers. An indication of the variety of grounds used can be found in the columns of the *SWDN* during November 1890. These recorded matches played that month at Sophia Gardens, Maindy Barracks, Cathays Recreation Ground,

---

42   *SWDN* 5 Oct. 1892; *County Borough of Cardiff Reports of Council and Committees*, Nov. 1891 to Nov. 1892, p. 589.

The flimsy nature of the goal posts can be glimpsed on the right of this early photograph. The player waiting to receive the ball is Charles Taylor (HMS Marlborough) who won nine Welsh caps between 1884 and 1887. He was killed in action in 1915. John Taylor

Roath Park, Llandaff Fields, Canton Common (later Jubilee Park); and on a variety of pitches now lost to us in Market Gardens Field (Canton), Atlas Ground (Canton), Saltmede (Grangetown), East Moors (Splott), Tynycoed Field (Roath), and Leckwith Common.

We do not know whether clubs had specific pitches at public parks. Given the number of teams playing at the Gardens, it seems unlikely, though one match report does refer to Mackintosh playing "on the patch of ... the Ely [Rovers] in the Sophia Gardens."[43] The marking of pitches was probably the responsibility of the home club. There are occasional references to this not having been carried out, such as when Penygraig complained that Llandaff had failed to mark out touch-lines and goal-lines.[44] The absence of barriers frequently resulted in spectators encroaching onto the field. Commenting favourably on the arrangements at Penarth's ground, "Old Stager" wrote in 1886 that he had expected to see supporters interfering with the players: "the sort of thing ... to be witnessed any Saturday at that happy hunting ground of Cardiff district clubs, the Sophia Gardens."[45]

---

43   *SWDN* 25 Nov. 1889.
44   *SWDN* 30 Dec. 1889.
45   *SWDN* 20 Sept. 1886.

What arrangements there were for erecting goal posts can only be guessed at. They may have been kept in situ but the likelihood is they were erected each week. Reminiscing some years later about the first ever South Wales Challenge Cup final held in 1879 at Newbridge Fields cricket ground outside Bridgend, Walter Clifford Phillips recalled that he and his fellow Newport committeemen arrived early to check out the ground. It was just as well they did, as it was deserted and no preparations had been made for the match. They discovered "some poles and sticks in the ditch" which they decided to erect and they then "measured out the ground ... [before] returning to Bridgend to greet the Newport team."[46] Goal posts were much smaller and lighter than today and so it would have been relatively easy to carry them from the corner of the field or from the local pub and erect them for each match. If every spare part of Sophia Gardens was used, as it almost certainly must have been, then something like this must have happened. Timber cross bars were not always standard in the early years of the game and tape was often used for this purpose. Sometimes, though, they were dispensed with altogether. When St. David's defeated Bridgend in 1892 at the Barracks, there were no cross bars and therefore no goal attempts.[47]

There were few on-field facilities for the players. Press correspondence in 1885 throws light on the inadequate conditions at Sophia Gardens and on the pilfering which went on.

[There is a] lack of a proper place ... for the players' clothes, bags etc. The dressing-rooms pertaining to public-houses in the neighbourhood of the Sophia Gardens Field are quite inadequate for the number of our local clubs which play ... there every Saturday and Wednesday ... players [have to] deposit their clothes in a wash-house ... which might accommodate four persons at the most, and on the open field ... pilfering goes on at an alarming rate. A few weeks ago the members of one club alone lost ... over £2 ... Such trifling articles as a spare football, hats, mufflers ... disappear with annoying frequency. One player recently had his bag and contents "lifted" ... owing to the nuisance of either having to come to the field dressed and go back dirty, or to dress on the field and have your things stolen, many men will not "turn up". What is wanted is a good large erection in the Sophia Gardens field ... with conveniences for washing ... This would be an incalculable boon to the football community.[48]

---

46   *SWDN* 4 March 1878 (Newbridge Fields), 21 Nov. 1892 (Phillips).
47   *SWDN* 31 Oct. 1892.
48   *SWDN* 10 Feb. 1885.

Another correspondent complained that thefts from players were common. He suggested a Cardiff v District match should be arranged to raise funds for a building, with a trough for washing.[49] It is not known whether the authorities responded to these complaints. It seems unlikely that much was done. Some years later, there were calls for the attendance of police at matches to deal with the "roughs" who robbed players' clothes and even stole their footballs.[50] Even after the First World War, there was little accommodation at Sophia Gardens. Bleddyn Williams recalled playing there for Cardiff Schoolboys around 1934, when the teams stripped under the trees and washed off with water from the river.[51]

There were occasions, of course, when Sophia Gardens was unavailable for sport. Nevertheless, despite its being "half a foot deep in snow" in February 1895, Canton and Grangetown Stars still managed to complete their fixture. Even when Buffalo Bill's Wild West Show

Typical kit bags in the 1890s.

colonised the ground for a week in September 1891, "Some of the Junior teams ... took advantage of the stretches of unoccupied land and had 'a kick or two' on them." If the locals had been able to persuade the Americans to play, the visitors might have turned out a decent front row, comprising "Kicking Bear", "Short Bull" and "No Neck". When players arrived at the Gardens in September 1895, this time their matches had to be abandoned because "the Band of Hope demonstration ... occupied the field." No doubt

---

49   *SWDN* 14 Feb. 1885.
50   *WM* 12 Oct. 1894.
51   Gareth Edwards and Don Llewellyn, "The Williams Family: More Than a 'Rugby Dynasty' ", *Garth Domain*, 26, (2004), p. 11.

Located opposite the Millennium Stadium, the City Arms is one of Cardiff's best known rugby pubs. During the nineteenth century too, it was a popular venue for supporters and local clubs, including Cardiff and Cardiff Rangers.   Siân Prescott

many happily retaliated in time honoured rugby tradition by returning to their local pub to celebrate a free afternoon.[52]

Public houses were, after all, vitally important to the game as social gathering places and club headquarters. Because of this, it soon became apparent to the sport's critics that rugby would have little "reforming" influence on the working class.[53] As Tony Collins and Wray Vamplew astutely put it, "Rather than football being an adjunct of the pub, the pub almost became an adjunct of football." They note that breweries recognised that a location near a major football ground was an important asset which increased takings.[54]

---

52   *WM* 4 Feb. 1895 (snow); *Welsh Athlete* 21 Sept. 1891 (Junior teams); *WM* 21 Sept. 1891 (No Neck); *SWDN* 30 Sept. 1895 (Band of Hope).

53   Gareth Morgan, "Rugby and Revivalism: Sport and Religion in Edwardian Wales", *IJHS*, 22, 3 (2005), p. 435.

54   Tony Collins and Wray Vamplew, *Mud, Sweat and Beers: A Cultural History of Sport and Alcohol* (Oxford, 2002), pp. 13-15; Alan Metcalfe, "The Control of Space and the Development of Sport: A Case Study of Twenty Two Sports in the Mining Communities of East Northumberland, 1800-1914", *Sports Historian*, 15, (1995), p. 27.

This must have been true in Cardiff. With their close proximity to both Cardiff Arms Park and Sophia Gardens, town centre pubs, hotels and restaurants were well placed to respond in a variety of ways to the needs of the rapidly increasing numbers of players and supporters.

The Cardiff club used the nearby *Grand Hotel* and *Angel Hotel* as their headquarters and for changing; while in 1886, they also hired a room in the equally convenient *Cattle Market Tavern* (familiar today to supporters from around the world as the *City Arms*) for training purposes. Cardiff did not possess their own private accommodation until a club pavilion was constructed at the Arms Park in 1904.[55]

The nature of the close relationship in Victorian times between rugby and the public house, particularly those in the town centre, can be glimpsed in the advertisements in local football handbooks published during the

WHEN IN CARDIFF GIVE

Ye Old Cardiff Cottage, St. Mary St.,

A CALL.

WINES, SPIRITS & BURTON BEERS OF THE BEST QUALITY.

Free House.

ALFRED E. WILLIAMS - Proprietor.

Headquarters of Grange Stars and Town Quarters of Cathays.

TELEGRAPHIC FOOTBALL RESULTS.

THE **7** PRINCIPAL MATCHES IN SOUTH WALES.

ONE WIRE, **1/6** PER WEEK.   TWO WIRES, **2/2**

PRINTED SHEETS SENT FRIDAY NIGHT'S POST

Licensed Houses—Advertisement Free.

MORTIMER & Co., Rotunda Buildings, Cardiff.

Advertisements in the 1894-5 handbook for the Cardiff Cottage, headquarters of two teams; and for Mortimer's telegraphic service which kept pub users informed of match results.

1890s. For example, in 1894-5, the *Cardiff Cottage* in St. Mary Street, still a popular rugby meeting place today, offered accommodation to the Grange Stars and Cathays clubs.

In 1890-1, the *Three Horse Shoes*, which was located in High Street, hosted St. David's; while a year later it accommodated four other clubs rugby clubs and provided telegraphic match results for customers. In 1894-5, the regulars at "the favourite resort of football enthusiasts", the *Philharmonic Restaurant* in St. Mary Street, could receive football results every Saturday; while in the same season, the publishers Mortimer & Co. offered free advertising to all licensed houses which used their telegraphic results service.

Another modern favourite with rugby supporters, the *Blue Bell* (now the *Goat Major*) in High Street promoted itself in 1891-2 as being only one

---

55   Arthur, *Cardiff Rugby*, p. 75; Davies, *Cardiff Rugby Club*, p. 52.

This 1890-1 advertisement for the Three Horse Shoes made a strong appeal to rugby followers. Penygraig, whose fixtures are shown alongside, became the first valleys club to achieve senior status for a while.

minute from both the Arms Park and (presumably if you could run fast) Sophia Gardens. It boasted first class accommodation for visiting teams and it was also where the Cardiff and District Football Union held its meetings.

"The Home of Athletes" was the claim made by the proprietor of the *New Market Hotel* (which has recently become an *Old Market Tavern*) in Trinity Street. It too was one minute from the Arms Park and a rather more realistic five minutes from the Gardens. It was the headquarters of St. David's in 1891-2 and provided the players with free hot and cold baths. It was here that the Cardiff and District Football Union was founded in 1892, though no blue plaque yet commemorates this significant contribution to the sporting history of Cardiff.

However, it was its strategic location in Westgate Street overlooking the Arms Park, which gave the fifty bedroom *Grand Hotel* its particular advantages. In 1891-2, its proprietors advertised facilities for football dinners, concerts and meetings; plunge and swimming baths; and special accommodation

An 1891-2 advertisement for the "centrally located" Blue Bell (renamed the Goat Major). The adjoining page demonstrates that Cardiff Harlequins had an impressive fixture list by this season, though the Cardiff club was a notable absentee.

for touring teams. The *Grand Hotel*'s unique attraction, however, was what may well be the earliest ever example of the hospitality suite: season tickets could be purchased to view matches from the hotel balconies, which can still be seen today. This was an innovative and enterprising society, after all.[56]

It could be a risk for hoteliers to welcome visiting teams, however. The Harlequins celebrated losing by six tries at the hands of Cardiff in 1886 by disrupting the performance at the Philharmonic Music Hall and then causing damage at the *Angel Hotel*, which included drop-kicking a tea service

---

56 *Cardiff and South Wales Footballer's Companion: 1890-91* (Cardiff, 1890), p. [18] (*Three Horse Shoes*); *The Welsh Athlete and West of England Cycling News Football Handbook 1891-2* (Cardiff, 1891), pp. [56] (*Blue Bell*), [54] (*New Market*), [42] (*Three Horse Shoes*), [52] (*Grand*); *Mortimer's Football Guide for South Wales and Monmouthshire: Season, 1894-95* (Barry, 1894), pp. 22 (*Philharmonic*), [49] (*Cardiff Cottage* and results service).

An 1891-2 advertisement for the rugby-friendly New Market Hotel which reveals that Thomas Mallett was then the proprietor. The accompanying fixture list was Penarth's most ambitious so far.

across the floor. The *SWDN* reported that the "London Harlequins ... have written offering to make good the damage occasioned by them at several Cardiff hotels during their stay in the town. The Cardiff match committee may discontinue fixtures with the Quins following their rowdy conduct." They did. Cardiff did not renew fixtures for twenty-five years. No doubt it was also alcohol which fuelled the boorish behaviour of Blackheath's players at the Theatre Royal in December 1896, where they "made idiots of themselves to the general annoyance of the house". The press was generally critical of such incidents but "Dagon" of the *Western Mail* described Cardiff's apparently uneventful stay in Burton in 1888 in rather ambiguous terms.

The practical jokes which are a proverbial indication of the presence of a football team in any hotel were of a rather mild and timid character. An uneventful night – a rare incident – was passed and in the morning

Among the many facilities offered in this 1891-2 advertisement for the Grand Hotel were season tickets to view the matches from the balconies. Alongside is Llanelli's fixture list, which included eight matches with North of England teams.

a visit was made to one of the many breweries in the town, where the team had the opportunity to inspect the works.[57]

It sounds as though "Dagon" was rather disappointed.

The 1890-91 football handbook provides further insights into the interdependence of pubs and Welsh rugby. It contains the fixture lists of twenty-six clubs in the Cardiff area and for nineteen of these it notes the location of their "dressing rooms". Details are shown in Table 6. Seventeen were based in pubs or hotels, one in a coffee tavern and one in a church institute.[58] These are similar to Tony Collins's findings for Yorkshire in 1885-6, where only five out of eighty rugby clubs did not use a pub as

---

57 *WM* 1 Feb. 1886; *SWDN* 1 Feb., 26 Apr. 1886 (Harlequins); *WM* 1 Jan. 1897 (Blackheath); *WM* 22 Oct. 1888 (Burton).

58 *Cardiff and South Wales Footballer's Companion: 1890-91* (Cardiff, 1890), pp. 15-66.

Over a hundred and twenty years later, the balconies of the former Grand Hotel in Westgate Street are still in place.

Siân Prescott

headquarters.[59] Though they relate to two seasons just outside the period covered by this book, the official handbooks of the Cardiff and District Rugby Union for 1905-6 and 1908-9 reveal that clubs then still relied heavily on the public house. Of the twenty-two teams in 1905 which gave details of their headquarters, twenty used pubs; while in 1908, seventeen of the twenty senior clubs did so.[60]

Several authors have referred to the practice of football clubs playing on land attached to public houses.[61] There is no evidence for this in the built-up areas of Cardiff but it was probably different in the less densely populated districts. For example, in the village of Whitchurch, the local club played on fields adjoining both the *Hollybush* and the *Fox and Hounds*, their headquarters for many years.

Whilst it was common in the north of England for well-known footballers to runs pubs, there is little indication of this happening in Cardiff at the time.[62] One exception was Syd Nicholls (Cardiff and Wales) who became manager of the *Grand Hotel* in 1894-5, with his brother and future international Gwyn Nicholls acting as his under-manager.[63] Syd Nicholls had finished playing then, but when Viv Huzzey became the licensee of the *Windsor Arms* in Stuart Street in the Docks in 1899, he was

---

59 Tony Collins, *Rugby's Great Split: Class, Culture and the Origins of Rugby League Football* (London, 2006 edn.), p. 27.

60 *Cardiff and District Rugby Union: Official Handbook, Season 1905-6* (Cardiff, 1905), pp. 4-7; *Cardiff and District Rugby Union: Official Handbook, Season 1908-9* (Cardiff, 1908), pp. 5-8.

61 Tony Mason, *Association Football and English Society 1863-1915* (Brighton, 1981), p. 27; Collins and Vamplew, *Mud, Sweat and Beers*, pp. 11-22; Metcalfe, "Control of Space", p. 24.

62 Mason, *Association Football and English Society*, pp. 118-119; Collins and Vamplew, *Mud, Sweat and Beers*, p. 13.

63 David Parry-Jones, *Prince Gwyn: Gwyn Nicholls and the First Golden Era of Welsh Rugby* (Bridgend, 1999), p. 32.

Table 6: Cardiff and District Clubs' Dressing Rooms 1890-1[64]

Club	Dressing Room	Playing Field
Canton	*Rover Hotel*, Wellington Street	Sophia Gardens
Cardiff	*Angel Hotel*, Castle Street	Cardiff Arms Park
Cardiff Cyclists	*Maindy Hotel*, [*North Star*], North Road, Maindy	Barracks
Cardiff Harlequins	*Washington Hotel*, GWR Station, Canal Wharf West/Penarth Road	Penarth Road
Cardiff Juniors (16 years)	*Coldstream Hotel*, Brook Street, Riverside	Sophia Gardens
Cardiff Rangers	*Cattle Market Tavern*, [*City Arms*], Quay Street	Sophia Gardens
Cardiff Rovers	*Bristol and South Wales Hotel*, Penarth Road	Penarth Road
Cardiff Star	*Coldstream Hotel*, Riverside	Sophia Gardens
Cardiff United	*Grand Hotel Vaults*, Womanby Street	Sophia Gardens
Cathays Rangers	*Maindy Hotel*, [*North Star*], North Road, Maindy	Barracks
Cathays Star	*St. Andrew's Institute*, George Street	Cathays Rec'n. Ground
Clyde Rovers (15 years)	*Lord Wimborne Hotel*, Portmanmoor Road, Splott	East Moors
Cogan	*Cogan Hotel*, Hewell Street, Cogan	Not known
Ely Rovers	*Half-Way Hotel*, Penhill Road	Sophia Gardens
Llandaff	*Malsters Arms*, Llandaff	Mill Field
St. David's	*Three Horse Shoes*, High Street	Sophia Gardens
St. Peter's	*Flora Hotel*, Cathays Terrace	Barracks
Star Juniors	*Anchor Coffee Tavern*, Custom House Street	Not known
Taff Vale Wanderers	*Woodville Hotel*, Woodville Road, Cathays	Barracks

---

64   Compiled from *Cardiff Footballer's Companion: 1890-91*, pp. 15-66.

Alcohol was not the only product popular with the followers of rugby in 1890-1.

still a Cardiff and Wales player. Reporting this, the *Western Mail* noted that, whilst it was very common in the Northern Union to become a licensed victualler, "yet it is only on very [rare] occasions that Welsh players get these chances." This arrangement was probably an unsuccessful attempt to keep Huzzey in Wales, for a year later he turned professional and joined Oldham in the Northern Union.[65]

The members of rugby clubs based in coffee taverns were not necessarily teetotal. There are references in the press to clubs using coffee taverns on some occasions and pubs at other times. In some cases, it was perhaps just a matter of convenience. Some teams used neither public house nor coffee tavern as their headquarters. In Grahame Lloyd's history of Cardiff City, there is an interesting account of the facilities used by the Riverside soccer club. Their clubhouse was a disused stable at the rear of a house, where members could play billiards and cards. As it was a short walk from Sophia Gardens, the team presumably also changed here.[66]

---

65 *WM* 23 Jan. 1899.

66 Grahame Lloyd, *C'Mon City! A Hundred Years of the Bluebirds* (Bridgend, 1999), pp. 21-2.

Players and Administrators

Having explored aspects of how rugby in Cardiff was organised, it would be appropriate to consider now who played and administered the game. It is widely accepted that the overwhelming majority of the first rugby players came from the middle and upper classes. As Gareth Williams has written, "The role of the middle class in establishing rugby clubs in Wales is clear".[67]

Cardiff provides an opportunity to test this with a limited study of the social background of the town's early players during the 1870s. Charles Arthur's 1908 history records the names of many of these and it also includes lists of members for Cardiff's first two seasons.[68] Additional names were obtained from press match reports of the period. As a result, the names of 150 men involved up to 1878 were identified. Census returns, directories, biographies and the internet were then consulted to try to identify individuals. In many cases, this proved impossible, not least because of the large number of players with common Welsh surnames. Sometimes only a surname was available, making a positive identification difficult. Nevertheless, information was traced on fifty-four, over a third of the known members and players associated with Cardiff and its predecessor clubs up to 1878. This is a sufficiently large sample to provide a reliable indication of the typical background of Cardiff's first players. Whilst this exercise largely confirms traditional views about the social class of early rugby players in Wales, it is the first detailed empirical investigation of a Welsh club's playing membership from this period.

Those identified included all the leading players and officials. Some came from families prominent in the commercial and civic life of the locality like Cory, Duncan, Hood, Batchelor, Riches and Vachell. None was working class, whether judged by occupation, father's occupation, residence or education. The majority were employed in mercantile occupations connected with the coal trade rather than the professions. Some were businessmen in their own right, including a newspaper proprietor, a timber merchant, a shipowner and a chain manufacturer. Many were employed in family enterprises such as shipping, timber importing, coal exporting and fuel manufacture. There were mining engineers, colliery agents, land agents, draughtsmen, teachers, students and a dentist. Finally, there was a large group of clerks employed by shipbrokers, solicitors, banks and the post office as well as by coal, railway and insurance companies. Towards the end of the decade, there are indications of an increase in the number of lower status clerks, suggesting perhaps the

---

67 Gareth Williams, "Community, Class and Rugby", p. 10.
68 Arthur, *Cardiff Rugby*, pp. 7-21.

A bowler hatted touch judge calls a line-out in an early match.

beginning of the downward shift in the social class of membership. Of course, it is possible that, amongst the unknown two-thirds, there were some working-class players, since they are generally less likely to have left some record of their lives. However, the overwhelming evidence is that in the 1870s Cardiff was predominantly, if not entirely, a middle-class club.

There is also some contemporary evidence which supports this view of an initially narrow social base. In 1878, the club captain, Raoul Foa, wrote to the press about his fellow players, "being *most of them engaged in business*, [they] are unable to absent themselves from the office more than one afternoon a week."[69] Another correspondent suggested that all members could be guaranteed games if internal matches were organised, involving Lloyd's v Coal Trade and Business in Docks v The Rest amongst others, suggesting that players were predominantly office workers.[70] In March 1879, Cardiff met the holders Newport in the final of the South Wales Challenge Cup. Attempting to excuse Cardiff's defeat, the *SWDN* declared that "while the members of [Cardiff] … are *many of them connected with the offices of commercial and railway companies*, many of the members of the Newport club are artisans and the difference in point of strength was considerable."[71]

This appears to confirm that the club was still largely socially exclusive at the end of the decade, though the *SWDN* was quite wrong about the involvement of working-class players in the Newport team at this time, as has been shown earlier. However, the match report also referred to the many thousands of spectators present and the keen interest which they displayed. Such levels of support would soon entice clubs to overcome any initial reluctance they may have had about selecting working men. It was inevitable that, amongst the growing numbers drawn to these exciting contests, there would have been workers who fancied giving the game a

69   *WM* 29 Nov. 1878 (italics added).
70   *WM* 2 Dec. 1878.
71   *SWDN* 10 Mar. 1879 (italics added).

try. Certainly, within two years of that 1879 cup final, working men were appearing in the Cardiff First XV.

Further evidence of the essentially middle-class nature of the game in the 1870s is revealed by the existence of the 10th Glamorgan Rifle Volunteers (GRV) club. There were also two other volunteer units in Cardiff at the time, the 16th GRV and the 3rd Glamorgan Artillery Volunteers (GAV). According to a local historian writing in 1918, when these were formed, the 16th GRV were known as the "People's Rifle Corps" and had "more moderate and less restrictive terms of entry than the 10th." He added that the 3rd GAV comprised "artisans, shipwrights and other stalwart working men".[72] It is revealing, therefore, that of these three units, it was only the more socially elite 10th GRV which formed a rugby club during the 1870s.

This research into players' backgrounds also provides clues about the process of the early growth of rugby in the town. Schoolmasters may have been instrumental in introducing the game. Then there were the products of rugby playing public schools. In Cardiff these included Rugby, Cheltenham, Marlborough, Clifton, Sherborne, Christ College Brecon and Monmouth. In addition, old boys of the private schools, Monkton House, Cardiff Collegiate and Bridgend, as well as Cowbridge Grammar School were crucially important. Whilst students are often credited with spreading the game, apart from a few who may have played at university or teaching hospital, their influence in Cardiff does not appear to have been particularly strong.

The game, however, *was* enhanced by the presence of talented newcomers. William Grave was already an established player when in 1872 he arrived from Manchester – where his father was a former Lord Mayor – to manage a family chain works. He had previously played for Cheltenham College, Manchester and Lancashire and had kicked the winning goal against Yorkshire in the first ever Roses Match in 1870. He later came close to winning an England cap. Marshall described him as "a half back … of great trickiness and wonderful drop kicking". Although Grave's time in Cardiff was brief, there is little doubt that he had a considerable impact. He was a leading light of the Arms Park pioneers, not only helping to get the game underway there but also coaching the less experienced players. Appointed vice-captain of Glamorgan FC in their first season 1874-5, he was described as "pre-eminent … his running, dodging and drop-kicking [were] a treat to watch". Some years later, "Welsh Athlete" recalled that Grave was "the most prominent" rugby player in the locality at the time. He might even have become the first Glamorgan/Cardiff player to win representative honours

---

72   W.J. Trounce, *"Cardiff in the Fifties": The Reminiscences and Historical Notes of Alderman W.J. Trounce J.P. 1850-1860* (Cardiff, 1918), pp. 88-9.

Cardiff Cricket Club 1875. William Grave is third from the left in the back row, looking to his left. Standing on the steps is EW Jones, who took part in the 1868 matches at the Arms Park.   *Courtesy of Cardiff Council Library Service*

when he was invited to play for the North of England but he declined because of his commitments in Cardiff. However, after one season with Glamorgan, he returned to Manchester and was immediately selected for the North against the South in January 1876. He later became secretary of Manchester and Lancashire, though his contribution to early Welsh rugby has long been forgotten. The influence of gifted individuals like William Grave should not be underestimated.[73]

However, by the early 1880s, Cardiff could no longer depend on its own resources to maintain its growing status in the sport. The club's initial function of merely providing enjoyment for members was giving way to the much stronger need of upholding the town's reputation.[74] In so doing, the club increasingly began to rely on players produced by the newly emerging local "junior" clubs, such as Bute Dock Rangers, Canton, Cardiff Quins,

---

73   *WM* 29 Mar. 1893; Hunter, *Cheltenham College Register 1841-1889*, p. 187; *Sheffield and Rotherham Independent* 29 Mar. 1870 (Lancashire), 31 Jan. 1876 (North); C. Stewart Caine (ed.), *John Wisden's Rugby Football Almanack for 1924-25* (London, 1924), pp. 229, 234 (North); F. Marshall (ed.), *Football: The Rugby Union Game* (London, 1894 edn.), pp. 399-400; *Evening Express* 27 August 1892 (Welsh Athlete).

74   See also Collins, *Rugby's Great Split*, p. 15.

Cardiff Rangers and Windsor. Both working-class and middle-class players joined Cardiff from these clubs who must, therefore, have drawn their players from across the social boundaries. If working men had reached a good enough standard to represent Cardiff by 1881, they probably began playing in local clubs at least by the end of the 1870s. The arrival of the working class, not only in Cardiff but throughout Welsh rugby, came at a time when clear signs of political change in Wales were also emerging. With nine gains in the general election of 1880, Liberal MPs now held twenty-nine of the thirty-three Welsh seats.[75] The movement towards a more democratic Wales in both politics and rugby was underway.

Given the major impact which they subsequently had on the wider game, it is interesting to note the number of former local club players who represented Cardiff in Hancock's record-breaking year. At the end of 1885-6, the *SWDN* published a list of the men who played under Hancock.[76] By searching the press in earlier seasons, it is possible to show that, of the seventeen who appeared most frequently in Hancock's team, *at least* eleven had played for local clubs before joining Cardiff. Seven of those eleven went on to win Welsh caps. Former Canton players included Billy Douglas, Albert Hybart, Dick Kedzlie, David Lewis, William Stadden (all Welsh internationals) and Arthur Emery, John Sant and Wyndham Jarman; while Hugh Hughes and George Young (both Welsh internationals) had played for Cardiff Harlequins and Jimmy Mahoney for Cardiff Rangers. Details of the seventeen players are shown in Table 7.

Reminiscing wistfully and perhaps rather fancifully in 1892 about the Cardiff club of 1884-5, "Old Stager" discussed the process of working-class players joining from local junior clubs.

> The game, by that time, had fairly caught on, and became the pursuit of the masses, who in earlier days had been content merely to look on from outside the ropes. Clubs were springing up all over the town, composed mainly of lusty youths many of them working lads or sons of working men, sound of wind and limb, and brimful of pluck and ambition ... [the Cardiff second XV was] recruited almost entirely from one of those minor clubs ... Canton ... [and they] ... upset in a pitched encounter the first fifteen. The result was the precipitate retirement of many of the older members.[77]

---

75   Kenneth O. Morgan, *Rebirth of a Nation: Wales 1880-1980* (Oxford, 1982 edn.), pp. 12-13.

76   *SWDN* 21 Apr. 1886.

77   *Cardiff Times* 10 Sept. 1892. See Croll, *Civilizing the Urban*, pp. 245-6 for a different interpretation from that presented here.

Table 7: Cardiff First XV Players 1885-6[78]
(See team photograph on page 6)

Name	Games Played	Occupation	Former Club(s)	Place of Birth	Honours
Hugh Hughes	27	Carpenter	Star, Cardiff Quins	Meirionydd	Wales
Wyndham Jarman	27	Decorator	Canton	Cardiff	
Alexander Bland	27	Solicitor		Pembs	Wales
William "Buller" Stadden	26	Labourer	Canton, Bute Dock Rangers	Cardiff	Wales
Quinton Dick Kedzlie	26	Blacksmith	Windsor, Canton	Scotland	Wales
Frank Hancock	26	Brewery Director	Wiveliscombe	Somerset	Wales
Arthur Emery	25	Merchant's Clerk	Canton	Cardiff	
James Mahoney	24	Labourer	Cardiff Rangers, Canton, Bute Dock Rangers	Cardiff	
William Douglas	23	Colliery Official	Windsor, Canton	Barry	Wales
Charles Arthur	22	Schoolmaster Estate Agent	Newton College Devon, Winchester, Dorchester, Cheltenham	Norfolk	Wales
Angus Stuart	22	Draper's Assistant		Scotland	GB & NZ
David Lewis	22	Clerk	Canton, Cardiff Quins	Cardiff	Wales
Henry Simpson	22	Chartering Clerk		Durham	Wales
John Sant	13	Architect	Canton	Cardiff	
Frank Hill	12	Solicitor	Monkton House, Clifton College	Cardiff	Wales
George Young	11	Shipowner's son	Monkton House, Cardiff Quins	Tyneside	Wales
Albert Hybart	10	Timber Exporter	Cardiff Collegiate, Canton, Cardiff Quins	Cardiff	Wales

78   Compiled from the *South Wales Daily News*, the *Western Mail*, directories, census returns and biographies.

Nicknamed the "Dancing Dervishes", Canton retained the District League Championship in 1906-7. GA Bird (with the ball) was the captain. Sitting next to him, sixth from left is WJ (Billy) Jenkins, who won four Welsh caps in 1912 and 1913.   *Canton RFC*

Using census returns, biographies and press articles, it is possible to establish the social background of Hancock's side.[79] Examination of Cardiff teams in match reports reveal that the process of working-class participation began *earlier* and was more *gradual* and less dramatic than implied in "Old Stager's" recollections. Of the six men who were working class, Dick Kedzlie (blacksmith) played as early as 1881-2; while Jimmy Mahoney (labourer), Wyndham Jarman (decorator) and William Stadden (labourer) all appeared in 1882-3. Angus Stuart (draper's assistant) first played in 1883-4 and Hugh Hughes (carpenter) early in 1884-5. Moreover, the inclusion of Mahoney is evidence that there was no bar to players from Cardiff's Irish Catholic community. There is no doubt, therefore, that during the 1880s, the composition of the Cardiff XV gradually became more socially mixed than the largely exclusive teams of the 1870s. Playing ability was now clearly more important than social standing. Wing three-quarter Angus Stuart was

---

79   Anon, *Contemporary Portraits: Men and Women of South Wales and Monmouthshire: Cardiff Section* (Cardiff, 1896), pp. 34-5; Jenkins, Pierce and Auty, *Who's Who of Welsh International Rugby,* passim.

Angus John Stuart, the Cardiff winger, who later played at forward for Great Britain and the All Blacks.

a well-known local professional sprinter. Together with Stadden, in 1886, he joined Dewsbury, where both were found employment as mill hands. In one of the most remarkable playing careers of any era, Scottish-born Stuart, had a Welsh trial on the wing and later played at *forward* for Great Britain (1888) *and* New Zealand (1893).[80] The contribution of these working men to the success of Hancock's team was important, perhaps crucial, and it is noteworthy that of the eight players who appeared most frequently in the First XV in that record breaking season, five were working class. However, the involvement of working-class players was neither sudden nor total.

A strong case can be made for the argument that Cardiff were only able to enjoy and maintain their dominant position in British rugby from the 1880s onwards because they sat at the apex of a large pyramid of local clubs from which they were constantly able to renew their teams. During Hancock's year, Swansea resolved to institute a cup competition to stimulate clubs in their area because it was "generally thought that the unbroken success achieved by the Cardiff first and second fifteens is due in measure to the large number of clubs they can draw from".[81] The frequently asserted and, it is contested, somewhat distorted view that Welsh rugby is essentially valleys rugby ignores the important contribution which these clubs – some now almost entirely forgotten – made to the game. From the very earliest days, local Cardiff clubs were producing players who would help to change not only the social character of Welsh rugby but also the way in which the Welsh, and later the rest of the world, would play rugby.

However, importantly, the participation of working men in the Cardiff club did not extend to its management. Arthur's history records the committee members for each season up to 1906 and it is clear that the control of the club was retained firmly by the middle class throughout. For 1899-1900, the final season in this study, eighteen officers are listed. They were all former players but, of the sixteen who can be identified, only one was working

---

80 *SWDN* 31 Mar., 3 Oct. 1886 (Stuart); R.H. Chester and N.A.C. McMillan, *The Visitors: The History of International Rugby Teams in New Zealand* (Auckland, 1990), p. 41.

81 *SWDN* 1 Feb. 1886.

class and he was on the committee because he was the club vice-captain. Two of the Second XV committee were lower middle class. All the remainder were solicitors, other professionals or businessmen of substance. It was also this class which dominated the WFU and other senior clubs at the time.[82]

Two clubs, from time to time, attempted to challenge Cardiff's dominance as the area's "premier" club. These were Cardiff Harlequins and Penarth.[83] It is a demonstration of the remarkable strength of Cardiff rugby that, for several seasons, these clubs were regarded as being amongst the handful of elite Welsh clubs and they were quite capable of defeating some of the strongest teams in the kingdom. But neither was ever able to break the powerful grip which the Cardiff club had on the Cardiff public: it was the "town" team and therefore the focus of enormous civic pride and, as such, it represented the town in a way in which no other team could hope to challenge. As the regional capital of a large hinterland, too, it drew its support from a much wider area than just the borough. When the "premier" team was playing away, neither the Quins nor Penarth could ever attract crowds like Cardiff, even if the opposition were Llanelli, Newport or Swansea.

Cardiff Harlequins were a socially mixed club, which emerged from the obscurity of district rugby in the late 1870s via a series of name changes and mergers. By 1890, together with their close rivals Penarth, the Quins were recognised as one of the seven leading Welsh clubs alongside Cardiff, Llanelli, Neath, Newport, and Swansea. Sometimes Penygraig – the first valleys club to reach this level, albeit for a brief period – were also included in this select group.[84] That the Quins had achieved such an elevated position in the game was due in no small measure to the efforts and financial support of their energetic secretary, Alfred J Davies, a Cardiff stockbroker. A very influential but now forgotten administrator, Davies served on the WFU for many years and also represented Wales on the IRB. No doubt hoping to lock-in the Quins' position as a senior club, at the WFU AGM in 1892, he moved that the Union should introduce a twelve team league, but was overwhelmingly defeated. In 1896, Davies stood unsuccessfully for the post of WFU secretary. He was largely responsible for establishing the Glamorgan County Football Union, and became its first secretary. A prominent referee, Davies officiated in the 1896 English County Championship final and took charge of the Somerset v New Zealand match shortly before his death in

82   Arthur, *Cardiff Rugby*, passim. For the 1899-1900 officers see p. 147.
83   Hignell and Prescott, *Cardiff Sporting Greats*, pp. 158-9 (Cardiff Quins); Musselwhite, *Penarth R.F.C.*, pp. 7-39.
84   *SWDN* 8 Apr. 1890, *WM* 9, 12 Apr. 1890.

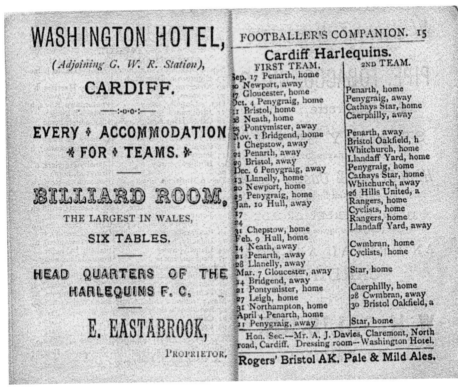

The advertisement and fixture list read:

WASHINGTON HOTEL,
(Adjoining G. W. R. Station),

CARDIFF.

—:-o-o-:—

EVERY ✦ ACCOMMODATION ✦ FOR ✦ TEAMS. ✦

BILLIARD ROOM,

THE LARGEST IN WALES,

SIX TABLES.

HEAD QUARTERS OF THE HARLEQUINS F. C.

E. EASTABROOK,

PROPRIETOR.

FOOTBALLER'S COMPANION. 15

Cardiff Harlequins.

FIRST TEAM.	2ND TEAM.
Sep. 17 Penarth, home	
10 Newport, away	
27 Gloucester, home	
Oct. 4 Penygraig, home	Penarth, home
11 Bristol, home	Penygraig, away
18 Neath, home	Cathays Star, home
25 Pontymister, away	Caerphilly, away
Nov. 1 Bridgend, home	
8 Chepstow, away	Penarth, away
22 Penarth, away	Bristol Oakfield, h
29 Bristol, away	Whitchurch, home
Dec. 6 Penygraig, away	Llandaff Yard, home
13 Llanelly, home	Penygraig, home
20 Newport, home	Cathays Star, home
25 Penygraig, home	Whitchurch, away
Jan. 10 Hull, away	26 Hills United, a
17	Rangers, home
24	Cyclists, home
31 Chepstow, home	Rangers, home
Feb. 9 Hull, home	Llandaff Yard, away
14 Neath, away	
21 Penarth, away	Cwmbran, home
28 Llanelly, away	Cyclists, home
Mar. 7 Gloucester, away	Star, home
14 Bridgend, away	
21 Pontymister, home	Caerphilly, home
27 Leigh, home	28 Cwmbran, away
31 Northampton, home	30 Bristol Oakfield, a
April 4 Penarth, home	
11 Penygraig, away	Star, home

Hon. Sec.—Mr. A. J. Davies, Claremont, North road, Cardiff. Dressing room—Washington Hotel.

Rogers' Bristol AK. Pale & Mild Ales.

In 1890-1, Cardiff Harlequins had a strong and varied fixture list, which included all the leading Welsh clubs except Cardiff.

1906. He was also active in Welsh athletics.[85] Despite his high profile in the game, he was never involved with the Cardiff club and, on the contrary, AJ Davies was sometimes regarded as being hostile to the Arms Park interest.

Under his leadership, the Quins were able to record victories over Swansea, Neath and Llanelli, though after beating Newport in 1888, their opponents decided they hadn't sent their First XV after all.[86] They also defeated many English sides including Bath, Bristol, Leicester and Northampton. Indeed, in 1888, Bristol's first ever fixture, which they lost, was with Cardiff Harlequins.[87] However, the Quins never bettered Cardiff, despite seven attempts between 1885-6 and 1888-9; and Cardiff refused to grant them a fixture

85 *SWDN* 12 Sept. 1892 (league); *SWDN* 21 Sept. 1896 (secretary); *WM* 21 Feb. 1896 (County Championship); *SWDN* 26 Apr. 1906 (obituary).

86 *WM* 26 Mar. 1888; *WM* 14, 17 Apr. 1888 (Newport).

87 *WM* 30 Jan. 1888. Some accounts of Bristol RFC incorrectly give their opponents that day as Cardiff.

Glamorgan v New Zealand 1905. Alfred J Davies (secretary) is standing back row first left. Local players included: Dai Westacott (Cardiff) back row fifth from left; John Dyke (Penarth) middle row second left; Reggie Gibbs (Cardiff) middle row fourth left; Johnny Williams (Cardiff) middle row fifth left; Jack Powell (Cardiff) middle row six left. All played for Wales.

Swansea RFC

thereafter.[88] Unfortunately the drawn match between the clubs in 1882-3 shown in the official Cardiff records is an error, as Cardiff actually played (London) Harlequins that day.[89] Nevertheless, Cardiff Quins produced two Welsh internationals in Percy Bennett (four caps between 1891 and 1892) and Fred Nicholls (one cap in 1892), as well as several Welsh trialists and county players. Despite these successes, however, they found it difficult to retain many of their more promising players. Amongst those who turned out for the Quins and later won caps for Wales as Cardiff players were: Syd Nicholls, WEO Williams, Hugh Hughes, William Elsey, Hugh Ingledew and Norman Biggs. Even Gwyn Nicholls had a couple of games for the

---

88   *SWDN* 8 Sept. 1890.
89   *SWDN* 19 Feb. 1883; *WM* 19 Feb. 1883. Arthur Gould guested for London Harlequins in this match.

*The Harlequins Ground, Roath, being used by Cardiff High School cricketers in 1899.
Cardiff Harlequins defeated many leading clubs here.*

Courtesy of Cardiff Council Library Service

club though he was never a regular player as is often claimed. It was both the constant drain of players to Cardiff and heavy financial burdens which eventually led to the club's decline.

In 1892, the Quins took over and developed a new ground in Roath, still known today as "The Harlequins", but they severely overstretched themselves financially in doing so.[90]

"Old Stager" thought it "as prettily situated a bit of ground as could be found anywhere in the vicinity of Cardiff".[91] However, despite beating Swansea, Llanelli, Neath, Bath and Bristol there, the crowds were never large enough to sustain this venture and following a major row with Cardiff over yet another transfer of a player, the rugby club virtually folded in 1895, playing only as a Wednesday team for a while. The Quins were later revived on a regular basis but they never regained their former prominence and only played as a local Cardiff and District club at Splott Park without much success up to the First World War. A club (or clubs) called Cardiff Harlequins existed sporadically between the wars and the name was again resurrected briefly in the early 1950s before disappearing but none of these later teams enjoyed any prominence in Cardiff and District. There is no connection between the original Quins and the current WRU League One

90   *SWDN* 10 Oct. 1892.
91   *SWDN* 4 Apr. 1892.

Penarth 1886-7. John Hayes, who later became club secretary, was captain (with the ball). Also in the team were future Welsh internationals Dickie Garrett (seated third from left) and George Rowles (seated seventh from left).   *Penarth RFC*

side Cardiff Harlequins, who changed their name from Cardiff High School Old Boys in 2011, although there is a tenuous and sentimental link in that The Harlequins ground was the home of both the High School and the Old Boys club for many years.

Formed in 1880 partly on the initiative of Cyril Batchelor, the son of a well-known Cardiff businessman and radical politician, Penarth were perhaps the most socially inclusive of all Welsh clubs of the period. Players in their earliest teams came from the across the very wide range of social classes found in the town. Engine fitters, boatmen, carpenters, railwaymen, boilermakers, coal-trimmers and labourers, as well as clerks, insurance agents, shop assistants and shopkeepers could be found playing alongside the public school educated sons of wealthy ship and coal magnates. The Penarth club provides strong evidence that, by the early 1880s, Welsh rugby was becoming socially open. Like Cardiff, however, the management of the club was controlled largely by the middle class, though there were perhaps fewer professionals and more small businessmen involved, while John Hayes the secretary from 1881 to 1887 was a docks foreman.[92] Writing to the *SWDN* in 1890 to refute arguments for a merger with Cardiff, a later secretary claimed that many of the town's leading residents were members:

---

92   1881 and 1891 Census; Penarth RFC archive; Musselwhite, *Penarth R.F.C.*, p. 7-8.

"we have a couple of hundred members ... including many of the aristocracy of Penarth".[93]

Under the guidance of stonemason Dickie Garrett and boilermaker George Rowles, both of whom captained the club and were capped by Wales, Penarth enjoyed a dramatic rise to prominence. Garrett won eight Welsh caps between 1888 and 1892; while Rowles played once in 1892. By the 1890s, the club had recorded victories over Cardiff and all the other leading Welsh clubs, apart from Swansea, as well as over London Welsh, Bath, Bristol, Devonport Albion, Gloucester, Leicester, Moseley, St. Helens and Wakefield Trinity. However, as with Cardiff Quins, the club found it difficult to prevent players from moving to their more powerful neighbour in Cardiff. By the end of the century, Penarth were struggling to maintain their previously high standard but, unlike the Quins, they managed to survive, mainly due to their being a town team with strong support from the local community. Hence, in the early 1900s, Penarth's fortunes revived and they were able to record three successive victories over the Barbarians between 1904 and 1907 and maintain an unbeaten home record in 1906-7.[94]

Apart from these senior clubs, it is virtually impossible to determine the social background of the administrators and players belonging to the majority of Cardiff's local teams, as no membership records survive. Team lists in the press are of limited use, since without addresses it is difficult to identify individuals with any certainty, especially given the size of Cardiff and the prevalence of common Welsh surnames. However, a limited investigation was undertaken using the 1891 census and the addresses of local club secretaries. These were found in the football handbooks for 1890 and 1891 and in the local press between 1889 and 1891.[95] Of the fifty-three identified this way, thirty-eight were traced in the census and their details are shown in Appendix 5.

The age of most of these secretaries was remarkably low. The majority were teenagers and only one was over twenty-five. This suggests that the officers of local clubs may have been drawn largely from the playing membership or their immediate friends and, if so, grassroots teams, at least, did not rely to any great extent on older enthusiasts to run their affairs. The lack of a committee composed of former players might perhaps partly explain the fragility of many of the clubs.

---

93   *SWDN* 22 Nov. 1890.

94   Chris Thau, *The Spirit of Penarth: One Hundred and Thirty-One Years of Seaside Rugby 1880-2011* (Penarth, 2012) pp.1-56; Musselwhite, Penarth R.F.C. pp. 7-39.

95   *WM* and *Evening Express* 1889-1891 passim; *Cardiff Footballer's Companion 1890-91*, pp. 3-67; *Welsh Athlete Football Handbook 1891-2*, pp. 43-130.

Cardiff had only one player, while Penarth had two in the Welsh XV which lost 17-0 to England in 1892. Back: W Watts (Newport), T Deacon (Swansea), F Mills (Swansea), CB Nicholl (Llanelli and Cambridge University), TC Graham (Newport), J Hannan (Newport); Middle: T Pearson (Cardiff), Richard Garrett (Penarth), W McCutcheon (Oldham), JA Gould (Newport) (captain), RL Thomas (Llanelli), W Bancroft (Swansea), AW Boucher (Newport); Front: George Rowles (Penarth), HP Phillips (Newport). WRU

An example of a prominent and yet very youthful administrator was Wilson Tunley, who at seventeen years was the secretary of two clubs, Cardiff Juniors and the very successful St. David's. Whilst still a teenager, he was actively involved in setting up the Cardiff and District Football Union, which he served for some years before joining the committee of Cardiff rugby club.

Seventeen of the thirty-eight secretaries who were traced were born in Cardiff and six elsewhere in south Wales. Of the rest, six came from the west country, eight from other parts of England and one from Scotland. They were predominantly clerks or tradesmen. Two-thirds had white collar occupations. Sixteen were clerical workers and there were also three shop assistants, a commercial traveller, a proof-reader's assistant and an eighteen year old teacher. One was a schoolboy. There was also a hardware merchant

Cardiff Reserves 1897-8. Wilson Tunley is standing second from left. The captain (with the ball) is AM Ricketts, formerly of Cardiff Northern. A young Bert Winfield, who had previously played for St. Andrew's, is sitting second from left.   Cardiff RFC

who seems to have been employed in his father's business and who was probably middle class. The remaining third comprised thirteen working men. Their occupations were plumber (three), plumber's apprentice, compositor, printer's apprentice, coach trimmer, coach painter, baker, currier, hairdresser, plasterer and telegraph messenger. Apart from the hardware merchant, none of the thirty-eight was obviously a member of the professional or business middle classes or lived in the more fashionable areas of the town. Neither were any from the unskilled labouring classes. It is interesting to compare this with the study by Martin Johnes and Ian Garland, who researched seventeen Welsh soccer club secretaries from 1880 and found that they had a predominantly lower middle-class profile, dominated by clerks with an age range of nineteen to thirty-eight.[96]

If this group is representative of the wider Cardiff rugby community around 1890, then it can be argued that the organisation of the game at

---

96   Martin Johnes and Ian Garland, "'The New Craze': football and society in north-east Wales, c. 1870-90", *Welsh History Review,* 22, 2 (2004), pp. 286-7.

the local level was largely dominated by young members of the skilled and semi-skilled working class and lower status middle class. This supports the views of earlier researchers, who believe that the growth of football in England in the late nineteenth century came substantially from within the working class rather than from the efforts of the middle class. The evidence above is admittedly limited, but when combined with that on the sheer level of participation across the town, it does suggest that most workers in Cardiff also arranged their own rugby, rather than having it organised for them. It is unlikely that there were very many middle-class reformers in the ranks of the secretaries of Cardiff's clubs.[97] Whilst the officials of the WFU and the leading clubs were largely members of the professional and business classes, this was generally not the case at the grassroots of the game.

By 1911, Cardiff had one of the highest proportions of adult males born outside the United Kingdom.[98] However, apart from the Irish and, to a much lesser extent, possibly the Scottish (e.g. Caledonians, Grange Thistles, Penarth Thistles), no other ethnic groups formed their own clubs. Surprisingly, given the very large number of Cardiffians who had roots in the west country, there were no teams with names which obviously connected them to Gloucester, Somerset, Devon or Cornwall. This may be an indication of the extent to which newcomers became quickly assimilated into the local rugby community. Of course, that is not to say that players from a particular area of England did not continue to socialise together by playing for the same club. Occasionally, foreign players can be identified in team lists. For instance, Raoul Foa, Cardiff's captain in 1878-9 who later became a highly successful City banker, was half Italian and half French. He was also Jewish. How much black participation there was in nineteenth-century Cardiff rugby is impossible to establish reliably. It is certain that at least one black player, Charles Lewis had a few games in the centre for Cardiff First and Second XVs, following some fine displays in District rugby. He scored four tries and two conversions for Grange Stars ("The Bricklayers") when they defeated Cathays United 19-0 in the final of the 1898-9 Union Shield and he also represented Cardiff and District. Whilst recognising his undoubted talents, some match reports referred to him in terms which would be completely unacceptable today. It is highly likely, though no evidence has yet been found to prove it, that other members of Cardiff's black community also played for local clubs.[99]

---

97   Richard Holt, *Sport and the British: A Modern History* (Oxford, 1989), p. 135.
98   1911 census.
99   *WM* 26 Sept., 5 Apr.1898; *SWDN* 26 Sept. 1898, 5 Apr., 18 Sept., 23 Oct. 1899 (Lewis).

Raoul Hector Foa, captain of Cardiff 1878-9.

To summarise then, until the early 1880s, the game in Cardiff was dominated by the middle class. Towards the end of the 1870s, however, changes began to take place. New clubs, which working men were able to join, were emerging and these soon became socially mixed by the first half of the 1880s. Even the Cardiff club admitted workmen by 1881-2 and, by the middle of the decade, they comprised a substantial part of the First XV. By 1890, local clubs were largely dominated by the working and lower middle classes. However, the administration of the senior clubs, including Cardiff, and of the WFU continued to remain in the control of the professional and business middle class. This, and the previous chapter, therefore, provides a detailed confirmation of Gareth Williams's description of Welsh rugby:

> Though an educated middle-class elite dominated the higher echelons of the game, lower down the scale clubs were run by working men for working men. Welsh rugby cannot be portrayed merely as a middle-class salvage operation, rescuing a sullen working class from the aimless and morally damaging attractions of the pub or gin-palace. Administered by the few it [was] played and watched by the many.[100]

---

100 Gareth Williams, "Community, Class and Rugby", p. 11.

6

RUGBY'S WIDER IMPACT:
'Football or Life in Cardiff'

Sport has always had a capacity to attract crowds and business. When George Owen described the game of cnapan in sixteenth-century Pembrokeshire, he recognised that the matches were also great social occasions, surrounded by commercial activity.

> … greate nomber would most usuallye meete, and therefore against these matches there would alsoe resorte to the place diverse victualers with meate, drinke and wyne of all sortes, also marchauntes, mercers, and pedlars would provide stalls, and booths, to shewe and utter [shout] their wares, and … some [came] to playe, some to eate and drinke, some to buye, and some to sell, others to see and others to be seene (you know what kinde I meane) greate multitudes of people would resorte beside the plaiers.[1]

Similarly, the popularity of rugby in Victorian Cardiff had an impact which went beyond the mere game itself. The large numbers playing and attending matches in the town, for instance, opened up many new opportunities for a range of businesses. Though it is impossible now to provide precise details, there are still numerous indicators of the general economic effect on Cardiff.

Sport was transformed in the nineteenth century by the improvements in transport which greatly extended the range of support and participation.[2] Transport operators were quick to recognise the commercial attractions of rugby. As soon as large crowds began to attend major matches, rail companies responded with cheap excursions. For instance, in 1886 – only five years after Wales's first ever international – the GWR ran a special day excursion from Cardiff to Blackheath for the England match, "leaving time to visit a

---

1   George Owen, *The Description of Penbrokeshire* [sic] [1603] (London, 1892), p. 272.
2   Neil Tranter, *Sport, Economy and Society in Britain, 1750-1914* (Cambridge, 1998), p. 34.

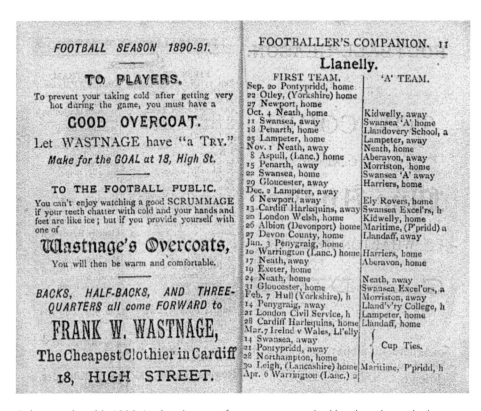

To boost sales, this 1890-1 advertisement for overcoats worked hard on the rugby imagery.

theatre."[3] It became a regular practice to run special trains for Cardiff's home and away fixtures, not only with their main rivals Newport and Swansea but also with less powerful opponents like Penygraig.[4] For a Newport v Cardiff game in 1894, attended by 15,000, GWR ran two special trains each with forty coaches and added sixteen extra ones on the regular 1.30 service.[5] The only way that supporters could realistically travel to matches outside their immediate locality was by rail. Fortunately south Wales had one of the most densely developed railway networks in the world and Cardiff was at its centre.[6] The game could not have expanded as it did without this rail infrastructure but it was a mutually beneficial relationship for both rugby and the railway companies.

---

3   *SWDN* 21 Dec. 1885.

4   *SWDN* 30 Oct. 1890.

5   *SWDN* 15 Jan. 1894.

6   John Williams, *Was Wales Industrialised? Essays in Modern Welsh History* (Llandysul, 1995), p. 42.

This was also true for local transport providers. The outward spread of tram and bus services made it much easier for players and supporters to get to matches, whilst at the same time the operators benefited from the increased takings. All the main Cardiff tram routes in the 1880s and 1890s ran close to the Arms Park and Sophia Gardens.[7] One of the reasons why Cardiff Harlequins chose their new ground in Newport Road in 1891 was that it was near a tram terminal at the *Royal Oak*.[8] There was also increased trade for the town's cabmen, ferrying players and supporters between stations, grounds and pubs. In 1896, one Swansea-based company advertised that it offered "special terms to football teams" for "cabs, carriages, phaetons, brakes, hansoms".[9] Spectators at Penarth-Cardiff games not only travelled by bus and train but they also used the boat service across what is now Cardiff Bay.[10] Not every town possessed adequate transport facilities for

19

EMPIRE PALACES—Cardiff, Newport & Swansea.

Cardiff and District Rugby Union.
SEASON, 1896-97.

OFFICIALS.

President :
T. H. MALLETT, Esq.

Vice-Presidents :

C. R. CRAWLEY.	A. M. RICKETTS.
G. W. PARSONS.	A. H. WILLIAMS.

Hon. Secretaries :
C. R. CRAWLEY and R. W. JOHN,
171, Penarth Road, Cardiff.

Hon. Treasurer :
A. H. WILLIAMS, 68, Railway Street, Cardiff.

LL. & T. BULLIN,
Heathfield Street and Ffynone Mews,
SWANSEA.
☞ **SPECIAL TERMS TO FOOTBALL TEAMS.**
Wedding Carriages with suitable Horses. Cabs, Open and Closed Carriages. Funeral Carriages, Phaetons, Brakes, Hansoms, &c. Cabs always ready.

The Right Hon. W. E. Gladstone has drunk **DUNVILLE'S " V,R,"**

The officials of Cardiff and District in 1896-7; and an advertisement for the Swansea carriage proprietor who offered special terms to clubs, no doubt a common practice.

the exceptional demands created by big matches, however. Previewing the 1893 Ireland international, "Old Stager" complained that getting transport from Llanelli station to Stradey Park was virtually impossible and that most supporters had to make the long journey on foot. He added that there had

---

7   R.H. Morgan, "The Development of an Urban Transport System: The Case of Cardiff", *Welsh History Review*, 13, 2 (1986), pp. 178-181.

8   *SWDN* 1 Oct. 1891, 4 Apr. 1892.

9   *The Handy Football Guide (Mortimer's) For South Wales and Monmouthshire: 1896-97* (Cardiff, 1896), p. 19.

10   *SWDN* 1 Oct. 1891. Spectators travelled "by rail, 'bus, or boat" to the Penarth v Cardiff match.

22

THE FAVORITE RESORT

OF

FOOTBALL ENTHUSIASTS!

Philharmonic
Restaurant,

(A FEW DOORS FROM THEATRE ROYAL.)

St. MARY STREET, CARDIFF.

WINES AND SPIRITS.   BILLIARDS.

ACCOMMODATION FOR 500 GUESTS.

Football Results Every Saturday.

An example of a restaurant promoting itself to rugby followers in the 1894-5 handbook. Note match results were provided.

been similar problems at Swansea a few years earlier.[11]

As Cardiff developed into the regional capital of south Wales from the 1880s, its central area was transformed as a commercial and service quarter.[12] Pubs, restaurants, hotels and theatres close to the Arms Park and Sophia Gardens were readily able to attract the custom of players and supporters. We have already seen the close relationship which existed between clubs and pubic houses. Of the 274 pubs in the borough in 1903, 131 were located in the central area and well over half of these were found in streets immediately surrounding the Arms Park.[13] The existence of this service industry was vital to the development of the game in Cardiff. In 1891, "Old Stager" reported complaints from supporters that there were not enough pubs and hotels in Llanelli to cater for the crowds attending the Ireland international.[14] The Irish RFU unsuccessfully requested that the 1893 international be moved from Llanelli because of its inadequate hotel provision. However, this was the last international played by Wales at Stradey Park for over a hundred years.[15]

As in the twenty-first century, success in major matches was the occasion for a great deal of celebration in the town's pubs and hotels. After Cardiff's victory at Swansea in 1888, the team was met at the station by brass bands and carried to the *Angel* "and there was a deal of cheering *and much consumption of liquor.*"[16] "Old Stager" wrote after Wales's first ever home win over England at Cardiff in 1893:

---

11   *SWDN* 10 Mar. 1893.

12   M.J. Daunton, *Coal Metropolis: Cardiff 1870-1914* (Leicester, 1977), p. 54.

13   Licensed Premises (Alehouses and Beerhouses) in Cardiff: Report of the Chief Constable, 1903.

14   *SWDN* 9 Mar. 1891.

15   WFU minutes 11 Feb. 1893. Wales returned to Stradey in February 1998 when Italy were defeated 23-20.

16   *SWDN* 16 Jan. 1888 (italics added).

The players ... were borne away to the Angel shoulder high ... later on *every hotel bar along the main streets was blocked to the street doors*, and everywhere football was the main topic of conversation. The victory of Wales simply sent the population of Cardiff, plus the thousands of visitors, off their blessed chumps.[17]

Certainly, then, the proprietors of such establishments had every reason to support and encourage this new trade. Tom Mallett was undoubtedly a lover of rugby, but when he presented a cup for competition to the Cardiff and District Football Union in 1893, it was also a smart business move. He had just left the *New Market Hotel* to become the landlord of the *Blue Bell*, and the Union's headquarters went with him.[18]

Sports outfitters and photographers were other local entrepreneurs who benefited greatly from the growth of the game. By 1878, one retailer in Queen Street was already advertising shin guards, bladders and "Foot Balls (Rugby Shape)" – interestingly there was no mention of any other shape available for purchase.[19] Another local retailer, T. Page Wood, originally specialised in supplying middle-class and upper-class customers with shooting and fishing equipment, but he swiftly recognised the new lucrative sports goods market offered by football. In 1886, he shrewdly donated a cup for competition amongst local clubs and, as a direct result, the first, but short-lived, Cardiff District Football Union was set up and he was appointed its president.[20] That Page Wood saw this as essentially a business venture, however, may be confirmed by the reactions of one disgruntled correspondent to the *SWDN* who was rather suspicious of his motives. "One would imagine the Union

Theatre Royal

CARDIFF.

1890-91.

The Home of Burlesques
The London Gaiety Companies
D'Oyley Carte's Opera Companies
Augustus Harris's Venus Companies
The Carl Rosa Companies.

The Christmas Pantomime

THIS YEAR WILL ECLIPSE
ALL OTHER EFFORTS.

Where do Footballers go?
Why, to the Royal, don't you know?
Don't be late, but be in time
To see the ROYAL PANTOMIME.

Theatres also recognised the potential custom that rugby offered.

---

17   *SWDN* 9 Jan. 1893 (italics added).
18   *SWDN* 9 Nov. 1893. The Mallett Cup is still the premier competition for Cardiff and District clubs.
19   *WM* 24 Dec. 1878.
20   *SWDN* 28 Aug. 1886; *Cardiff District Football Union Handbook 1886-87* (Cardiff, 1886), p. [3].

With Tom Mallett as landlord of the Blue Bell in High Street, it became the headquarters of the C&DFU and was known as the "The Cardiff Football House".

Courtesy of SA Brain and Co.

existed as an advertising medium."[21] Describing the astonishing popularity of rugby, the weekly *Cardiff Argus* commented in 1888:

> There is no kind of out-door amusement which has become so thoroughly popular during the last few years, in South Wales, as Football ... A glance at the stock of "Footballs" just received by [Page Wood] would lead to the conclusion that they were stored there for a century, but they are only "this season's goods", and are of all kinds and sizes, from the "match" balls to the small ones used in the junior clubs connected with our educational establishments.[22]

T. PAGE WOOD & Co.

ATHLETIC OUTFITTERS, CARDIFF.

The G.G.B.	11/6
The GLAMORGAN (patent)	10/6
The CAMBRIAN	7/6
The IMPERIAL (Registered)	10/6
The INTERNATIONAL	8/6
The JUNIOR MATCH	5/6

Boys' Footballs 1/-, 2/-, 2/6, 3/6, and 4/6.
Rugby and Association.

Every Requisite for Athletes.
Boxing Gloves, Dumb Bells, Indian Clubs,
&c., &c.

T. PAGE WOOD & CO.,
21, CASTLE STREET, CARDIFF.

FOOTBALLER'S COMPANION. 33

Cardiff Crusaders.

LIST OF MATCHES.

Sept.	13..	Penarth Albion, away
	20..	Canton 'A' away
	27..	Cardiff United 'A' home
Oct.	4..	Cogan 'A' away
	11..	Whitchurch, home
	18..	Splott Rovers 'A' away
	25..	Cathays Star, home
Nov.	1..	
	8..	Llandaff Juniors, home
	15..	Canton 'A' home
	22..	Roath Juniors, home
	29..	Cathays Star, away
Dec.	6..	Caerphilly 'A' home
	13..	Cardiff Juniors, away
	20..	Ely Rovers 'A' away
	27..	Cardiff Star 'A' away
Jan.	3..	Roath Windsor, home
	10..	Splott Rovers 'A' home
	17..	Caerphilly 'A' away
	24..	Cogan 'A' home
	31..	Llandaff Juniors, away
Feb.	7..	Cardiff Star 'A' home
	14..	Whitchurch, away
	21..	Ely Rovers 'A' home
	28..	Penarth Albion, home
Mar.	7..	Cardiff United 'A' away
	14..	Roath Juniors, away
	21..	Roath Windsor, away

Hon. Sec.—Mr. F. J. Bosley, 11, Penarth road, Cardiff.

Rogers' Bristol AK. Pale and Mild Ales.

T Page Wood promoted his footballs in his 1890-1 handbook, alongside the fixture list of a typical neighbourhood club, Cardiff Crusaders, who played all their matches in the Cardiff area.

---

21   *SWDN* 28 Apr. 1890.
22   *Cardiff Argus* 26 Sept. 1888.

ANDERSONS,

The . . .

Waterproofers

————

FOOTBALL

REQUISITES.

Head Protector.

Shin Guard.

❊ ❊ ❊ ❊

Wholesale and

Retail Warehouse,

Only Welsh Address,

8, QUEEN STREET, CARDIFF.

Items every rugby player needed, according to an Andersons' advertisement in 1896-7.

Another of Page Wood's sporting initiatives was the publication of an annual football handbook, which ran to at least seven editions by 1891-2.[23] These contained fixture lists and club details but they were also an imaginative way of promoting his goods which now included balls, bladders, jerseys, caps, gloves, shin guards, ankle guards and football insurance policies.[24] Such was the success of these handbooks that he even extended his publishing activities in 1891-2, by launching *The Welsh Athlete*, a weekly sports journal, overwhelmingly devoted to rugby. Sadly for future sports historians, however, this business enterprise was a financial failure and it folded before the end of the season. Other Cardiff outfitters followed Page Wood's lead. Evans and Co, of the Royal Arcade, sold footballs, jerseys, shorts, badges and presentation caps, while Andersons in Queen Street not only supplied jerseys, boots and bags but also donated gold medals for the Mallett Cup winners.[25]

It was a common practice to photograph teams before major matches. This was regarded as a tedious and time-consuming business and was invariably described in match reports as an ordeal. There was clearly a market for the products of the photographers' efforts though and this sometimes led to friction between them on match day as they competed for the best positions from which to set up their cameras.[26] These photographs were not only purchased by clubs and players. A football handbook for 1896-7 included

---

23 *The Welsh Athlete and West of England Cycling News Football Handbook 1891-2* (Cardiff, 1891), p. [5]. The preface refers to its being the seventh edition of the "Football Handbook". Later versions were produced by other publishers.

24 *Cardiff and South Wales Footballer's Companion: 1890-91* (Cardiff, 1890), pp. 28, 30, 32; *Welsh Athlete Football Handbook 1891-2*, p. [2].

25 *Welsh Athlete Football Handbook 1891-2*, p. [47] (Evans); *Mortimer's Football Guide for South Wales and Monmouthshire: Season, 1894-95*, p. 42 (Anderson's); *SWDN* 24 Oct. 1896 (medals).

26 *WM* 8 Feb. 1892 (Wales v Scotland).

advertisements for Goldie of Cardiff and Dando of Newport, and both reveal that they also specialised in selling team photographs to the general public.[27] Also, pub landlords often purchased them for display in the bars and front widows of their premises. Around the turn of the century, enterprising photographers began taking pictures of the spectators at the Arms Park and these were then sold as post-cards in local shops. Judging by the number which still survive, they must have been very popular.

Some, however, found other ways of using images to cash in on the sport. These were not always welcomed. "Old Stager" was aghast at the activities of one local insurance agent in 1889:

It has come at last. The ingenious advertiser, noting the popularity of football, has commenced to turn even it to account. On Saturday men were distributing at the Park ... portraits of [Cardiff players] Charley Arthur and [Wyndham] Jarman, on the back of which our friend Mr. Henry Perkins, of Cardiff invited all ... to ensure with him against sickness and accident. What next, I wonder?[28]

The long-gone Three Horse Shoes in High Street in the 1890s. Note the team photos in the window. A close-up view reveals at least one is of Cardiff at the Arms Park.
Courtesy of Cardiff Council Library Service

---

27   *Handy Football Guide: 1896-97*, pp. [20] (Goldie), [16] (Dando).
28   *SWDN* 14 Oct. 1889.

Alexander Duncan. An official of the WFU for many years, he probably used his influence as a proprietor of the South Wales Daily News to promote the game in its columns.

Kenneth O. Morgan argues that the *South Wales Daily News* generally gave little prominence to cultural affairs.[29] Nevertheless, on the whole, this Liberal daily tended to cover the game in rather more depth than the Tory *Western Mail*. This may have been partly due to the influence of one of the *SWDN*'s proprietors, Alexander Duncan, a former Cardiff player who served on the committees of both Cardiff and the WFU at the time. Both papers were Cardiff based but they also enjoyed a much wider regional circulation. In the maelstrom of Welsh club rivalry, this could sometimes cause tensions within their readership, a problem which didn't usually arise with their more locally based competitors in Llanelli, Newport, Swansea and elsewhere. This sometimes created a conflict of interest which could never really be satisfactorily resolved. Following the reporting of a major dispute involving Cardiff, William Wilkins, the secretary of Llanelli, complained, probably justifiably, "Both the [Cardiff] daily papers, while professing to cater for South Wales, hold a brief for Cardiff first."[30]

As the game's popularity grew, columnists like "Old Stager", "Welsh Athlete", "Forward", "Dagon", "Freelance", "Goal Post", and "Touchstone" became regular contributors. Their articles would sometimes include highly provocative views on WFU conduct, team selection, player performance and the behaviour of clubs, players and spectators. This would often stimulate much correspondence. Indeed, the press provided a vital forum for participants and supporters to voice their opinions, initiate ideas and resolve disputes of all kinds. Some journalists even became directly involved in the game; for example, as we have seen, HW Wells ("Welsh Athlete") was instrumental in setting up the Cardiff and District Football Union and became its first president.[31] The local press, therefore, could be viewed as an unofficial but important branch of the sport, helping to promote the game even at the grassroots level.

---

29   Kenneth O. Morgan, *Rebirth of a Nation: Wales 1880-1980* (Oxford, 1982 edn.), p. 51.

30   *WM* 17 Nov. 1892.

31   *WM* 9 Nov. 1892.

After being relatively indifferent to rugby in the very early years, the Cardiff press soon began to recognise the commercial advantages of increasing its coverage of the sport. Looking back at this period, the *SWDN* in 1892 recalled that "Pressmen of the old school seemed to have tumbled to the fact that a game which was attracting the attention of thousands week after week was worth shedding ink over."[32] The first accounts of what were clearly rugby matches appeared in the early 1870s but these were very sporadic and brief, and usually appeared under "District Intelligence" or "District News" columns, alongside reports of petty crimes, fire brigade suppers and meetings of the Highways Board and the like.[33] Reflecting the growing numbers playing the game though, by the mid-1870s, reports began to appear more frequently and in greater detail and eventually they were given more prominence.[34] As early as February 1877, what might be described as the first Monday sports page emerged, when the *Western Mail* published four match reports together. Lists of all the players were included. The clubs involved represent an interesting spread: Llandovery College v Carmarthen Wanderers; Roath v Ely; Pontypool v Aberdare; and Newport v Hereford.[35] Further evidence of the game's increasing hold is revealed a year later when rugby was mentioned in a *Western Mail* editorial for the first time.[36] Events beyond mere on-field activities were now regularly commented on, such as the banquet given in honour of the victorious Newport cup team of 1878.[37] By the end of the decade, both Cardiff papers were full of detail about the game: regular and comprehensive match accounts, team lists, reports of meetings, cup draws, disputes, complaints, letters and dedicated columns in Monday editions. A close study of the Cardiff dailies, therefore, demonstrates just how rapidly interest had grown during the 1870s. Gradually the number of columns devoted to rugby football in the Monday edition increased, so that by 1896 rugby reports and analysis sometimes took up nearly two of the *SWDN*'s eight pages. As Andrew Croll points out, the greater press coverage being given to sport by this time meant that it was difficult for readers – even those with little interest – to ignore it.[38]

---

32   *SWDN* 7 Nov. 1892.
33   See for example, *WM* 9 Nov. 1871, *SWDN* 29 Nov. 1872.
34   See for example, *SWDN* 24 Nov. 1874, 18 Jan. 1875.
35   *WM* 26 February 1877.
36   *WM* 4 Mar. 1878.
37   *WM* 25 Apr. 1878.
38   Andrew J. Croll, *Civilizing the Urban: Popular Culture, Public Space and Urban Meaning, Merthyr c.1870-1914* (PhD thesis, University of Wales, Cardiff, 1997), p. 257.

Some journalists find a better view than from the press box to report a match at the Arms Park.

A surprisingly large amount of coverage was devoted to the results and even accounts of grassroots matches. The *SWDN* even provided a special form for local clubs to send in match reports post free.[39] In the last decades of the century, the two main papers' evening and weekly titles (*South Wales Echo, Evening Express, Cardiff Times, Weekly Mail*) also dealt with the game more frequently. The evening papers, in particular, began to take on more regular day-to-day coverage with, for instance, further commentary by sports columnists like "Old Stager". The special late Saturday edition was another device adopted to cash in on the seemingly limitless interest in rugby. An early example was the special Saturday edition of the *South Wales Echo* printed for the 1885 international in Edinburgh.[40] The publication of the forthcoming week's fixtures became a regular practice in the 1880s, as did that of local team selections in the 1890s. Money prizes for predicting the results of leading Welsh club matches were also sometimes offered.[41] The use of photography would have to wait until the twentieth century but artists' drawings of the scenes at the game occasionally accompanied major match reports, whilst sketch portraits of leading personalities became a regular feature of the sports columns from the mid-1880s.[42] However, by the turn of the century the amount of space devoted to rugby began to diminish somewhat, mainly to accommodate the greater coverage being given to soccer, particularly English Football League matches and subsequently local ones. The most affected by this development were *local* rugby clubs, who were less frequently reported than before, though senior rugby was still covered with the same enthusiasm.[43] The amount of space devoted to the South African War between 1899 and 1902 inevitably meant that the reporting of all sport, including important matches, was reduced significantly.

The great interest in rugby in Wales inevitably led to an increased commercialisation of the game itself. By the 1890s, Cardiff had become

---

39   *SWDN* 13 Sept. 1887.

40   *SWDN* 12 Jan. 1885.

41   *WM* 13 Nov. 1895.

42   For examples of pen pictures, see *WM* 8 Feb. (Alex Duncan) 1886, 20 Feb. 1886 (Frank Hancock).

43   For example, *SWDN* 16 Jan. 1899.

a major gate-taking club, with a substantial annual income. It was now effectively a business in its own right and this was recognised in 1892, when the club secretary began to be paid for his services.[44] According to "Old Stager" in 1898, a game which should have been a pastime was fast becoming a business.[45] During this decade, five figure attendances at the Arms Park were frequently reported. Commenting on various press estimates of the crowd at the Llwynypia v Cardiff match in 1897, which varied from 6,000 to 16,000, "Welsh Athlete" reminded readers, "Popular estimates of the sizes of football crowds are, as a rule, far too large ... [But it] is a significant fact of the extreme interest taken in football by the masses." Therefore, whilst such figures may have been exaggerations, they do indicate that there was a substantial and growing following for the club game.[46] If the reported figures are accepted at face value, then throughout the 1890s, Cardiff often played in front of crowds in excess of 10,000, while key games, especially with Newport, could attract as many as 20,000 supporters. The *Western Mail* even claimed that such was the rivalry between these two clubs that the passion aroused for their games sometimes exceeded that of international matches. "Whatever may be the interest attached to international ... games, so far as Cardiff and Newport are concerned, it pales before the fierce fire of enthusiasm that burns on the occasion of matches between the towns." After all, the two clubs were, at least according to the *Western Mail*, Britain's "leading exponents" of the game.[47] Fixtures against Blackheath and against Christmas and Easter touring sides were also highly popular and could draw crowds of over 15,000. In 1899, 20,000 were reported to have attended Cardiff's matches with Swansea and the Barbarians.[48]

The social composition of these match crowds is difficult to determine precisely, though given their size and the character of local participation in rugby, there must have been very many working-class spectators. As early as 1885, "Old Stager" was sneering at "the 'great unwashed' [who were] devoted adherents of football and patronise it liberally". He piled on the insults by adding, "As the effect of this is to cause a number of sixpences to flow into the coffers of the [Newport] club which might otherwise be spent on beer, *these people* are worthy of encouragement."[49]

---

44 *SWDN* 25 July 1892.
45 *SWDN* 21 Feb. 1898.
46 *WM* 20 Oct. 1897.
47 *WM* 25 Nov. 1895.
48 Match reports *SWDN* and *WM* 1891-1900 passim.
49 *SWDN* 21 Sept. 1885 (italics added).

Some of "these people" on the Arms Park terrace at a match with Newport in the early 1900s. Several women can be identified near the back.

References to the mixed social character of the crowds were often made in the press. "Spectators at local games are derived from all classes of society".[50] Workmen's tickets were introduced by Cardiff in 1890 when 968 were sold, equal to the number of members' and season tickets.[51] By 1892, out of 2,700 members' and season tickets sold, nearly 1,700 were workmen's.[52] In 1897, club membership was the largest in Wales at 1,200 and by 1899 this had grown to 2,000.[53] One Cardiff supporter clearly believed the club belonged to the whole community, and not just the elite, when he wrote in 1892 about the "general public, who are in reality the shareholders [of Cardiff]".[54] This is an interesting viewpoint and it contrasts with today's acceptance that modern professional rugby teams can be owned and controlled by a small number of very wealthy patrons.

---

50   *WM* 27 Jan. 1897.

51   C.S. Arthur, *The Cardiff Rugby Football Club: History and Statistics, 1876-1906* (Cardiff, 1908), p. 102.

52   *WM* 18 July 1892.

53   *SWDN* 20 Oct. 1897; *WM* 29 July 1899.

54   *WM* 5 Jan. 1892.

Throughout the period, there were frequent references in the press to supporters who attempted to view the matches at the Arms Park without paying. This involved several ruses, all demanding some athleticism on the part of the evaders: scaling the high boundary wall near the Cardiff and County Club on Westgate Street; wading through the river Taff on the western side of the Arms Park; or climbing nearby trees and telegraph poles.[55] No doubt serving the prejudices of a predominantly middle-class readership, it was usually implied that "these people" were members of the feckless lower orders. Unruly and sometimes violent spectators were also becoming a worrying problem and working-class "hobbledehoy rowdies" were often blamed. During the last five years of the century, crowd disturbances forced the WFU to close the grounds of the Aberavon, Abertillery, Brynmawr, Ferndale, Maesteg and Neath clubs.[56] At the Cardiff v Newport match in 1897, the referee was attacked and consequently the Arms Park was also suspended for five weeks.[57]

There is also little doubt about whom the *SWDN* had in mind when it reported on the behaviour at the Cardiff and District cup finals in 1897.

> [There was] no excuse for the disgraceful language used by a number of roughs who had ensconced themselves at the back of the stand and who, notwithstanding the presence of several ladies, criticised the play of the teams in brutal 'Billingsgate' [language].[58]

The reference to women attending matches was not at all unusual. They are mentioned in the very earliest match reports, for example, "several ladies and gentlemen favoured the players with their presence" at a Glamorgan FC game at Sophia Gardens in 1874.[59] By 1880, when Swansea defeated

Agile spectators avoid paying by making use of a telegraph pole outside the Arms Park.

55   For example, *SWDN* 20 Mar. 1899; D.E. Davies, *Cardiff Rugby Club: History and Statistics, 1876-1975: "The Greatest"* (Cardiff, 1975) p. 17.

56   WFU Minutes 1895 to 1899.

57   *SWDN* 15 Feb. 1897; WFU Minutes 22 Feb. 1897.

58   *SWDN* 15 Mar. 1897.

59   *WM* 26 Oct. 1874.

Lampeter College in the cup final, the *SWDN* was pleased to record the growing interest amongst women:

> Thousands of people [today] witness a good match, and the ladies, despite wind and weather, give countenance to the game by attending in large numbers, whereas two years ago, if a gentleman had the temerity to ask a lady to accompany him to a football match, the request would be provocative of the well-known feminine expression – The idea! But now, if a gentleman ventures to traduce football in the presence of ladies as being too dangerous, he is at once designated a "muff". Young men who join in the game are looked upon as heroes in their respective towns, and find a host of friends.[60]

When Wales played their first ever away match in Dublin in 1882, *The Irish Times* revealed that two Welsh women had travelled to watch the game.[61] Early references to female supporters may have been made to challenge the belief, widely held at the time, that rugby was an "uncivilised" activity. Numbers are always difficult, if not impossible, to estimate but, for example, "hundreds of ladies" were reported to have been at the 1891 Cardiff v Gloucester fixture which was attended by 7,000.[62] It was customary for women to sit in the stands free of charge. By 1898, there were complaints at the Cardiff AGM that they were monopolising the grandstand. Nevertheless, the policy of allowing women to attend for free so long as they were accompanied by a member, was continued, despite a (presumably jocular) criticism that their hats were too large.[63] The popular post-cards of the period, depicting the crowds at the Arms Park, confirm that many women did indeed attend matches there. Whilst those using the grandstand are likely to have been mostly middle class, women can also be spotted amongst the supporters in the predominantly working-class standing areas. Such press reports and images therefore, demonstrate that watching rugby in Cardiff was certainly not a totally male preoccupation.

As a result of growing membership and attendances, the Cardiff club's income also rose steadily, although reports of its increasing prosperity were not necessarily always well received. In 1889, there was some falling-out with the Marquess of Bute over match entrance fees. He had become concerned about rumours that Cardiff were using this income on lavish dinners and

---

60   *SWDN* 8 Mar. 1880.
61   *Irish Times* 30 Jan. 1882.
62   *WM* 16 Nov. 1891.
63   *SWDN* 30 July 1898.

Many women attended matches at the Arms Park around the turn of the century, as is clearly demonstrated by this post-card image in which at least fifty can be identified.

other benefits for members but he was assured by the committee that the money was needed to maintain and develop the ground in the wider interests of the town's prestige. "The club [is] not an individual enterprise. It was for the honour of the town that they charged for admission."[64] Whatever the truth of this pious argument, it seems to have been accepted by the Marquess. No doubt it was largely for his benefit that it was announced at the 1897 AGM that the club was run purely in the interest of sport and that no other club in Britain could boast of such a good record in charitable donations.[65] There does seem to have been some substance in this last claim, as will be seen.

Cardiff *did* have considerable financial liabilities in maintaining a ground suitable for first-class club and international matches. The pitch was a particular and a recurring problem. The ancient course of the Taff had been diverted from what became the Arms Park only a few years earlier, so the playing surface and surrounding areas were frequently muddy and occasionally flooded.[66] After the Llanelli match in 1884, "Old Stager" complained of having to wade through "a dreary expanse of mud and slush" to get to

---

64   *SWDN* 29 Aug. 1889.
65   *SWDN* 31 July 1897.
66   Gareth Williams, *1905 and All That: Essays on Rugby Football, Sport and Welsh Society* (Llandysul, 1991), pp. 56-7. The river was diverted between 1848 and 1856.

the pitch which was covered in "numerous miniature lakes".[67] In another game the following season, the whole of one side of the playing area was under water and the players' struggles in the wet caused great amusement for the spectators.[68] When Cardiff defeated the Maoris in 1888, the ground was "in a deplorable state, wet, muddy, with pools of water on the pitch."[69] As late as the Thursday before the Scotland match in 1890, the pitch was still entirely under water.[70] In the depth of winter, it was often necessary to lay a covering of straw to protect the playing surface from freezing; whilst the arrangements to ensure that the 1893 England international could go ahead have become part of rugby's folklore and these are discussed later.[71] Eventually in 1895, the poor conditions necessitated taking up the whole of the playing surface, laying new drains and re-turfing the pitch at a cost of over £1,000.[72] This did not permanently solve the problem, while as recently as 1960 the Arms Park suffered from very severe flooding when the entire ground was covered by a metre of water.[73]

With the growing numbers of spectators came increasing demands to improve facilities. There was constant pressure for new accommodation, such as grandstands and standing areas, press boxes, fencing to replace ropes around the pitch, footboards and paths etc.

In 1888, the erection of steel fencing "to keep the street urchins from getting into the grounds" set the club back £148 and it did not succeed.[74] After 20,000 attended the 1894 Newport game, "Old Stager" warned that the club could not afford to be complacent and recommended the building of yet another stand. "That the expenditure on accommodation for visitors ... has been lavish everyone will admit, but the committee must keep in mind the fact that football is increasing in popularity and that the population of the town is growing."[75]

Charles Arthur was secretary of Cardiff at the time and his 1908 history details the continual annual expenditure on improvements, reflecting the growing support for the club. For instance, the first grandstand was erected

---

67 *SWDN* 22 Dec. 1884.

68 *SWDN* 12 Oct. 1885.

69 Gareth Williams, 'Taffs Acre: The Pre-1900 Years', in David Parry-Jones, *Taffs Acre: History and Celebration of Cardiff Arms Park* (London, 1984), pp. 43-4.

70 *SWDN* 3 Feb. 1890.

71 Williams, *Taffs Acre*, p. 43.

72 Arthur, *Cardiff Rugby*, p. 122.

73 Davies, *Cardiff Rugby Club*, p. 141. Most of Cardiff RFC's early records were lost in these floods.

74 Arthur, *Cardiff Rugby*, p. 86.

75 *SWDN* 22 Oct. 1894.

Ground problems were a constant problem. This close-up of an 1870s photograph reveals the marshy nature of the Arms Park. This particular area was the site of the original course of the river Taff, which had been diverted only twenty years earlier.
Courtesy of Cardiff Council Library Service

in 1881 for £50. This soon had to be replaced in 1885 with a new stand costing £362; and two wings were added eight years later at a cost of £437, providing seating for 1,200. In 1890, new standing areas were constructed along the entire length of the ground for £254 and these were enlarged in 1893 for £106 and again in 1894 for £194. Another £103 was spent on repairing stands and erecting new ones in 1896.[76] More care had to be taken with the standard of construction following the collapse of a standing area at the river end during a match with Swinton in 1893, which resulted in compensation payments being made to several injured spectators.[77]

As a result of all this expenditure, the club chairman was able to boast – clearly with the WFU in mind – that only three other grounds in the kingdom, "Crystal Palace, Aston Villa and Everton", could have accommodated the crowd of perhaps 40,000 which attended the Ireland international in March 1899.[78] However, the events that day revealed that even the Arms Park was not sufficiently up to the job of catering for such numbers. So many wanted to get into the match that the gates were rushed and forced open and thousands poured in, while others swarmed over the walls. Consequently the facilities in the ground were completely overwhelmed and

76   Arthur, *Cardiff Rugby*, pp. 43-138; *SWDN* 27 Oct. 1890.
77   *SWDN* 29 July 1893.
78   *WM* and *SWDN* 29 July 1899.

Rugby at the heart of Cardiff. The Arms Park in the 1890s from Westgate Street, showing the 1885 grandstand and its extensions, together with the recently constructed standing areas around the ground. Note the press box facing the goal-line in the left-hand corner.

there was an "absolute breakdown of the arrangements", with spectators streaming on to the pitch. According to the *Western Mail*, "the popularity of football has outgrown all the provision that can be made for it." At their very next meeting, the WFU discussed the question of an international ground and resolved to improve facilities at Cardiff and Swansea. So in 1900, the Cardiff club entered into an agreement to increase standing and seating accommodation, with the Union bearing three-quarters of the cost and Cardiff contributing £481. This increased the capacity to 35,000 and it began the process which eventually led to the Welsh Rugby Union taking over the ownership of the ground in 1968 when the Cardiff club moved onto to its present site on the adjacent former cricket area. Because of the central location of the Arms Park, these ground developments added a prominent and distinctive new feature to the townscape of Victorian Cardiff.[79]

Improvements to the ground and accommodation, therefore, were a constant drain on the club's resources, but at the same time they provided occasional business for local architects, builders, contractors and suppliers, as well as employment for local tradesmen and casual workers. Although it was the WFU, rather than the Cardiff club, which met the bill, the scale of the arrangements for ensuring the pitch was playable for the 1893 England

79 *WM* and *SWDN* 20 Mar. 1899; WFU minutes 27 Apr. 1899, 26 Apr. 1900; Arthur, *Cardiff Rugby*, p. 157. See Hignell and Prescott, *Cardiff Sporting Greats*, pp. 31-3, 184-6, 211-12 for the history of developments at Cardiff Arms Park.

match is worth mentioning. Some fifty-eight men were employed for five days before the match attending the 500 coal-fired braziers and the thirty hot boiler plates placed around the ground. At noon on match day another fifteen men were taken on to clear the pitch. Around eighteen tons of coal were burned and the total cost of the operation amounted to over £200. This remarkable event is indicative of the importance of coal in the Welsh economy and in the making of Cardiff in particular. It was worth all the effort. Wales won the match 12-11 and went on to win their first Triple Crown.[80]

The 1893 Triple Crown commemorative medal presented to Arthur Gould. Siân Prescott. Courtesy of Robert Gould

For some clubs, the financial burden of ground costs could be too great to sustain. After Cardiff Harlequins took a lease from the Tredegar Estate on two swampy and uneven brick fields in Roath, they spent (according to press reports) a massive £2,000 draining, levelling and preparing the football field and cycling track and erecting stands, changing accommodation and fencing.[81] This over-ambitious expenditure certainly contributed to the club's eventual demise, though their enterprise was not totally wasted, as the "The Harlequins" has been a venue for rugby ever since. It hosted a Welsh trial in 1892, the WFU Challenge Cup final in 1893, the first ever Cardiff and District Mallett Cup final in 1894 and a county match between Glamorgan and Lancashire in 1895. For over seventy years, it served as the Cardiff High School sports field, while from 1947 to 1961 it was the Cardiff High School Old Boys rugby ground and has now been the home of St. Peter's RFC since the late 1970s.[82]

In an age when the State took little responsibility even for the most disadvantaged in society, it is not surprising that Welsh rugby was actively

---

80   Williams, *Taffs Acre*, p. 43; *SWDN* 9 Jan. 1893; *WM* 5, 7 Jan. 1893.
81   *WM* 8 Sept. 1891; *SWDN* 4 Apr., 10 Oct. 1892.
82   Hignell and Prescott, *Cardiff Sporting Greats*, pp. 158-9.

involved in supporting charities and relief funds. Given the appalling frequency and scale of industrial disasters of the time – which no doubt involved many participants and supporters of the game – rugby could hardly stand aside. So the practice of clubs donating match takings began very early in the game in Wales. In 1878, for instance, following the catastrophic loss of 268 men and boys in an explosion at the Abercarn colliery, the proceeds of matches at Cardiff, Swansea and Newport were all given to the relief fund. And neither were international tragedies ignored. In 1877, Newport donated all the takings from their first ever game held at Rodney Parade to the Indian Famine Fund.[83]

Notwithstanding the heavy burdens mentioned above, Cardiff's steadily improving financial position enabled the club to make generous annual contributions to a variety of local charities. Arthur's history shows that from 1890-1 onwards, large donations, often of several hundreds of pounds, were made out of club income each year.[84] For instance, in 1892, the club endowed a scholarship at Cardiff University; while in 1898 the new seamen's hospital received £100 and a further £400 a year later. Other beneficiaries in 1899 included Cardiff Infirmary, Nazareth House Orphanage, Porthcawl Convalescent Rest Home, the Shipping and Port Labourers Relief Fund, the Deaf and Dumb Institute and Missions, the Blind Asylum, the Cardiff Merciful Society, the St. Vincent de Paul Society, the Nurses Institute, the Girls Home, and the Society for Prevention of Cruelty to Children. A total of £680 was donated this year.

Sometimes special matches might be arranged, such as that with a Cardiff District XV in 1890 for the families of the 176 miners killed in the Llanerch colliery explosion. Alternatively, the whole proceeds of the gate from a major regular fixture might be handed over, as happened, for example, with the 1886 Swansea match takings, following the death of seven seamen when a ship blew up at Cardiff docks. Again in 1892, it was the receipts from the lucrative Swansea match which were given to the relief fund set up after the Tondu Park Slip colliery explosion when 112 died. By 1897, the Cardiff club had donated over £3,000 to charity which was claimed to be a record for a sports club anywhere in Britain.[85] Even the *Sheffield Daily Telegraph* picked

---

83 *WM* 21 Sept. 1878 (Cardiff), 7 Oct. 1878 (Swansea), 29 Oct. 1878 (Newport); *SWDN* 17 Oct. 1877 (Indian Famine).

84 Arthur, *Cardiff Rugby*, pp. 102-151.

85 Arthur, *Cardiff Rugby*, pp. 96, 113, 217; Davies, *Cardiff Rugby Club*, p. 46 (1898-9); *WM* 29 Mar. 1886; *SWDN* 20 Oct. 1897. See, however, Tony Collins, *Rugby's Great Split: Class, Culture and the Origins of Rugby League Football* (London, 2006 edn.), p. 83 for details of northern clubs' donations to charity.

up the story and wrote, "There is a good deal to admire in a club which can be so openhanded as this ... a somewhat refreshing oasis in a dreary wilderness."[86] As well as distributing club funds, Cardiff regularly allowed teams of boilermakers, cabmen and the like, to use the Arms Park for charitable and good causes. These matches were often organised to provide financial help for injured or sick work colleagues or their widows, but not always. The gate proceeds from the "coal-trimmers and dockers derby" between Cardiff and Newport, for instance, went to the Welsh National Museum.[87] Leading players would often turn out in these games to help boost the takings. The WFU too also contributed to a variety of Cardiff charities – including the Infirmary and Nazareth House – usually by direct donation but occasionally by handing over the proceeds from representative matches, as happened with the South Wales v United Hospitals game in 1888.[88] Several local Catholic organisations were beneficiaries of all this philanthropy, which may, in part, reflect the anxiety of rugby's administrators to keep on good terms with the owner of the Arms Park, the Marquess of Bute, a prominent convert to Roman Catholicism. That the game was able to display such generosity not only reveals that it was in a healthy condition from the late 1880s, but also that it saw itself as an integral part of the social fabric. Such charitable contributions were also important in cementing the wider perception of sports organisations in general, and Cardiff rugby club in particular, as community and civic institutions.

It is sometimes alleged that the commercialisation of the game must have inevitably led to the payment of players. There is no doubt that broken time payments were being paid in Wales, though even the most successful valley clubs did not have huge resources for this. Arranging employment at the local pit may have been as common as making direct cash payments, though it was still a breach of the professional regulations. Eric Dunning and Kenneth Sheard, however, imply that Cardiff must have paid their players during the 1890s, given the substantial sums which the club received from gate money. They draw on the details of Cardiff's gate receipts (though these were hardly representative of Welsh clubs in general as claimed) which were published in *Report on Rugby* (1959) by Morgan and Nicholson.[89] These authors obtained the figures unacknowledged from

---

86   Quoted in *SWDN* 26 Oct. 1897.
87   *WM* 20, 25 Apr. 1907.
88   *WM* 19, 22 Mar. 1888 (United Hospitals); *SWDN* 14 Apr. 1896 (direct donations).
89   Eric Dunning and Kenneth Sheard, *Barbarians, Gentlemen and Players: A Sociological Study of the Development of Rugby Football* (London, 2005 edn.), p. 191; William J. Morgan and Geoffrey Nicholson, *Report on Rugby* (London, 1959), p. 78.

THE MERCANTILE ACCIDENT & GUARANTEE INSURANCE COMPANY, LIMITED.

RATES FOR FOOTBALL TEAM POLICIES.

These Rates are approximate and subject to revision should there be exceptional circumstances to necessitate an increased rate.

BENEFITS ASSURED.				PREMIUM PER PLAYER.	
Sum at Death.	Permanent Total Disablement.	Permanent Partial Disablement.	During temporary total Disablement, as per Schedule.	For Six Months.	For each Additional Month.
£200	£200	£100	£3 per week	£1 1/	3/6 per play'r
150	150	75	2 „	15/	2/6 „
100	100	50	1 10/ „	12/	2/ „
50	50	25	1 „	9/	1/6 „

SPECIAL RATES FOR ATHLETES (INDIVIDUAL POLICIES).

These Rates will cover all Accidents sustained while engaged in any ONE of the following Sports:—Football, Cricket, Tennis, Cross Country Running, Skating, Cycling, Gymnastics, Shooting, Boating, etc.

Agent: WILLIAM PAGE WOOD,

21, CASTLE STREET, CARDIFF.

Details of player insurance cover advertised in the 1890-1 handbook.

Charles Arthur's 1908 club history. Dunning and Sheard quote from *Report on Rugby* that "clubs were soon making enough money to pay players' ... expenses, if not more." Because Cardiff had enough income to pay players, the argument seems to run, they must have done so.

What this does not take into account, however, are – as Charles Arthur clearly shows – the very substantial expenditures which Cardiff regularly incurred in charitable donations, support for local and schools rugby, player insurance, match expenses, guarantees, visitor entertainment and, importantly, ground maintenance and development. Whilst there is no doubt that Cardiff players were looked after very well indeed, not least because an ambitious fixture list involved very heavy travelling and hotel expenditures, there is no *evidence* that the club regularly made direct cash payments and Morgan and Nicholson do not provide any. In 1895, "Welsh Athlete" commented, somewhat critically, that since wealthy Welsh clubs could afford to pay for boots, jerseys, rail fares and hotels and "every tittle tattle of expenses", players were more or less professional compared to earlier times. But he did not accuse clubs of directly paying players, though he did prophesise correctly that while it "may not come for some time" one day it would happen.[90]

---

90   *WM* 12 Aug. 1895.

There are a number of reasons which suggest that it is unlikely that Cardiff regularly paid players as a matter of course. There was the risk that the Marquess of Bute might reconsider their use of the Arms Park, if it became known that they were not operating as an essentially amateur operation. In addition, Dunning and Sheard argue that rugby in Wales was controlled by men who did not "adhere to the amateur ethos". There may be some truth in this but the example of Cardiff is a not a good one. Most of the senior officials who controlled the club at this time probably would not have accepted the regular payment of players. Around the time of the Northern Union breakaway, some leading Welsh club officials, including WH Gwynn the WFU secretary, *were* undoubtedly sympathetic to, or even in favour of, broken time payments; but Cardiff and Newport were known to be strongly opposed to, or "dead against", the practice "and were determined to have none of it."[91] An article in the *Evening Express* in 1901 appears to confirm that Cardiff did not pay players as a matter of course. This suggested that "veiled professionalism" was so rampant in south Wales that some believed that even Cardiff was not "free from the taint." But if players *were* being paid, it argued, this would simply have led to the resignation of leading members of the committee. The *Express*, however, did take a more pragmatic view of the matter: "Other clubs [do it], why not Cardiff?"[92] Finally, the number of working-class Cardiff players who signed for professional Northern Union clubs at this time suggests that there was no great financial benefit for them to remain in Cardiff.

A Popular Urban Culture

Clearly, in many ways then, rugby had a much greater impact on the urban life of Victorian Cardiff than has previously been acknowledged by historians of the city. Discussing Cardiff's cultural amenities around the 1850s to the 1870s, Professor William Rees, in his history of Cardiff, refers to the Cardiff Athenaeum, the Classical Society, the Blue Ribbon Choir, the Cardiff Naturalists Society and many other similar worthy organisations. However, apart from a brief reference to the formation of Cardiff Cricket Club, he entirely ignores the new popular culture of sport which, as we have seen, was beginning to develop such a powerful hold on many of the town's citizens. Admittedly, in a footnote, Rees adds, "More organised sport was at this time becoming popular" but the only example he is able to provide of this popularity is a

---

91   *SWDN* 25 Sept. 1893.
92   *Evening Express* 20 April 1901.

brief account of two Cardiff climbers who died on Mont Blanc.[93] Yet, just as in Yorkshire and Lancashire in the late nineteenth century, rugby became one of the major forms of mass entertainment in the town.[94] In a society where the quality of civic life may have been limited compared to that in older and more prestigious cities, success in sport would have been enthusiastically embraced.

Mitchell and Kenyon's recently discovered films, which portray British urban life around the turn of the century, vividly reveal how important and lively street society was at the time.[95] Therefore, the presence of large numbers of footballers and supporters congregating on public parks or trudging back to their headquarters every Saturday must have been a familiar part of the urban scene to everyone, even the uninterested. In his history of Cardiff RFC, Danny Davies recalled, too, the sight, smells and sounds of street vendors, irresistibly drawn by the match-day crowds in Westgate Street:

> some selling hot chestnuts and potatoes from their coke fires, their stands a magnet for urchins in winter ... others sold sweets, peppermints, bulls-eyes, brandy snaps and pasties from their baskets ... Their cries were well known in and around the Cardiff Arms Park.[96]

The huge crowds of merry, money-spending supporters of all classes, regularly converging on the town centre for major club matches and internationals, quickly became a distinguishing characteristic of life in Cardiff, as it remains to this day.

For the Llanelli game in 1894, "Cosmopolitan Cardiff ... was thoroughly Welsh on Saturday afternoon", while a month later, "Half the male population of Cardiff, and not a few of the gentler sex ... seemed to have found their way to the Park and its neighbourhood" to watch the match against their keenest rivals Newport.[97] In 1895, when Ireland were the visitors to the Arms Park:

> On the roofs of the neighbouring business premises, warehouses etc. were hundreds of sightseers; in the trees a large number perched themselves,

---

93   William Rees, *A History of Cardiff* (Cardiff, 1969 edn.), pp. 326-7, footnote 116.
94   Tony Collins, *A Social History of English Rugby Union*, (London, 2009), p. 27.
95   *The Lost World of Mitchell and Kenyon*, (DVD), (BBC, 2005).
96   Davies, *Cardiff Rugby Club*, pp.17-18.
97   *SWDN* 12 Feb. 1894 (Llanelli), 5 Mar. 1894 (Newport).

In Westgate Street "the crowd were packed wall to wall".

while some were even daring enough to plant themselves on the roof of the press box.[98]

The *SWDN*'s description of the atmosphere in Cardiff, on the occasion of the 1899 Triple Crown decider against Ireland, is still entirely recognisable in the twenty-first century. "Westgate Street presented an extraordinary appearance. The road would have done credit to a Continental thoroughfare on a fete day ... The crowd were packed from wall to wall." [99] The composition of these crowds reflected Welsh society. At the Scotland match in 1896, the *Western Mail* noted the presence of colliers, tinplaters, Cardiff workmen ("not always Welsh"), Cardiff "mashers", coal-trimmers, "pale young" curates and ladies, who were "beyond description". There were even dissenting ministers, for "all the chapels in the world would not keep folks from the match." [100]

---

98   *SWDN* 18 Mar. 1895.

99   *SWDN* 20 Mar. 1899.

100 *WM* 27 Jan. 1896. A "masher" was someone who dressed or behaved in a way to attract susceptible young women.

This close-up of the photograph of the 1903 international match shows the proximity of the Grand Theatre to the Arms Park. It can be seen immediately behind the well-dressed referee.

Daryl Leeworthy

David Smith and Gareth Williams perceptively reveal how Welsh rugby had become the people's theatre.[101] Perhaps it is not surprising, then, that the theatre itself was quick to reflect this new popular culture. To promote their annual pantomimes, the casts of both the Theatre Royal and the Grand Theatre regularly played each other at "rugby" on the Arms Park. The 1890 pantomime at the Grand included a song about the "bold blue and black" as well as a "Great Football Ballet ... the sensation of Cardiff", in which the dancers performed in costumes decorated in the colours of the leading Welsh clubs.[102] The Whitsun production at the Theatre Royal in 1886 was even *set* in the Arms Park during a match, and was called *Football or Life in Cardiff*.[103] The *SWDN* announced that "For once the national winter pastime of Wales has changed both its habitat and its season, for during the present week "Football" occupies the boards of the Theatre Royal instead of the Cardiff Arms Park." The play's hit comic song was a version of the old favourite, *Crawshay Bailey's Engine*,

---

101 David Smith and Gareth Williams, *Fields of Praise: The Official History of the Welsh Rugby Union 1881-1981* (Cardiff, 1980), p. 75; see also David Smith, "People's Theatre – A Century of Welsh Rugby", *History Today*, 31, March (1981), pp. 31-6.

102 *SWDN* 27 Dec. 1890, *WM* 27 Dec. 1890. The "bold blue and black" was a nickname for the Cardiff club at the time.

103 *SWDN* 17 June 1886.

with the verses adapted to the members of Hancock's record-breaking Cardiff team. It was received with such "enthusiastic acclamation" that several encores had to be given.[104] Here is another vivid example of just how far rugby had entered into the lifeblood of Victorian Cardiff.

Barely fifteen years after the arrival of the sport, the Welsh press were regularly referring to rugby football as the national sport. Before the England international in Swansea in 1885, "Old Stager" claimed that the game had increased so greatly in popularity over the previous three or four years that it was "now recognised as a national pastime."[105] After the match, which Wales lost, he wrote of "the strong hold football has secured on the affections of a large portion of the inhabitants of South Wales", adding that it monopolised conversation so much that people forgot all about General Gordon's safety at the siege of Khartoum and the Fenian bombing campaign in London.[106] In Cardiff's pubs and hotels, too, rugby football was often the main topic of conversation, sometimes involving those who weren't even regular followers of the game. As early as 1890, the *SWDN* detected what has become a perennial characteristic of Welsh life. "Football strongly affects our social barometer – one week very stormy, another set fair."[107] When the team to play England in 1891 was announced, the same paper recognised another familiar Welsh speciality:

The Theatre Royal in Wood Street. Courtesy of SA Brain and Co.

---

104 *SWDN* 15 June 1886.
105 *SWDN* 2 Jan. 1885.
106 *SWDN* 5 Jan. 1885.
107 *SWDN* 24 Nov. 1890.

Cardiff 1893-4. Norman Biggs (with the ball) was the captain.   *Cardiff RFC*

It has been said that every Britisher considers himself qualified to lead an army, edit The Times, or be Prime Minister, and to these gifts must be added in Wales the ability to pick a football team.[108]

On the morning of the 1891 England match in Newport, the *SWDN* memorably declared, "football in South Wales ... has now become the one great popular pastime of the people".[109]

After he had turned out for Richmond against Liverpool in 1893, the Welsh international Norman Biggs made some revealing remarks about the attitudes to rugby in Cardiff compared to those in some other parts of Britain. "What is the great difference between the London match and a Cardiff game? ... At Richmond there was no need to exert myself, and nobody cared much who won – that's the difference."[110] Nobody cared! But

108 *SWDN* 22 Dec. 1890.
109 *SWDN* 3 Jan. 1891.
110 *WM* 28 Oct. 1893.

not everyone was necessarily impressed with this obsession with mere sport. The *SWDN* columnist "Cosmos" was one such critic, though his remarks are still worth repeating in full as they reveal a great deal about the place rugby enjoyed in the new popular urban culture. When visiting the *Pier Head Restaurant* at Cardiff docks after the 1891 England international match, he stopped to listen to the conversations of "the usual crowd of loafers" and had this to say about the encounter:

> It was not the slackness of times; it was not Parnell; it was not the Disestablishment of the Church; it was not the utilization of the Welsh language, though from their accent, they were purely Welsh; it was not the strike in Scotland; it was not the selection of the head-constable of Glamorganshire; it was not intermediate education; it was not total abstinence; it was not the lowness of freights or the price of coal; it was not the severity of the weather – but what I heard was something about the backs being absolutely superior, and the forwards heeling out.
>
> I knew then the most absorbing topic of interest ... there are twelve vessels laid up [idle] in Cardiff Docks ... wages are declining ... arts, industry may fade, *but who cares as long as there is a football match, and sixpence with which to see it?*[111]

"The most absorbing topic".

---

111 *SWDN* 6 Jan. 1891 (italics added).

7

CONCLUSIONS:
'The noble game is not totally unknown here.'

The last three decades of the nineteenth century, therefore, witnessed nothing less than a transformation in the sporting life of Cardiff and south Wales. By the end of the century, the interest and participation in rugby had reached a level which would have been unimaginable to the pioneers of only thirty years earlier.

Informal kick-abouts and folk, street and Shrovetide football were not uncommon in mid nineteenth-century Wales, but to what extent – if any – these may have influenced the later adoption of rugby remains unknown. During the 1860s, more organised versions of football were occasionally played in south Wales but these were sporadic events and hybrid rules were the norm. The evidence suggests that the participants in these games were middle and upper class. The comparatively late arrival of rugby is partly explained by the relatively small Welsh middle class and by the absence in the main urban centres of any large public schools and universities, which helped to establish and stimulate the game elsewhere. Rugby was eventually introduced mainly by old boys and masters from the major rugby playing public schools, especially those located in the west country. Locally, private and grammar schools were probably as important as the Welsh public schools.

The arrival of the game coincided with the demographic and industrial transformation of Wales and, during the 1870s, Welsh rugby too changed out of all recognition. What had been a minority and elite leisure pastime at the beginning of the decade was becoming, ten years later, a consuming passion enjoyed across the community. By this time, there were well over a hundred teams in existence in south Wales.

The first organised rugby clubs began to emerge around 1870. One of the earliest, if not *the* earliest, was located in Cardiff, thereby placing the town – in contrast to the prevailing view – at the very heart of the origin of the game in Wales. Within a few years, rugby became the established form of football played in south Wales. By the mid-1870s, all the major Welsh clubs had been formed; local organisation of the game was improving; and interest was beginning to spread beyond the game's original narrow social base. For the next two decades, association football remained very much a minority activity. It was, however, mainly in the coastal towns of Cardiff, Newport, Swansea and Llanelli, and not the coalfield valleys as is sometimes assumed, that Welsh enthusiasm for the game first materialised.

The demand for representative and competitive rugby emerged very early and in response to this the South Wales Football Club was founded in 1875 and the South Wales Challenge Cup inaugurated in 1877. Despite the infancy of the game in Wales, this appears to have been the first major open cup competition in Britain. It had an immediate and lasting effect and was widely acknowledged by contemporaries as one of the main reasons for the game's subsequent popularity in Wales. Its early introduction reveals that competitiveness and inter-town rivalry was emerging even *before* the arrival of the working man. This was fuelled by the growing economic and political rivalry between the leading Welsh towns and it resulted in an increasing incidence of match disputes and disruption, sometimes involving violence by both players and supporters. As the events at the Newport-Cardiff cup clash in 1880 show, this was happening before participation by working-class players was significant.

The first clubs were founded by the social elite for their own recreation. However, this soon changed. For instance, the merger of Cardiff Wanderers and Glamorgan in 1876 had the specific objective of creating a team which would be more representative of Cardiff in its matches with its rivals. Though hard evidence is difficult to locate, it seems that by the end of the 1870s, Welsh working men were beginning to take up rugby.

Increasing competitiveness, especially in the cup, was matched by growing attendances. The two fed on each other. By the end of the decade, crowds of thousands were being reported at major games. This was probably how many working men were drawn into the sport, first as spectators, then as players. The middle class in Wales was relatively small, so as new clubs sprang up, they could not afford to turn potential players away simply because of their social background. Similarly, if senior clubs wished to compete successfully, particularly with strong English teams, they *had* to select from a wider pool. This was a decisive turning point in the history of the Welsh game. Had working-class players been shut out, as happened elsewhere, then rugby in Wales would have stagnated and would never have risen much above English county standard, as was experienced in other sports. But crucially, civic and national pride was more important than social exclusivity. Before long, of course, workmen offered more than just making up the numbers. It was soon recognised that they possessed new and valuable qualities which could enhance the Welsh game. It was such players who would eventually provide sufficient fire and muscle to the pack to enable Wales to unleash Cardiff's four three-quarter system with such effect during the first "Golden Era" of 1899 to 1911 when, following the victory over New Zealand, they were regarded as the unofficial world champions.

The 1880-1 season was a vitally important one as it saw the formation of the Welsh Football Union which could now harness the game's enormous potential and, at the same time, control the wilder excesses of the growing number of its adherents. The same year also saw the first appearance of the Welsh international team. This at last gave a national focus around which the game – in south Wales at least – could coalesce and, within a year, rugby was already being described as the national sport. The Cardiff club was closely involved in both these developments.

The growth in interest in both playing and watching rugby was as strong in Cardiff as anywhere in Wales. Whilst popular sport in the Victorian period has been largely ignored by the city's historians, it is clear that it had a major influence on the life of Cardiff. The emergence of rugby as a popular pastime, enjoyed by all classes in Cardiff, cannot be divorced from the huge economic, demographic and social changes experienced by the town in the second half of the nineteenth century. These were to influence markedly the particular character of rugby in Cardiff.

In *some* respects, Cardiff's sporting culture was different from that of many other towns in Britain, though as Tony Collins has pointed out, it was by no means atypical in the period. In the late 1870s and early 1880s in Liverpool and Manchester and in Leeds, Bradford and Hull in the 1890s, rugby was still the most popular game, despite the growth of soccer.[1] Nevertheless, rugby dominated nineteenth-century Cardiff; it enjoyed cross-class support; and, at the neighbourhood level, social improvers were not particularly prominent. Within Wales, Cardiff stood out in several ways. There was the sheer number of its clubs and players. Though working-class participation was strong, there was still a notable middle-class involvement. The archetypal Welsh club team, comprised entirely of hard-bitten colliers, so beloved of some writers, simply did not exist in Cardiff, though there were plenty of teams which included equally tough dockers and coal-trimmers. The pronounced attachment to the game of the town's Catholic schools and parishes was another distinguishing aspect of the local game. These features,

---

1   Tony Collins, "Book Review: This Spellbound Rugby People", *Sport in History*, 32, 3 (2012), pp. 454-7.

and others touched on below, helped to create the distinctive character of Cardiff "district" rugby.

Cardiff became the largest town in Wales from the 1870s, mainly by attracting large numbers of migrants. Given the town's growing industrial and commercial prominence, these newcomers included many members of the mercantile and professional classes. It should not be a surprise, therefore, that Cardiff was a focus for early Welsh rugby. What is surprising, however, is that occasionally some commentators have suggested that Cardiff lagged behind other centres in Wales in taking up the game. Even in 1878, the Cardiff captain, Raoul Foa, was forced to respond to a letter in the local press which suggested that there was no club in the town. Evidently irritated by this, he felt it necessary to reply somewhat understatedly that "the noble game is not totally unknown here."[2]

A close study of local newspapers has revealed a previously unrecognised scale of participation in rugby during the years 1870 to 1900. Whilst the research was largely confined to the Cardiff area, it does strongly suggest that the extent of rugby's penetration into nineteenth-century Wales was even greater than has previously been assumed. Therefore, simply relying on the number of clubs in membership of the WFU as an indication of the game's popularity clearly grossly underestimates the actual extent of the popularity of the game.

Whilst many of the "clubs" identified were short lived or transient, their existence nevertheless provides a measure of the depth of interest in the game. During the first eight years of the 1890s, there were, on average, over 200 teams each season in the Cardiff locality. The large numbers involved in playing and administering the game in the town, therefore, calls into question the often expressed contention that Welsh rugby was essentially a valleys phenomenon. Only by the late 1890s are there signs of a decline in participation in Cardiff. This occurred partly because soccer at last began to penetrate the sporting culture of the town, largely the result of the introduction of the game in elementary schools and the arrival of migrants from regions where soccer was the established sport.

Rugby had become firmly entrenched as the main sporting interest of the town's middle and working classes by the 1880s. It provided an accessible means by which many newcomers could identify with their host community, show allegiance to it and enter into its social life. In so doing, it acted as a "social cement", helping to develop a sense of neighbourhood, civic and national identity amongst a diverse population.

---

2   *Western Mail* 14 Oct. 1878.

The detailed analysis of the background of clubs contrasts with the results of research into English soccer at this time. Though there *were* many church, workplace and pub teams in Cardiff, their overall importance was much less marked. They comprised only around a quarter of all teams, which was considerably lower than suggested in some studies of English soccer. In addition, with the notable exception of a few Catholic parish clubs, they rarely featured amongst the strongest local adult teams.

The relatively smaller number of church teams may be partly explained by the general opposition to sport and its associated activities by Welsh nonconformists and by the antipathy towards "uncivilised" rugby by religious organisations in general. Catholic authorities seem to have been rather less concerned about this, recognising no doubt that rugby could act as a useful bridgehead for the assimilation of Irish Catholics into the wider community. The relatively low number of workplace teams is partly a reflection of the nature of Cardiff's industrial economy, where there was little manufacturing and where many workers were employed in casual waterfront occupations. Neither case of church nor workplace, therefore, suggests that there was a strong element of middle-class "social control" in the establishment and organisation of rugby in Cardiff. The number of pub teams was insignificant though since most clubs used public houses as their headquarters, their contribution to the game was, nevertheless, still immense.

On the other hand, neighbourhood and street teams were clearly the overwhelming choice of most players. Research into early rugby in Rochdale produced similar findings, which may perhaps indicate there were different emphases in club formation in the two branches of football but clearly this requires much further investigation. In one of the most rapidly growing towns in Britain, the popularity of neighbourhood teams was probably a response to the need to accommodate newcomers quickly into the game, avoiding the necessity of having to be a member of a pre-existing organisation, such as a church.

The evidence from local newspapers suggests that large numbers of youngsters were involved in school, street and junior rugby. Most of these teams appear to have been largely organised by the boys themselves. Even with adult clubs, it was apparent that club officials were often very young and certainly predominantly of a playing age.

The investigation into the background of Cardiff's players in the 1870s confirms the widely held view that the game was introduced and initially played by a social elite, largely drawn from the mercantile and professional classes, at least some of whom had been educated at public school. However, this dominance first began to erode by the end of the decade with the arrival of lower status middle-class and working-class players. By the early 1880s, new neighbourhood clubs, in which working men appeared, were springing up. Cardiff were including working men by 1881-2 and by the middle of the decade they comprised a substantial proportion of the First XV. It is significant that the very first working-class Welsh international, William Stadden, came through this system.

Thus, from the mid-1880s, Cardiff sat at the apex of a growing pyramid of local clubs from which it was constantly able to renew its teams. In one sense, then, even though the club was still technically a private organisation, Cardiff can be seen as a "representative" team, embracing the "region" of Cardiff and district. It was certainly regarded as an institution which represented the whole of Cardiff by its many supporters. In this respect, Cardiff was no different from any of the other leading Welsh clubs, all of which acted as the focus of deep civic pride for the various communities which they represented.

Growth at the local club level was stimulated by the continued success of the Cardiff team, playing with a revolutionary new style which it had pioneered. Cardiff now had one of the best club sides in Britain. Since the team was essentially a representative one, local players could aspire to progress via an extensive and comprehensive network of junior and neighbourhood clubs. Though class barriers undoubtedly still existed, the over-riding demand from spectators, the general public and the press was for success on the field, so working-class players could and did find themselves representing their town and even their country.

By 1890, grassroots clubs were largely administered by young members of the skilled and semi-skilled working class and lower status middle class. Amongst the huge number of teams in Cardiff, only a few appear to have been exclusively middle class and many middle-class players belonged to socially mixed clubs. This provides strong evidence that the game was largely played and administered by ordinary working people and not the well intentioned middle class. Rugby in Victorian Cardiff was at the centre of working-class culture and this demonstrates that, in Wales, at least, it was, above all, a game of the urban working class. However, it was a different story when it came to the administration of the WFU and the senior clubs, as there it was the professional and business classes who continued to control the game and they ensured that it did not fall into the hands of a more democratic representation. With the major gate-taking clubs dominating the Union, by restricting membership and by operating a cartel in the election of officers, they managed to retain overall control of the game in Wales. So with membership of the WFU becoming ever more restrictive, the Cardiff and District Football Union was set up in 1892 to govern and nurture the game at the grassroots level. This was an immediate success and "the District" quickly became one of the defining components of "Cardiff rugby".

However, the majority of teams which appeared in this period never belonged to any union nor participated in any formal competitions. Even of those local clubs which did join the Welsh Football Union or the Cardiff and District Football Union in the 1890s, most enjoyed only a brief existence. There was a very high rate of annual turnover. The condition of the local club game in the period was one of chronic instability, with even successful teams disappearing as quickly as they rose. While financial and ground problems were contributory causes, the main reason seems to have been the frequency with which players and officials moved on. By the late 1890s, district clubs often lost players as a result of financial inducements made by other Welsh clubs or by those in the Northern Union.

The success of the Challenge Cup inspired the establishment of numerous other competitions across south Wales. By the 1890s, the thirst for competition had also extended to the formation of leagues, though not for the senior Welsh clubs. This was as true in Cardiff as elsewhere in Wales. An early district cup was discontinued in 1890 after only four years but it was soon replaced by the new Cardiff and District Football Union's Mallett Cup – still in existence – from 1893-4. Later, cups for less strong clubs and for youth teams were successfully inaugurated by the District Union and a two division league was established in 1894 with a third youth division added in 1899. Similar developments occurred widely throughout the towns and valleys of south Wales, though these competitions were never co-ordinated nationally.

Daryl Leeworthy has argued that, with the arrival of modern sport in the nineteenth century, "the landscape of towns and cities ... has been altered by the needs of players and spectators."[3] This was certainly true in Cardiff, where rugby was facilitated by a range of convenient playing areas. In particular, Sophia Gardens, centrally located and close to pubs and transport routes, provided accommodation for countless teams and players and was even the Cardiff club's home for its first three years. The strategic location of the Arms Park had an even wider significance for the game in Wales and it still helps to sustain its popularity to the present day. Easily accessible from both within and without the town, it rapidly became – as it remains today in the form of the Millennium Stadium and the Cardiff RFC

---

3   Daryl Leeworthy, *Fields of Play: The Sporting Heritage of Wales*, (Aberystwyth 2012), p. 159.

ground – a conspicuous statement about the importance of rugby football to Cardiff and to Wales.

The level of interest in club and international rugby generated financial benefits for a range of businesses and organisations in the town, including transport operators; public house, hotel, restaurant and theatre proprietors; sports goods suppliers; photographers; newspaper proprietors, publishers and printers; builders and contractors; and charities. Cardiff's new and rapidly expanding role as the regional centre for south Wales meant that the level and range of its transport, commercial and recreational infrastructure was better able to respond to the new demands from rugby than anywhere else in Wales. The close proximity of the Arms Park and Sophia Gardens to the commercial centre only reinforced this. Attendances at club matches at the Park regularly reached five figures by the 1890s and on occasion rose to 20,000. International matches could attract substantially more spectators. These crowds reflected the composition and character of Welsh industrial society – cosmopolitan, socially inclusive, disputatious and sometimes disruptive and disrespectful of authority.

The income of the major clubs rose substantially during the 1890s and this was particularly true of Cardiff. However, the club also incurred high costs in maintaining the playing surface which was especially prone to flooding. In addition, significant sums were spent on continual ground improvements to meet the growing demands of spectators. The club was also very generous in making regular donations to local charities and junior rugby. Players were looked after extremely well in terms of equipment, travel and hotel expenses but there is no firm evidence that direct cash payments were regularly made. This is not to say that it never happened, but given the views of the committee and the possible opposition of the club's ground landlord, it is unlikely that such payments ever became standard in the period. If they were, the evidence so far remains elusive.

For a whole generation of Victorians, rugby union was *the* Cardiff sport. Its early introduction gave it a seemingly unassailable lead over its rivals. The absence of any serious competition from any other team or mass spectator sport for over twenty-five years allowed rugby to become entrenched in the local popular culture. The success of the town team was not only the focus for the expression of great civic pride, irrespective of class or even gender, but it also stimulated the growth in participation at a neighbourhood level. As the dominant sport in Cardiff, rugby provided a diverse and uprooted population, whether players or spectators, with a sense of belonging. Just as *Fields of Praise* argues that the sport contributed to a newfound sense of nationhood, it can be claimed that, at a local level, rugby also contributed to a new sense of citizenship.[4] Rugby in Cardiff was a highly visible feature of the urban landscape. Whether it was the central prominence of the Arms Park, the presence of players on public parks and streets, or the large crowds regularly descending on Cardiff for major matches, it would have been difficult for its Victorian citizens to be completely unaware of the game's place in the life of the town.

Victorian Cardiff was a brash and thrusting newcomer on Britain's urban scene. It had a lot of catching up to do. Often compared to Chicago, it was an upstart, with no great history or distinguished institutions. "Cardiff was no Edinburgh or Athens of the west".[5] However, success in sport provided one way for Cardiff to make its presence felt, apart, that is, from merely being recognised as the country's "Coal Metropolis". Ordinary citizens, businessmen, journalists and politicians – many of them born elsewhere – identified themselves with what was now "their" rugby team, which regularly recorded victories over the representatives of Britain's older and more prestigious cities. Just as the town of Cardiff had ascended from obscurity to become the world's most important centre for the export of coal, so too had its innovative rugby representatives risen to the very forefront of the game.

This study has revealed, for the first time, the extent of involvement in rugby in one locality in Victorian Wales. Cardiff was the largest town by the period but how different its experience was from that of other south Wales urban places needs to be examined in further research. Each town had its own context, of course, which helped to determine its particular rugby character. Cardiff's geographic, demographic, economic, social, educational and religious structure all influenced the particular way in which rugby developed in the town. In a vibrant, competitive and innovative society, Cardiff's aspiring mercantile and professional class introduced the game and continued to control it at the highest level. The location and extent of the town's recreational and commercial infrastructure provided the physical environment in which the game could flourish. A massively expanded and diverse working class embraced the game enthusiastically. They dominated it at its lower levels, took the level of participation to unprecedented heights and thereby contributed strongly to the creation of the socially inclusive version of rugby football which has thrived in Wales ever since. Cardiff was

---

4   David Smith and Gareth Williams, *Fields of Praise: The Official History of the Welsh Rugby Union 1881-1981* (Cardiff, 1980) passim.

5   Kenneth O. Morgan, *Rebirth of a Nation: Wales 1880-1980* (Oxford, 1982 edn.), p. 22; John Davies, *A Pocket Guide: Cardiff* (Cardiff, 2002) p. 48.

a crucible of the game in Wales. It remained at the very heart of Welsh rugby throughout the Victorian period. Rugby was also at the heart of the life of Victorian Cardiff.

APPENDICES

Appendix 1
Welsh Rugby Teams 1880-1

Compiled from the *South Wales Daily News* and the *Western Mail*

Aberavon 1&2
Aberdare
Albion, Cardiff
Alexandra Rangers, Newport
Arnold College, Swansea 1&2
Blaenavon Scarlet Runners
Blaina Ironsides
Bloomfield, Swansea
Brecon
Bridgend 1&2
Builth Wells
Burry Port Juniors
Bute Dock Rangers, Cardiff 1&2
Cadoxton, Neath
Cambrian, Aberdare
Canton Rovers, Cardiff 1&2
Canton Wanderers, Cardiff
Cardiff 1&2
Cardiff Proprietary Collegiate School
Carmarthen
Carmarthen Juniors
Carmarthen Training College
Cathays Rangers, Cardiff
Chepstow
Chepstow Grammar School
Christ College Brecon
Cwmavon 1&2
Dare
East Wales (Representative)
Excelsior, Newport
Green Institute, Neath
Haverfordwest
Hirwaun
Lampeter Town

Llandeilo
Llandeilo Academy
Llandeilo Grammar School
Llandovery College 1&2
Llandovery College Old Boys
Llanelli 1&2
Llanelli Juniors
Machen
Maindee, Newport 1&2
Melbourne, Swansea
Merthyr
Monmouth School
Monmouthshire (Representative)
Mountain Ash
Mountain Ash Temperance
Narberth
Neath 1&2
Neath Abbey
Neath Institute
Neath Proprietary School
Neath Rovers
Newport 1&2
Newport Crusaders 1&2
Newport Grammar School
Newport Rovers 1&2
Newport Wanderers
Oakfield, Cwmbran
Old Monmothians
Pembroke Dock
Penarth
Penarth Juniors
Pontardawe
Pontymister 1&2
Pontymister Rovers

Pontypool 1&2
Pontypridd
Porthcawl
Richmond, Cardiff
Risca Star
Roath, Cardiff 1&2
Roath Collegiate School, Cardiff
Roath Juniors ,Cardiff
South Wales FU (Representative)
St. Andrew's College, Swansea
St. David's College, Lampeter
St. Elvan's, Aberdare

Star, Aberdare
Star, Roath, Cardiff
Swansea 1&2
Swansea Juniors
Swansea Rovers
Tredegar
United Rhondda Valley
University College Wales, Aberystwyth
West Wales (Representative)
Windsor, Roath, Cardiff 1&2
Windsor, Swansea

Appendix 2
Cardiff and District Rugby Teams 1895-6

Compiled from the *South Wales Daily News* and the *Western Mail*

2nd GAV (Cardiff Artillery)
6th Cardiff Boys Brigade 1&2
7th Cardiff Boys Brigade
All Saints Church Lads Brigade
All Saints, Llandaff Yard
Anglo–Bavarian Rovers
Barry 1&2
Barry Barbarians
Barry Boilermakers
Barry Church Lads Brigade
Barry Coal Trimmers (Tippers)
Barry Crescents
Barry Dock Crusaders
Barry Dock Juniors
Barry Excelsiors
Barry Loco
Barry Moulders
Barry Stars
Belgrave 1&2
Belmonts
Bland's Deal Carriers
Bute Docks Workers
Bute Engineers
Cadoxton Crescents
Cadoxton/Stars
Cadoxton United
Caledonians 1&2
Cambrians
Canton 1&2
Canton Hornets
Canton United
Canton Wanderers1&2

Cardiff 1&2
Cardiff Albions
Cardiff Alexandras
Cardiff and District FU
    (Representative)
Cardiff Banks
Cardiff Barbarians
Cardiff Boilermakers
Cardiff Boys Brigade
Cardiff Chartering Clerks
Cardiff Clothiers
Cardiff Crescent
Cardiff Crusaders
Cardiff Electrics 1&2
Cardiff Harlequins 1&2&Wednesday
Cardiff Hibernians (Representative)
Cardiff Hornets
Cardiff (Roath) Marlborough
Cardiff Moulders
Cardiff Northern 1&2
Cardiff Old Westonians
Cardiff Postmen
Cardiff Rangers
Cardiff Saints
Cardiff Star
Cardiff Steam Joinery Men
Cardiff Telegraph Messengers
Cardiff United
Cardiff Villa
Cardiff (& South Wales) Wanderers
Cardiff Wednesday Star
Cardiff Windsor

Cardiff YMCA Wednesday 1&2
Carlton Juniors
Cathays 1&2
Cathays Crescents
Cathays Institute 1&2
Cathays Juniors
Cathays Primrose Juniors
Cathays Rovers (Wednesday)
Cathays Stars
Cathays Wednesday
Cefn Mably
Clifton Rovers
Craddock Juniors
Crescent Juniors
Crescent Stars
Crescent United
Depot, Welsh Regiment
Dinas Powys
Docks Cabmen
Docks Juniors
Docks Printers
Docks United
Dowlais Magpies/Stars
Duke Street Rovers
Eldon United/Rovers
Ely Paper Mills
Ely Paper Mills Beaters
Ely Paper Mills Binders
Ely Rangers 1&2
Empire Theatre
Glamorgan Police (E Division)
Gloucester Stars
Gloucester Wagon Works
Grange Albions
Grange Raglans
Grange United 1&2
Grangetown 1&2
Grangetown Harlequins
Grangetown Rovers
Grangetown Workingmen's Liberal
    Club

Grangetown Workmen's
    Conservative Club
Grasshoppers
GWR Crusaders
GWR Excelsiors
Great Western Rangers
Hamilton/Stars
Havelock Stars
Hayes Rovers
Heath Rovers
Holton Juniors, Barry
Howard Crescent
Iestyn Juniors
Inverness Juniors
Lincoln Harlequins
Lisvane
Llandaff 1&2&Past Players
Llandaff Blossoms/Wednesday
Llandaff Boys Brigade
Llandaff
    Church Lads Brigade
Llandaff Linton
Llandaff Rovers
Llandaff Stars 1&2
Llandaff Working Men's Club
Llandaff Yard
Llandaff Yard Boys Brigade
Loudoun Hornets 1&2
Loudoun Stars
Loudouns 1&2
Louisa Street Stars
Mackintosh
Mackintosh United
May Street Stars
Melingriffith
Merthyr (Street) Stars
Monkton House 1&2
Moorland Stars
North Central Filibusters/Rovers
Oakfield Stars
Old Monktonians

Park Rovers 1&2
Pearl Crusaders
Pearl Street Joinery
Penarth 1&2
Penarth Excelsior
Penarth Hornets (Wednesday)
Penarth Stars 1&2
Penarth Victorias
Penarth White Rose (Wednesday)
Pentyrch
Pentyrch Juniors
Pentyrch Rowdy Boys
Penylan 1&2&3
Penylan Juniors
Picton Stars
Radyr Stars
Red Rose
Rhymney Railway Cleaners
Richmond Crescents
Richmond Road Juniors
Riverside
Roath
Roath Albion (Wednesday)
Roath Albion Juniors (Saturday)
Roath Excelsiors
Roath Park Juniors
Roath Road/ Juniors/Stars
Roath Stars
Roath United
Roath Wanderers
Roath Wednesday
Roath Windsor
Romilly 1&2
Romilly Rangers
Romilly Victorias
Saltmede Crusaders
Sawmills Rovers
Spillers United
Splott Cruaders 1&2
Splott Raglans 1&2
Splott White Star

Spring Wanderers
St. Andrew's 1&2
St. Anne's Rangers
St. Anne's/ Stars
St. Catherine's
St. David's
St. David's Crusaders
St. David's Juniors
St. David's Rovers 1&2
St. Dyfrig's
St. Fagans
St. Fagans Juniors
St. John's
St. Mary's 1&2
St. Mary's Hall School 1&2
St. Michael's 1&2
St. Monica's
St. Paul's
St. Peter's 1&2
St. Peter's Stars
Steam Joinery Juniors
Sydenham Stars
Taffs Well
Taffs Well Juniors
Taffs Well Rovers
Talbot Stars/United
The Windsors
Theatre Royal
Tongwynlais
Tongwynlais Juniors
Tongwynlais Stars
Town Cabmen
Town Printers
Town Raglans
Tredegar Stars/Tredegars
Trinity Crusaders
Ty Mawr, Llandaff North
University College Cardiff 1&2
Victoria Stars
Wellington
Wells United, Canton

Western Wagon Works
Wharton 1&2
Wharton Juniors
Whitchurch 1&2
Whitchurch Harlequins
Whitchurch Juniors
Whitchurch Stars

White Lion Rovers
White Star
Windsor Juniors/Stars
Windsor Stars Penarth
Windsor United
Woodlands
Woodvilles

Appendix 3
Competitions in Cardiff[1]

(1) Cardiff District Football Union.

Cardiff District Challenge Cup				
Season	Winners		Runners-up	
1886-7	Cardiff Harlequins	35	Penarth	0
1887-8	Penarth	3	Cardiff Harlequins	1
1888-9	Penarth	39	Llandaff	1
1889-0	Penarth	63	Ely Rovers	10

Cardiff District Junior Cup				
Season	Winners		Runners-up	
1889-0	Cathays Rangers	By 1 point	Grangetown	

(2) Cardiff and District Football Union/Cardiff and District Rugby Union

Cardiff and District Mallett Cup				
Season	Winners		Runners-Up	
1893-4	Cardiff Reserves	8	Canton	0
1894-5[2]	Cardiff Northern	8	Canton	0
1895-6[3]	Roath	-	Canton	-
1896-7	Canton	10	St. Paul's	8

---

1   Compiled from the *Western Mail, South Wales Daily News, South Wales Echo, Football Echo,* other local newspapers and *Cardiff and District Rugby Union: Official Handbook, Season 1908-9,* (Cardiff, 1908), p. [1]. The scores in some finals are unknown.
2   Held on a league basis, with a play-off.
3   Held on a league basis.

Cardiff and District Mallett Cup				
Season	Winners		Runners-Up	
1897-8	St. Paul's	10	Canton	0
1898-9	Mackintosh	11	St. Paul's	3
1899-1900	St. Peter's	3	Roath	0
1900-1	Mackintosh	11	Cardiff Romilly	9
1901-2	Cardiff Romilly	10	Roath	0
1902-3	Grange Stars	7	Mackintosh	0
1903-4	Cardiff Romilly	6	Grange Stars	0
1904-5	Cardiff Romilly	4	Grange Stars	0
1905-6	Cardiff Romilly	3	Mackintosh	0
1906-7	Canton	3	Grange United	0
1907-8	Canton Wanderers	14	Cardiff Romilly	0
1908-9	Cardiff Romilly	6	Cardiff Harlequins	3
1909-0	Canton Wanderers	7	Canton	3
1910-1	Mackintosh	3	Canton Wanderers	0
1911-2	Cardiff Barbarians	9	Canton Wanderers	0
1912-3	St. David's	6	Canton	0
1913-4	Grangetown	6	Senghenydd	0
1914-5 to 1918-9	Not Held			
1919-0	St. David's	4	Canton	3
1920-1	Canton	11	Loudouns	3
1921-2	Mackintosh	7	Cardiff Gas	0
1922-3	Cardiff Gas	11	Cardiff Welsh	5
1923-4	Grange Baptists	3	Cardiff Gas	0

Cardiff and District Mallett Cup				
Season	Winners		Runners-Up	
1924-5	Grange Baptists	3	Loudouns	0
1925-6	Grange Baptists	7	Canton	5
1926-7	Grange Baptists	18	Canton	6
1927-8	Spillers	15	Senghenydd	0
1928-9	Cardiff Crusaders	8	Cardiff Romilly	3
1929-0	Grange Baptists	3	Cardiff Romilly	0
1930-1	St. Peter's	9	Cardiff Crusaders	3
1931-2	St. Peter's	6	Cathedral Club	0
1932-3	Spillers	3	St. Paul's	0
1933-4	Spillers	9	Romilly	0
1934-5	Melingriffith	3	Spillers	0
1935-6	Melingriffith	3	Canton St. Mary's	0
1936-7	Spillers	8	Canton St. Mary's	0
1937-8	Currans	5	Splott Old Boys	3
1938-9	Spillers	16	St. David's	8
1939-0 to 1945-6	Not Held			
1946-7	Old Sandonians	11	Central Harlequins	0
1947-8	Cardiff Dockers	10	Cardiff Exiles	3
1948-9	Old Sandonians	9	Canton St. Mary's	0
1949-0	Pentyrch	8	Llantrisant	3
1950-1	Pentyrch	6	Llantrisant	3
1951-2	Pentyrch	3	St. Clare's	0
1952-3	Guest Keen	6	Pentyrch	3
1953-4	Guest Keen	6	Canton	0

Cardiff and District Mallett Cup				
Season	Winners		Runners-Up	
1954-5	Guest Keen	3	Welch Regiment	0
1955-6	Guest Keen	3	St. David's	0
1956-7	St. David's	5	Guest Keen	0
1957-8	Currans	11	Canton	5
1958-9	St. David's	11	Guest Keen	0
1959-0	St. David's	12	Canton	3
1960-1	St. David's	5	Guest Keen	0
1961-2	Old Howardians	6	Canton	3
1962-3	CIACS	NK	St. Alban's	NK
1963-4	Canton	3	St. David's	0
1964-5	St. Joseph's	3	St. Alban's	0
1965-6	Canton	NK	Guest Keen	NK
1966-7	Rumney	17	St. Alban's	6
1967-8	St. Alban's	3	St. David's	0
1968-9	CIACS	15	St. Alban's	3
1969-0	CIACS	NK	St. David's	NK
1970-1	St. Joseph's	6	St. Alban's	3
1971-2	St. Joseph's	7	Rumney	4
1972-3	St. Joseph's	18	Cathays HSOB	6
1973-4	Fairwater	3	Llandaff Athletic	0
1974-5	CIACS	16	Fairwater	0
1975-6	St. Alban's	6	St. Joseph's	3
1976-7	CIACS	9	St. Joseph's	3
1977-8	CIACS	6	Caerau Ely	0

Cardiff and District Mallett Cup				
Season	Winners		Runners-Up	
1978-9	Rumney	22	Llanishen	3
1979-0	Rumney	30	St. Alban's	8
1980-1	Rumney	22	St. Joseph's	9
1981-2	Rumney	15	CIACS	6
1982-3	Rumney	9	St. Joseph's	6
1983-4	CIACS	16	Cathays HSOB	3
1984-5	CIACS	18	Rumney II	3
1985-6	CIACS	13	Llanishen	0
1986-7	St. Alban's	18	St. Peter's II	9
1987-8	CIACS	19	St. Alban's	13
1988-9	CIACS	13	Canton	0
1989-0	St. Alban's	18	CIACS	7
1990-1	CIACS	19	St. Alban's	9
1991-2	Whitchurch	16	CIACS	6
1992-3	Fairwater	17	Whitchurch	8
1993-4	Fairwater	10	St. Alban's	3
1994-5	Fairwater	11	St. Alban's	3
1995-6	Fairwater	27	St. Alban's	19
1996-7	Llanrumney	8	Fairwater	3
1997-8	Llanrumney	35	Rumney II	12
1998-9	Fairwater	19	Llanedeyrn	3
1999-0	Caerau Ely	19	Rumney II	5
2000-1	Rumney II	23	Fairwater	12
2001-2	Glamorgan Wanderers II	27	Llanrumney	8

Cardiff and District Mallett Cup				
Season	Winners		Runners-Up	
2002-3	Glamorgan Wanderers II	24	Rumney II	20
2003-4	Fairwater II	NK	Caerau Ely	NK
2004-5	Glamorgan Wanderers II	NK	Caerau Ely	NK
2005-6	Glamorgan Wanderers II	45	Pentyrch II	22
2006-7	Caerau Ely	17	St. Joseph's II	12
2007-8	UWIC II	22	CIACS	10
2008-9	UWIC II	12	Rumney II	3
2009-0	Rumney II	39	Clwb Rygbi	24
2010-1	Glamorgan Wanderers II	20	Caerau Ely	5
2011-2	Rumney II	17	Llanishen II	9
2012-3	Rumney II	39	Llanrumney	0
2013-4	Cardiff Met. University II	50	Glam. Wanderers II	14
2014-5	Llanishen II	29	St. Peter's II	17

Cardiff and District Union Shield				
Season	Winners		Runners-up	
1894-5[4]	Roath		Not Known	
1895-6[5]	Mackintosh		Not Known	
1896-7	St. Peter's	5	Adamsdown	3
1897-8	St. Mary's	14	St. Andrew's	0
1898-9	Grange Stars	19	Cathays United	0
1899-1900	Roath II	14	Canton Harlequins	0
1900-1	Cardiff Barbarians	10	St. Agnes	8

4   Held on a league basis.
5   Held on a league basis.

Cardiff and District Union Shield				
Season	Winners		Runners-up	
1901-2	St. David's	17	Empire United	0
1902-3	Llandaff Yard	9	Penarth United	8
1903-4	St. Teilo's	10	Penarth United	0
1904-5	Roath Hornets	6	Canton Wanderers	3
1905-6	St. Paul's	3	Canton Wanderers	0
1906-7	Not Held			
1907-8	Cardiff Fruiterers	13	Grange Institute	0
1908-9	Grange Harriers	6	Cardiff Welsh	0
1909-0	Cardiff Centrals	3	Cardiff Welsh	0

Cardiff and District Ninian Stuart Cup[6]				
Season	Winners		Runners-Up	
1910-1	Cardiff Nomads	4	Cardiff Welsh	0
1911-2	Senghenydd	4	Splott Crusaders	0
1912-3	Penarth United	3	Grange Stars	0
1913-4	Barry	6	Adamsdown	0
1914-5 to 1918-9	Not Held			
1919-0	St. David's II	8	St. Peter's	0
1920-1	St. Peter's	9	Lyndon Athletic	4
1921-2	St. Paul's	6	St. Peter's	0
1922-3	Grange Harlequins	5	St. Mary's Athletic	0

---

6   It is not always clear from match reports, whether a club was represented by their First, Second or even Third XV.

Cardiff and District Ninian Stuart Cup				
Season	Winners		Runners-Up	
1923-4	St. Peter's United	3	Senghenydd	0
1924-5	Senghenydd	3	Cardiff Foundries	0
1925-6	Grange Lyndons	6	Royal Engineers	0
1926-7	St. Paul's	20	Grange Baptists II	0
1927-8	Cardiff Supporters	9	St. Paul's II	3
1928-9	Currans Athletic	3	Grange Baptists II	0
1929-0	St. Peter's I	3	Cardiff Crusaders II	0
1930-1	St. Paul's	8	St. Joseph's	3
1931-2	St. Paul's	3	St. Joseph's	0
1932-3	St. Joseph's	6	Grange Hibernian	0
1933-4	St. David's	4	Central Harlequins	0
1934-5 to 1936-7[7]	Not Held			
1937-8	Hancocks Nut Brown	8	Dinas Powys II	0
1938-9 to 1949-9	Not Held			
1949-0	Canton Loco	5	Cory Hall Youth	0
1950-1	Guest Keen	6	Cardiff Wheatsheaf	3
1951-2	Currans	NK	Ely	NK
1952-3	Roath Park	8	Cardiff Harlequins	0
1953-4	CIACS II	NK	Melingriffith	NK
1954-5	Welch Regiment	9	St. Alban's II	6

---

7   As the cup was not held during these three seasons, the trophy was presented to the Mallett Cup runners-up.

Cardiff and District Ninian Stuart Cup				
Season	Winners		Runners-Up	
1955-6	St. Alban's II	NK	Guest Keen II	NK
1956-7[8]	Not Held			
1957-8	Caerphilly	NK	St. Alban's II	NK
1958-9[9]	Old Howardians II	-	Centurions	-
1959-0	Old Howardians II	3	Canton II	0
1960-1	St. Joseph's II	9	Cardiff HSOB II	3
1961-2	Cowbridge	3	St. Cadoc's	0
1962-3	CIACS II	NK	St. Alban's II	NK
1963-4	St. Cadoc's	9	St. Alban's II	0
1964-5	Rumney II	6	CIACS II	3
1965-6	Cowbridge II	9	Rumney II	6
1966-7	CIACS II	13	Cardiff Fire Service	3
1967-8	St. Joseph's II	NK	Not Known	NK
1968-9[10]	Pontyclun Athletic (Shared)	3	Rumney II (Shared)	3
1969-0	Rumney II	9	St. Alban's II	6
1970-1	Rumney II	8	St. Alban's II	0
1971-2	CIACS II	6	Rumney II	0
1972-3	Rumney II	6	St. Alban's II	3
1973-4	CIACS II	13	St. Alban's II	9
1974-5	CIACS II	4	St. Alban's II	3

8   As the cup was not held this season, it was retained by the previous season's winners St. Alban's II.

9   Centurions disbanded before the final could be played, so Old Howardians II were declared the winners.

10   Trophy shared between Pontyclun Athletic and Rumney II.

Cardiff and District Ninian Stuart Cup				
Season	Winners		Runners-Up	
1975-6	St. Alban's II	10	Fairwater II	9
1976-7	Rumney II	12	Clwb Rygbi II	7
1977-8	St. Joseph's II	6	Rumney II	3
1978-9	Rumney II	15	St. Alban's II	3
1979-0	St. Alban's II	NK	CIACS II	NK
1980-1	Rumney II	20	St Joseph's II	0
1981-2	St. Alban's II	6	Rumney II	3
1982-3	Rumney II	21	Rhiwbina III	3
1983-4	Rumney III	12	St. David's II	7
1984-5	CIACS II	19	Rumney III	0
1985-6	CIACS II	23	Llanishen II	3
1986-7	CIACS II	9	Caerau Ely II	0
1987-8	CIACS II	28	St. Albans II	11
1988-9	CIACS II	9	Rumney III	3
1989-0	CIACS II	7	Whitchurch II	0
1990-1	St. Alban's II	32	CIACS II	3
1991-2	CIACS II	7	St. Alban's II	3
1992-3	St. Peters III	20	Fairwater II	14
1993-4	St. Peters III	10	Rumney III	0
1994-5	Fairwater II	12	Llanrumney II	3
1995-6	St. Peters III	13	Fairwater II	3
1996-7	Rumney III	6	Llanrumney II	3
1997-8	Rumney III	13	Fairwater II	5
1998-9	Rumney III	15	Fairwater II	13

Cardiff and District Ninian Stuart Cup				
Season	Winners		Runners-Up	
1999-0	Rumney III	21	Fairwater II	7
2000-1	St. Peters III	20	Llanishen III	10
2001-2	Llanrumney II	10	Rumney III	6
2002-3	Rumney III	12	Llanishen III	6
2003-4	Llanishen III	30	Clwb Rygbi II	0
2004-5	Llandaff North III	15	Caerau Ely II	11
2005-6	Cardiff Saracens II	25	Cardiff HSOB III	20
2006-7	St. Peters III	17	Caerau Ely II	12
2007-8	St. Peters III	43	Llandaff North III	0
2008-9	Clwb Rygbi II	28	Rumney III	27
2009-0	Rumney III	43	Clwb Rygbi II	31
2010-1	Caerau Ely II	42	Llandaff North III	10
2011-2	Careau Ely II	7	Llanrumney II	6
2012-3	Rhiwbina III	8	Llanrumney II	6
2013-4	Rhiwbina III	27	Clwb Rygbi III	6
2014-5	Caerau Ely II	20	St. Peter's III	17

Cardiff and District Senior League to 1900	
Season	Winners
1894-5	Cardiff Northern
1895-6	Roath
1896-7	Not Held
1897-8	St. Peter's
1898-9	St. Paul's
1899-1900	Roath

Cardiff and District Junior League to 1900	
Season	Winners
1894-5	Roath
1895-6	Mackintosh
1896-7	Not Held
1897-8	St. Andrew's
1898-9	Grange Stars
1899-1900	Canton Harlequins

Cardiff and District Second Junior League to 1900	
Season	Winners
1899-1900	Cardiff Barbarians

(3) Cardiff Football Club

Cardiff FC Junior Cup to 1900				
Season	Winners		Runners-up	
1896-7	Canton Crescents	9	Roath Crescents	3
1897-8	St. Peter's Reserves	5	Canton Crescents	0
1898-9	Penarth United	3	Grange Stars Reserves	0
1899-1900	Canton Crusaders	3	St. Mary's Juniors	0

Appendix 4

South Wales Football Union/Welsh Football Union Competition[1]

South Wales Challenge Cup					
Season	Winners		Runners-up		
1877-8	Newport 1 goal		Swansea nil		
1878-9	Newport 1 goal 2 tries		Cardiff nil		
1879-0	Swansea 2 tries		Lampeter College nil		
1880-1	Cardiff 1 try		Llanelli nil		
1881-2	Newport 1 try 4 minors		Llanelli 1 try 2 minors		
1882-3[2]	Newport 1 goal 2 tries		Swansea 1 goal 1 try		
1883-4	Llanelli 1 try		Newport nil		
1884-5	Newport 1 try		Neath nil		
1885-6	Llanelli 2 dropped goals 1 try		Newport nil		
1886-7	Swansea 1 goal		Llanelli nil		
1887-8 to 1888-9	Not Held				
1889-0[3]	Penygraig	2	Llanelli A	0	
1890-1	Newport Seconds	6	Swansea Harlequins	0	
1891-2	Llandaff	8	Llanelli A	0	
1892-3	Pontymister	14	Neath A	0	
1893-4	Llanelli A	10	Pontymister	0	

1   Compiled from the *Western Mail* and *South Wales Daily News* and David Smith and Gareth Williams, *Fields of Praise*, pp.485-6.
2   This was the last season in which Cardiff competed in the cup. C.S. Arthur, The Cardiff Rugby Football Club: History and Statistics 1876-1906, (Cardiff, 2008), p.52.
3   Reintroduced for less strong clubs and second teams.

South Wales Challenge Cup				
Season	Winners		Runners-up	
1894-5	Neath A	5	Crumlin	0
1895-6	Pontymister	6	Llandeilo	0
1896-7	Llanelli A	18	Risca	0
1897-8 to 1900-1	Not Held			
1901-2[4]	Cynon Stars	9	Neath Excelsiors	0
1902-3	Ystrad Stars, Rhondda	11	Felinfoel	0
1903-4	Halfway, Llanelli	15	Troedyrhiw	6
1904-5 to 1912-3	Not Held			
1913-4[5]	Aberavon	10	Blaina	0

4   Reintroduced for junior clubs.
5   Reintroduced for senior clubs in 1913-14. This was the last occasion the cup was held. The whereabouts of the trophy today is unknown.

Appendix 5
Cardiff and District Club Secretaries

Cardiff and District Club Secretaries 1889-91					
Name	**Age**	**Occupation**	**Place of Birth**	**Club**	**Source**
Frederick Barrass	17	Merchant's clerk	Newcastle	Kymin, Penarth	FH 91-2
Frederick Bosley	20	Railway clerk	London	Cardiff Crusaders	FC 90-1
Ernest Carder	19	Builder's clerk	Cardiff	Cathays	WM 91-2
Isaac Chorley	24	Plumber	Somerset	Footlights	WM 90-1
Henry Cypher	20	Clerk	Wilts	Taff Vale Wanderers	FC 90-1
Edward Davies	16	Clerk	Cardiff	Roath Windsor	FC 90-1
George Dyer	15	Clerk	Cardiff	Cardiff Albion	FH 91-2
Robert England	18	Teacher	Cardiff	Canton	FH 91-2
William Gardner	19	Office clerk	Sunderland	Splott Rovers	FC 90-1
Thomas Grant	20	Plumber	Lincs	Cardiff Star	FC 90-1
John Hall	25	Book-keeper	Cardiff	Cogan	FC 90-1
Samuel Hall	22	Currier	Llandaff	Llandaff	FC 90-1
Bertie Harris	14	Scholar	Newport	Canton Rovers (11-13)	EE 90-1

Cardiff and District Club Secretaries 1889-91

Name	Age	Occupation	Place of Birth	Club	Source
Henry Hayes	16	Office boy	Cornwall	Penarth Albion	FC 90-1
Fred Hodson	17	Proof-reader's assistant	London	Star Juniors (13-14)	FC 90-1
David Hopkins	22	Clerk	Llantrisant	Cardiff Rangers	FC 90-1
Eli Hopkins	18	Office clerk	Whitchurch	Whitchurch	WM 91-2
Francis John	18	Clerk	St Andrews	Barry	FH 91-2
William Johnston	16	Telegraph messenger	Scotland	Clyde Rovers (15)	FC 90-1
Richard Jones	19	Plumber's apprentice	Gloucester	Canton	FC 90-1
Thomas Jones	19	Hardware merchant	Llantrisant	Cardiff Cyclists	FC 90-1
Edward Lewis	21	Chartering clerk	Cardiff	Heath	FH 91-2
Thomas Lewis	16	Clerk	Swansea	Ely Juniors	FH 91-2
Arthur Lloyd	19	Coach trimmer	Cardiff	Cardiff United	FC 90-1
William Morgan	15	Printer's apprentice	Cardiff	Albany Stars (15)	WM 90-1
John Nelms	25	Compositor	Gloucester	Barry and Cadoxton	FH 91-2
George Parsons	21	Hairdresser	Dorset	Grangetown	FH 91-2
George Pawley	17	Grocer's assistant	Penarth	Penarth United	FH 91-2
Thomas Phillips	19	Travelling salesman	Pentyrch	Pentyrch	WM 89-0

Cardiff and District Club Secretaries 1889-91

Name	Age	Occupation	Place of Birth	Club	Source
Sidney Phillips	24	Ship chandler's assistant	Bath	Ely Rovers	FC 90-1
Anthony Proud	22	Plumber	North Shields	Wanderers	WM 90-1
John Richards	16	Coach painter	Cardiff	St. Germans	FH 91-2
William Rigby	31	Draper's assistant	Lancs	Cardiff Rovers	FC 90-1
Frank Seager	19	Book-keeper	Cardiff	Tyneside (16-20)	WM 89-0
Sidney Smith	22	Baker	Birkenhead	Cathays Stars	FC 90-1
Ernest Thomas	17	Plasterer and paper hanger	Cardiff	St. Peters	FC 90-1
John Thomas	18	Clerk	Pembs	Roath Windsor	FH 91-2
Wilson Tunley	17	Clerk	Cardiff	Cardiff Juniors (16), St. David's	FC 90-1

Key to Sources:

EE (*Evening Express*).

FC (*Cardiff and South Wales Footballer's Companion: 1890-91*).

FH (*The Welsh Athlete and West of England Cycling News Football Handbook 1891-2*).

WM (*Western Mail*).

Bibliography

Manuscripts

Cardiff Census Returns, 1881, 1891.
Cardiff Cricket Club Members Lists, 1883, 1884.
County Borough of Cardiff Reports of Council and Committees, Nov. 1891 to Nov. 1892.
Licensed Premises (Alehouses and Beerhouses) in Cardiff: Report of the Chief Constable, 1903. (Unpublished transcript).
Penarth RFC Archive 1885-1900.
Rodway, I.M.F., *History of Canton R.F.C.* (Unpublished transcript, n.d.).
Rugby Football Union Minutes, January 1871- March 1883.
Welsh Football Union (WRU) Minutes, September 1892 - September 1902.

Newspapers and Journals

Brecon County Times
Bridgend Chronicle
Bristol Mercury
British Medical Journal
Cambrian
Cardiff and Merthyr Guardian
Cardiff Argus
Cardiff Times
Evening Express (Cardiff)
Football Echo (Cardiff)
Football Express (Cardiff)
Glasgow Herald
Huddersfield Daily Chronicle
Leeds Mercury
Liverpool Mercury
Monmouthshire Merlin
Morning Post
North Wales Chronicle
North Wales Express
Pembrokeshire Herald
Potter's Electric News

Principality
Sheffield and Rotherham Independent
South Wales Argus
South Wales Daily News
South Wales Echo
Star of Gwent
Tenby Observer
The Irish Times
The Red Dragon
The Times
The Welsh Athlete
Weekly Mail (Cardiff)
Welshman
Western Mail
York Herald

Handbooks

Cardiff and District Rugby Union: Official Handbook, Season 1905-6 (Cardiff, 1905).
Cardiff and District Rugby Union: Official Handbook, Season 1908-9 (Cardiff, 1908).
Cardiff and South Wales Footballer's Companion: 1890-91 (Cardiff, 1890).
Cardiff District Football Union Handbook 1886-87 (Cardiff, 1886).
Cardiff Schools Rugby Union Handbook Season 1987-88 (Cardiff, 1987).
Mortimer's Football Guide for South Wales and Monmouthshire: Season, 1894-95
    (Barry, 1894).
The Handy Football Guide (Mortimer's) For South Wales and Monmouthshire:
    1896-97 (Cardiff, 1896).
The Welsh Athlete and West of England Cycling News Football Handbook 1891-2
    (Cardiff, 1891).
Welsh Districts Rugby Union 2000-2001 Handbook (Cardiff, 2000).
Welsh Football Union: Year Book, 1889-90 (Newport, 1889).
Welsh Rugby Union 2002-2003 Handbook (Cardiff, 2002).

Annuals

Alcock, C.W., (ed.), *John Lillywhite's Football Annual* (London, 1868).
Alcock, C.W., (ed.), *The Football Annual* (London, 1869-1895).
Jackson, N.L., (ed.), *The Football Handbook 1888-9* (London, 1889).
Owen, O.L. (ed.), *Playfair Rugby Football Annual* (London, 1950-1967).
Stewart Caine, C., (ed.), *John Wisden's Rugby Football Almanack for 1924-25*
    (London, 1924).

Directories

Butcher's Cardiff Directory (Cardiff, 1875-1883).
Daniel Owen and Co.'s Cardiff Directory (Cardiff, 1887-1895).
J. Wright and Co.'s Cardiff Directory (Cardiff, 1883-1886).
Slater's Post Office Directory of Cardiff and its Suburbs (Cardiff, 1882-1885).
Webster and Co.'s Postal and Commercial Directory of the City of Bristol and Counties of Glamorgan and Monmouth (London, 1865).
Western Mail Cardiff Directory (Cardiff, 1897-1900).

Books

Andrews, David, 'Sport and the Masculine Hegemony of the Modern Nation: Welsh Rugby, Culture and Society, 1890-1914', in Nauright, John and Chandler, Timothy J.L. (eds.), *Making Men: Rugby and Masculine Identity* (London, 1996).
Anon., *Contemporary Portraits: Men and Women of South Wales and Monmouthshire: Cardiff Section* (Cardiff, 1896).
Anon, *Marlborough College Register From 1843 to 1904 Inclusive* (Oxford, 1905).
Anon., *Sixty Years of Rugby 1887-1947: Ammanford R.F.C.* (Ammanford, 1947).
Anon., *Llandaff Rugby Football Club American Tour Souvenir* (Cardiff, 1968).
Anon., *Treherbert Rugby Football Club Centenary Year 1874-1974* (Treherbert, 1974).
Anon., *Merthyr Rugby Football Club Centenary Year 1876-1976* (Merthyr, 1976).
Anon., *Penygraig RFC: 100 Years of Valley Rugby 1877-1977* (Penygraig, 1977).
Anon., *The Blues: Loughor Rugby Football Club 1882-1982* (Loughor, 1981).
Arthur, C.S., *The Cardiff Rugby Football Club: History and Statistics, 1876-1906* (Cardiff, 1908).
Atkinson, Philip T., *One Hundred Years of Rhymney Rugby: The Centenary History of Rhymney R.F.C. 1877-1982* (Rhymney, 1982).
Bale, John, *Sport and Place: A Geography of Sport in England Scotland and Wales* (London, 1982).
Bassett, Michael G., *Games of Interchanging Praise: A Centenary History of Rugby Football in Barry* (Barry, 1988).
Beken, Paul and Jones, Stephen, *Dragon in Exile: The Centenary History of London Welsh R.F.C.* (London, 1985).
Billot, John, *History of Welsh International Rugby* (Cardiff, 1999 edn.).
Birley, Derek, *Sport and the making of Britain* (Manchester, 1993).
Birley, Derek, *Land of sport and glory: Sport and British society, 1887-1910* (Manchester, 1995).

Birley, Derek, *Playing the game: Sport and British society, 1910-45* (Manchester, 1995).

Boucher, David, *Steel, Skill and Survival: Rugby in Ebbw Vale and the Valleys (1870-1952)* (Ebbw Vale, 2000).

Breeze, Alan, *One Hundred Years of Abergavenny Rugby Football Club* (Abergavenny, 1975).

Broughton-Mainwaring, Rowland, *Historical Record of the Royal Welch Fusiliers* (London, 1889).

Brown, Mike, *Brewed in Northants* (Longfield, Kent, 1998).

Cary, A.D.L. and Stouppe McLance, S., *Regimental Records of the Royal Welch Fusiliers Volume II 1816-1914* (London, 1923).

Chester, R.H. and McMillan, N.A.C., *The Encyclopaedia of New Zealand Rugby* (Auckland, 1981).

Chester, R.H. and McMillan, N.A.C., *The Visitors: The History of International Rugby Teams in New Zealand* (Auckland, 1990).

Childs, D.F., *One Hundred Years of the "Rocks": the History of St. Peter's R.F.C. 1886/1986* (Cardiff, 1986).

Collins, John, Currie, Alan, Currie, Brenda, Walters, Mike and Williams, Clive, *The History of Welsh Athletics Volume I* (Llanelli, 2002).

Collins, Tony, *Rugby's Great Split: Class, Culture and the Origins of Rugby League Football* (London, 1998 edn.) (London, 2006 edn.).

Collins, Tony, 'Violence, gamesmanship and the amateur ideal in Victorian middle-class rugby', in Huggins, Mike and Mangan, J.A. (eds.), *Disreputable Pleasures: Less Virtuous Victorians at Play* (London, 2004).

Collins, Tony, *A Social History of English Rugby Union* (London, 2009).

Collins, Tony and Vamplew, Wray, *Mud, Sweat, and Beers: A Cultural History of Sport and Alcohol* (Oxford, 2002).

Collins, W.J. Townsend, (ed.), *Newport Athletic Club: The record of half a Century 1875-1925* (Newport, 1925).

Collins, W.J. Townsend, *Rugby Recollections* (Newport, 1948).

Corrigan, Peter, *100 Years of Welsh Soccer: The Official History of the Football Association of Wales* (Cardiff, [1976]).

Croll, Andy, *Civilizing the Urban: Popular Culture and Public Space in Merthyr, c1870-1914* (Cardiff, 2000).

Cunningham, Vanessa and Goodwin, John, *Cardiff University: A Celebration* (Cardiff, 2001).

Daglish, J.R.A., *Red, Blue & Black: The First 125 Years of Liverpool Football Club (Rugby Union)* (Manchester, 1983).

Dargavel, T., *Neath R.F.C. 1871-1971 Centenary Year* (Neath, 1971).

Daunton, M.J., *Coal Metropolis: Cardiff 1870-1914* (Leicester, 1977).

Daunton, M.J., 'Coal to Capital: Cardiff since 1839', in Morgan, Prys (ed.), *Glamorgan County History, Volume VI, Glamorgan Society: 1780-1980* (Cardiff, 1988).

Davidson, John Mcl., *International Rugby Union: A Compendium of Scotland's Matches* (Edinburgh, 1994).

Davies, D.E., *Cardiff Rugby Club: History and Statistics, 1876-1975: "The Greatest"* (Cardiff, 1975).

Davies, Iolo, *"A Certaine Schoole": A History of the Grammar School at Cowbridge Glamorgan* (Cowbridge, 1967).

Davies, John, *A History of Wales* (London, 1994).

Davies, John, *A Pocket Guide: Cardiff* (Cardiff, 2002).

Davis, Jack, *One Hundred Years of Newport Rugby 1875-1975* (Risca, 1974).

Dolan, J., (ed.), *Aberavon Rugby Football Club 1876-1976* (Port Talbot, 1976).

Donovan, Edward, Crane, Arthur, Smith, Allan and Harris, John, *Pontypool's Pride: The Official History of Pontypool Rugby Football Club 1868-1988* (Abertillery, 1988).

Dow, David, *"White Gold": The Story of Swansea R.F.C. 1872-1914.* (Working title) (Unpublished, in preparation).

Dunning, Eric and Sheard, Kenneth, *Barbarians, Gentlemen and Players: A Sociological Study of the Development of Rugby Football* (Oxford, 1979 edn.), (London, 2005 edn.).

Edwards, R. Wendell, *100 Years of Rugby Football in Bangor* (Bangor, 1980).

Ereaut, E.J., *Richmond Football Club: From 1861 to 1925* (London, 1925).

Evans, Barbara M., *Blaina Rugby Football Club 1875-1976: Memories of Mutton Tump* (Risca, 1976).

Evans, D. Gareth, *A History of Wales 1815-1906* (Cardiff, 1989).

Evans, Denver, *Bont: The Story of a Village and its Rugby Club, Pontarddulais* (Pontarddulais, 1980).

Evans, Howard, *Welsh International Matches 1881-2000* (Edinburgh, 1999).

Evans, Neil, "Regions, Nations, Globe: Roles, Representations and Urban Space in Cardiff, 1839-1928", in Fahrmeir, Andreas and Rembold, Elfie (eds.), *Representation of British Cities: Transformation of Urban Spaces, 1700-2000* (Berlin/Wien, 2003).

Evans, T.L., *Carmarthen Rugby Football Club Centenary Year 1874-1974* (Llandeilo, 1974).

Evans, W. Gareth, *A History of Llandovery College* (Llandovery, 1981).

Farmer, David, *The Life and Times of Swansea R.F.C.: The All Whites* (Swansea, 1995).

Farmer, Stuart and Hands, David, *The Tigers Tale: The Official History of Leicester Football Club 1880-1993* (Leicester, 1993).

Foster, Joseph, *Alumni Oxonienses 1715-1886* (4 Volumes) (London, 1887-1888).

Foster, T.J., *Floreat Howardia: The Story of Howard Gardens Schools Cardiff 1885-1990* (Cardiff, 1990).

Gane, Denis, *Cwmbran R.F.C. One Hundred Years of Rugby* (Cwmbran, 1980).

Gardiner, Duncan and Evans, Alan (eds.), *Images of Sport: Cardiff Rugby Football Club 1876-1939* (Stroud, 1999).

Gate, Robert, *Gone North: Welshmen in Rugby League, Volume 1* (Sowerby Bridge, 1986).

Gate, Robert, *Gone North: Welshmen in Rugby League, Volume 2* (Sowerby Bridge, 1988).

Gealy, D.I., 'Sport at Llandovery: Rugby Football', in Jones, R. Brinley (ed.), *Floreat Landubriense: Celebrating a Century and a Half of Education at Llandovery College* (Llandovery, 1998).

Glover, Brian, *Prince of Ales: The History of Brewing in Wales* (Stroud, 1993).

Godwin, Terry, *The International Rugby Championship 1883-1983* (London, 1984).

Godwin, Terry, *The Complete Who's Who of International Rugby* (Poole, 1987).

Green, Geoffrey, *The History of the Football Association* (London, 1953).

Griffiths, John, *The Book of English International Rugby 1871-1982* (London, 1982).

Griffiths, John, *The Phoenix Book of International Rugby Records* (London, 1987).

Griffiths, John, *Rugby's Strangest Matches: Extraordinary but true stories from over a century of rugby* (London, 2000).

Grigg, Russell, *History of Trinity College Carmarthen 1848-1998* (Cardiff, 1998).

Harragan, Bob (ed.), *Images of Wales: Llanelli Rugby Club* (Stroud, 1998).

Harragan, Bob and Andrew Hignell, *C.P. Lewis: The Champion Cricketer of South Wales* (Cardiff, 2009)

Harris, C.R.G., *The Statistical History of Cardiff Rugby Football Club 1876-1984* (Cardiff, 1984).

Harris, Gareth, *Amalgamation: Pontypridd R.F.C. at Taff Vale Park – The Early Days* (Pontypridd, 1999).

Harris, Gareth, *Taff Vale Park: Memories Lost in Time* (Pontypridd, 2000).

Harris, Gareth and Evans, Alan, *The Butchers Arms Boys: The Early Years* (Neath, 1997).

Harris, H.A., *Sport in Britain: Its Origins and Development* (London, 1975).

Harvey, Adrian, *Football: The First Hundred Years: The Untold Story* (London, 2005).

Hawkins, Frank C. and Seymour-Bell, E., *Fifty Years with the Clifton Rugby Football Club 1872-1922* (Bristol, 1922).

Hignell, Andrew, *From Sophia to SWALEC: A History of Cricket in Cardiff* (Stroud, 2009).

Hignell, Andrew K., *A 'Favourit' Game: Cricket in south Wales before 1914* (Cardiff, 1992).

Hignell, Andrew and Prescott, Gwyn (eds.), *Cardiff Sporting Greats* (Stroud, 2007).

Holt, R.J., 'Football and the Urban Way of Life in Nineteenth–Century Britain', in Mangan, J.A., *Pleasure, Profit, Proselytism: British Culture and Sport at Home and Abroad 1700-1914* (London, 1988).

Holt, Richard, *Sport and the British: A Modern History* (Oxford, 1989).

Hopkins, Bleddyn, *Images of Sport: Swansea RFC 1873-1945* (Stroud, 2002).

Huggins, M.J., 'Leisure and Sport in Middlesbrough, 1840-1914', in Pollard, A.J. (ed.), *Middlesbrough: Town and Community 1830-1950* (Stroud, 1996).

Huggins, Mike and Mangan, J.A. (eds.), *Disreputable Pleasures: Less Virtuous Victorians at Play* (London, 2004).

Hughes, Gareth (ed.), *One Hundred Years of Scarlet* (Llanelli, 1983).

Hughes, Gareth, *The Scarlets: A History of Llanelli Rugby Football Club* (Llanelli, 1986).

Hunter, A.A. (ed.), *Cheltenham College Register 1841-1889* (London, 1890)

Irving, Dennis, *One Hundred Years of Rugby at Narberth* (Narberth, 1982).

James, Danny and Rowlands, P.O.J., *Brecon Rugby Football Club: One Hundred Years of Rugby Football 1879-1979* (Brecon, 1979).

Jarvis, Bernard, *The Origin of Chepstow Rugby Football Club* (Chepstow, 1978).

Jefferies, Horace, *100 Years in Black and White: Cross Keys Rugby Football Club* (Pontypool, 1985).

Jenkins, D.G., *Blaenavon Rugby Football Club Centenary Brochure 1877-1977* (Blaenavon, 1977).

Jenkins, John M. (ed.), *A Rugby Compendium: An Authoritative Guide to the Literature of Rugby Union* (Boston Spa, 1998).

Jenkins, John M., Pierce, Duncan and Auty, Timothy, *Who's Who of Welsh International Rugby Players* (Wrexham, 1991).

Johnes, Martin, *Soccer and Society: South Wales, 1900-1939* (Cardiff, 2002).

Johnes, Martin, *A History of Sport in Wales* (Cardiff, 2005).

Johnson, Martin, *Rugby and All That* (London, 2001).

Jones, Desmond T. (ed.), *Pontypridd Rugby Football Club 1876-1976* (Pontypridd, 1976).

Jones, Elias, 'The Palmy Days of Welsh Rugby', (1935), reprinted in Hughes, Gareth (ed.), *One Hundred Years of Scarlet* (Llanelli, 1983).

Jones, Gareth E. and Smith, Dai (eds.), *The People of Wales* (Llandusul, 1999).

Jones, Ieuan, *The First 100 Years: The History of Mountain Ash Rugby Union Football Club 1875–1975* (Mountain Ash, 1975).

Jones, J.R., *The Encyclopaedia of Rugby Football* (London, 1960).

Jones, R. Brinley (ed.), *Floreat Landubriense: Celebrating a Century and a Half of Education at Llandovery College* (Llandovery, 1998).

Lawrie, W.A.D., *Bridgend Rugby Football Club: The First Hundred Years* (Bridgend, 1979).

Leeworthy, Daryl, *Fields of Play: The Sporting Heritage of Wales* (Aberystwyth, 2012).

Lewis, Steve, *Images of Sport: Newport Rugby Football Club 1874-1950* (Stroud, 1999).

Lewis, Steve and Griffiths, John, *The Essential History of Rugby Union: Wales* (London, 2003).

Llewellyn, Arthur and Llewellyn, Don, *Pentyrch R.F.C.: A Club For All Seasons 1883-1983* (Pentyrch, 1983).

Lloyd, Grahame, *C'mon City! A Hundred Years of the Bluebirds* (Bridgend, 1999).

Lowerson, John, *Sport and the English middle classes, 1870-1914* (Manchester, 1993).

Macrory, Jennifer, *Running with the Ball: The Birth of Rugby Football* (London, 1991).

Mangan, J.A. (ed.), *Pleasure, Profit, Proselytism: British Culture and Sport at Home and Abroad 1700-1914* (London, 1988).

Mangan, J.A., *Athleticism in the Victorian and Edwardian Public School* (London, 2000 edn.).

Mangan, J.A. (ed.), *A Sport-Loving Society: Victorian and Edwardian Middle-Class England at Play* (London, 2006).

Marshall, F. (ed.), *Football: The Rugby Union Game* (London, 1894 edn.).

Marshall, F and Tosswill, Leonard R., (eds.), *Football: The Rugby Union Game* (London, 1925).

Marshall, Howard and Jordan, J.P., *Oxford v. Cambridge: The Story of the University Rugby Match* (London, 1951).

Mason, Tony, *Association Football and English Society 1863-1915* (Brighton, 1981).

Mason, Tony, *Sport in Britain* (London, 1988).

Mason, Tony (ed.), *Sport in Britain: A Social History* (Cambridge, 1989).

Matthews, Brinley E., *The Swansea Story: A History of the Swansea Rugby Football Club 1874-1968* (Swansea, 1968).

McWhirter, Ross and Noble, Andrew, *Centenary History of Oxford University Rugby Football Club* (Oxford, 1969).

Meller, H.E., *Leisure and the Changing City, 1870-1914* (London, 1976).

Metcalfe, Alan, *Leisure and Recreation in a Victorian Mining Community: The Social Economy of Leisure in North-East England, 1820-1914* (London, 2006).

Michell, A.T. (ed.), *Rugby School Register, Volume II, From August 1842, To January, 1874,* (Rugby, 1904).

Moorhouse, Geoffrey, *At the George And Other Essays on Rugby League* (London, 1989).

Moorhouse, Geoffrey, *A People's Game: The Official History of Rugby League 1895-1995* (London, 1996).

Morgan, Dennis, *The Cardiff Story: A History of the City from its Earliest Times to the Present* (Cowbridge, 1991).

Morgan, Eifion, *Llandovery RFC Centenary 1881-1981* (Llandovery, 1981).

Morgan, Kenneth O., *Rebirth of a Nation: Wales 1880-1980* (Oxford, 1982 edn.).

Morgan, William J. and Nicholson, Geoffrey, *Report on Rugby* (London, 1959).

Morris, P.J. and Probert, W.G., *Builth Wells Rugby Football Club Centenary Booklet 1882-1982* (Builth Wells, 1982).

Moses, Anthony J. and Moses, Brenda C., *A History of Dinas Powys Rugby Football Club and its Associations with the Village, 1882-1982* (Risca, 1982).

Musselwhite, John, *The Butcher Boys of Donkey Island: An Historical Profile of Penarth R.F.C.* (Penarth, 1980).

Nauright, John and Chandler, Timothy J.L. (eds.), *Making Men: Rugby and Masculine Identity* (London, 1996).

Nicholls, E. Gwyn, *The Modern Rugby Game and How to Play It* (London, 1908).

O'Keefe, Bill and Young, Emyr, *The Arms Park: Heart of a Rugby Nation* (Talybont, Ceredigion, 2012).

O'Leary, Paul, *Immigration and Integration: The Irish in Wales, 1798-1922* (Cardiff, 2002 edn.).

Old Rugbeian Society, *The Origin of Rugby Football* (Rugby 1897).

Owen, George, (ed. Owen, Henry), *The Description of Penbrokeshire* [sic] [1603] (London, 1892).

Owen, O.L., *The History of the Rugby Football Union* (London, 1955).

Parry-Jones, David (ed.), *Taffs Acre: History and Celebration of Cardiff Arms Park* (London, 1984).

Parry-Jones, David, *The Rugby Clubs of Wales* (London, 1989).

Parry-Jones, David, *Prince Gwyn: Gwyn Nicholls and the First Golden Era of Welsh Rugby* (Bridgend, 1999).

Phillips, Glyn and James, Gwyn, *"The Old Parish", 100 Not Out 1882-1982: A History of Maesteg Rugby Football Club* (Maesteg, 1982).

Pike, W.T., (ed.), *Glamorgan Contemporary Biographies: Pike's New Century Series No. 20* (Brighton, 1907).

Plomer, William, (ed.), *Kilvert's Diary, 1870-1879* (London, 1973)

Pollard, Jack, *Australian Rugby: The Game and the Players* (Chippendale, Australia, 1994).

Powell, Terry (ed.), *An Illustrated History of Newbridge R.F.C.* (Risca, 1988).

Prescott, Gwyn, *"The Best and Happiest Team": A History of Cardiff High School Old Boys Rugby Football Club 1929-1978* (Cardiff, 1979).

Prescott, Gwyn, *"Call Them to Remembrance": The Welsh Rugby Internationals who Died in the Great War* (Cardiff, 2014).

Price, D.T.W., *A History of Saint David's University College Lampeter, Volume One: To 1898* (Cardiff, 1977).

Price, Mike, *Images of Sport: Neath RFC 1871-1945* (Stroud, 2002).

Reason, John and James, Carwyn, *The World of Rugby: A History of Rugby Union Football* (London, 1979).

Rees, J. Hywel, *The Gowerton Rugby Football Club 1884-1984: One Hundred Years On* (Gowerton, 1983).

Rees, William, *A History of Cardiff* (Cardiff, 1969 edn.).

Richards, Alun, *A Touch of Glory: 100 Years of Welsh Rugby* (London, 1980).

Richards, Huw, *A Game for Hooligans: The History of Rugby Union* (Edinburgh, 2006)Richards, Huw, *The Red and the White: The Story of England v Wales Rugby* (London, 2009).

Roderick, Alan, *Newport Rugby Greats* (Newport, 1995).

Ruddick, Ray (ed.), *Images of Sport: Pontypool Rugby Football Club* (Stroud, 2002).

Russell, Dave, *Football and the English: A Social History of Association Football in England, 1863-1995* (Preston, 1997).

Ryan, Greg (ed.), *Tackling Rugby Myths: Rugby and New Zealand Society 1854-2004* (Dunedin, New Zealand, 2005).

Ryan, Greg, *The Conquest for Rugby Supremacy: Accounting for the 1905 All Blacks* (Christchurch, New Zealand, 2005).

Samuel, Michael, *Lampeter Town Rugby Football Club 1875 Centenary Year Brochure* (Llanelli, 1975).

Sheers, Owen, *Calon: A Journey to the Heart of Welsh Rugby* (London, 2013).

Shepley, Nick, *The Story of Cardiff* (Stroud, 2014).

Smith, Dai, *Aneurin Bevan and the World of South Wales* (Cardiff, 1993).

Smith, Dai, *Wales: A Question for History* (Bridgend, 1999).

Smith, David and Williams, Gareth, *Fields of Praise: The Official History of the Welsh Rugby Union 1881-1981* (Cardiff, 1980).

Smith, Jed, *The Original Rules of Rugby* (Oxford, 2007).

Smith, Sean, *The Union Game: A Rugby History* (London, 1999).

Starmer-Smith, Nigel (ed.), *Rugby – A Way of Life: An Illustrated History of Rugby* (London, 1986).

Stephens, Meic (ed.), *New Companion to the Literature of Wales* (Cardiff, 1998).

Thau, Chris, *The Spirit of Penarth: One Hundred and Thirty-One Years of Seaside Rugby 1880-2011* (Penarth, 2012).

Thomas, E.T., White, V.T., et al. (eds.), *Glyncorrwg Rugby Football Club 1880-1980: A Brief Summary of the First Hundred Years* (Glyncorrwg, 1980).

Thomas, Irene and Thomas, Keith, *Abertillery Rugby Football Club 1883-1983: The Centenary Book* (Barry, 1983).

Thomas, J.B.G., *The Men in Scarlet: The Story of Welsh Rugby Football* (London, 1972).

Thomas, J.B.G., 'In the Beginning' in Western Mail in Association with the Welsh Rugby Union, *100 Years of Welsh Rugby* (Cardiff, 1980).

Thomas, J.B.G. and Harding, Rowe (eds.), *Rugby in Wales* (Swansea, 1970).

Thomas, W. Alan, *Cardiff Cricket Club: 1867-1967* (Cardiff, 1967).

Thomas, Wayne, *A Century of Welsh Rugby Players* (Birmingham, 1979).

Thorburn, A.M.C., *The Scottish Rugby Union: Official History* (Edinburgh, 1985).

Thorburn, Sandy, *The History of Scottish Rugby* (London, 1980).

Titley, Uel A. and MacWhirter, Ross, *Centenary History of the Rugby Football Union* (London, 1970).

Toulouse, H.C., *Monmouth School Rugby Football Club: One Hundred Years* (Newport, 1973).

Tranter, Neil, *Sport, Economy and Society in Britain 1750-1914* (Cambridge, 1998).

Trounce, W.J., *"Cardiff in the Fifties": The Reminiscences and Historical Notes of Alderman W.J. Trounce J.P. 1850-1860* (Cardiff, 1918).

Vamplew, Wray, *Pay up and play the game: Professional Sport in Britain 1875-1914* (Cambridge, 1988).

Van Esbeck, Edmund, *Irish Rugby 1874-1999: A History* (Dublin, 1999).

Venn, J.A., *Alumni Cantabrigienses Part II* (6 Volumes) (Cambridge, 1940-1954).

Vincent, Geoffrey T., ''To Uphold the Honour of the Province': Football in Canterbury c. 1854 - c. 1890', in Ryan, Greg (ed.), *Tackling Rugby Myths: Rugby and New Zealand Society 1854-2004* (Dunedin, New Zealand, 2005).

Walvin, James, *Leisure and Society 1830-1950* (London, 1978).

Westcott, Gordon, *A Century on the Rugby Beat: A History of Police Rugby Football in the South Wales Constabulary Area* (Bridgend, 1992).

Williams, Chris, *Capitalism, Community and Conflict: The South Wales Coalfield 1898-1947* (Cardiff, 1998).

Williams, Gareth, 'Taffs Acre: The Pre-1900 Years', in Parry-Jones, David, *Taffs Acre: History and Celebration of Cardiff Arms Park* (London, 1984).

Williams, Gareth, 'From Popular Culture to Public Cliché: Image and Identity in Wales, 1890-1914', in Mangan, J.A., *Pleasure, Profit, Proselytism: British Culture and Sport at Home and Abroad 1700-1914* (London, 1988).

Williams, Gareth, 'Sport and Society in Glamorgan 1750-1980', in Morgan, Prys (ed.), *Glamorgan County History, Volume VI, Glamorgan Society 1780-1980* (Cardiff, 1988).

Williams, Gareth, 'Rugby Union', in Mason, Tony (ed.), *Sport in Britain: A Social History* (Cambridge, 1989).

Williams, Gareth, *1905 and All That: Essays on Rugby Football, Sport and Welsh Society* (Llandysul, 1991).

Williams, Gareth, 'Popular Culture and the Historians', in Lambert, Peter and Schofield, Phillipp (eds.), *Making History: An Introduction to the History and Practices of a Discipline* (Abingdon, 2004).

Williams, John, *Digest of Welsh Historical Statistics*, Volume 1 (Cardiff, 1985).

Williams, John, *Was Wales Industrialised? Essays in Modern Welsh History* (Llandysul, 1995).

Articles

Adair, Daryl, "Competing or Complementary Forces: The 'Civilising' Process and the Commitment to Winning in Nineteenth Century English Rugby and Association Football", *Canadian Journal of History of Sport*, XXIV, 2 (1993), 47-67.

Anon., "Rugby Football in Wales: An Estimate", *Welsh Outlook*, 1, 1 (1914), 17-20.

Anon., "Some Famous Footballers: Cardiff Rugby Football Club", *St. Peter's Magazine*, V, 2 (1925), 43-5.

Bale, J., "Sport and National Identity: A Geographical View", *International Journal of the History of Sport*, 3, 1 (1986), 18-41.

Barlow, Stuart, "The Diffusion of 'Rugby' Football in the Industrialized Context of Rochdale, 1868-1890: A Conflict of Ethical Values", *International Journal of the History of Sport*, 10, 1 (1993), 49-67.

Burdsey, Daniel and Chappell, Robert, " 'And If You Know Your History …': An Examination of the Formation of Football Clubs in Scotland and their Role in the Construction of Social Identity", *Sports Historian*, 20, 1 (2001), 94-106.

Campbell, J.D., " 'Training for Sport is Training for War': Sport and the Transformation of the British Army, 1860-1914", *International Journal of the History of Sport*, 17, 4 (2000), 21-58.

Chandler, Timothy J.L., "Games at Oxbridge and the Public Schools, 1830-1880: The Diffusion of an Innovation", *International Journal of the History of Sport*, 8, 2 (1991), 171-204.

Collins, Tony, "Myth and Reality in the 1895 Rugby Split", *Sports Historian*, 16, (1996), 33-41.

Collins, Tony, "History, Theory and the 'Civilizing Process' ", *Sport in History*, 25, 2 (2005), 289-306.

Collins, Tony, "The Ambiguities of Amateurism: English Rugby Union in the Edwardian", *Sport in History*, 26, 3 (2006), 386-405.

Collins, Tony and Vamplew, Wray, "The Pub, the Drinks Trade and the Early Years of Modern Football", *Sports Historian*, 20, 1 (2000), 1-17.

Collins, Tony, "Book Review: This Spellbound Rugby People", *Sport in History*, 32, 3 (2012), 454-7.

Curry, Graham, "The Trinity Connection: An Analysis of the Role of Members of Cambridge University in the Development of Football in the Mid-Nineteenth Century", *Sports Historian*, 22, 2 (2002), 46-73.

Curry, Graham, Dunning, Eric and Sheard, Kenneth, "Sociological Versus Empiricist History: Some Comments on Tony Collins's 'History, Theory and the 'Civilizing Process' ", *Sport in History*, 26, 1 (2006), 110-123.

Dunning, Eric and Curry, Graham, "The Curate's Egg Scrambled Again: Comments on 'The Curate's Egg Put Back Together'!", *International Journal of the History of Sport*, 19, 4 (2002), 200-204.

Edwards, Gerald and Llewellyn, Don, "The Williams Family: More Than a 'Rugby Dynasty' ", *Garth Domain*, 26, (2004), 1-40.

Evans, A.L., "Some Reflections on Local Sport", *Port Talbot History Society Transactions*, 13, 2 (1981), 22-49.

Evans, Neil, "The Welsh Victorian City: The Middle Class and Civic and National Consciousness in Cardiff, 1850-1914", *Welsh History Review*, 12, 3 (1985), 350-387.

Finn, G.P.T., "Racism, Religion and Social Prejudice: Irish Catholic Clubs, Soccer and Scottish Society – I The Historical Roots of Prejudice", *International Journal of the History of Sport*, 8, 1 (1991), 72-95.

Finn, G.P.T., "Racism, Religion and Social Prejudice: Irish Catholic Clubs, Soccer and Scottish Society – II Social Identities and Conspiracy Theories", *International Journal of the History of Sport*, 8, 3 (1991), 374-397.

Gouldstone, John, "The Working-Class Origins of Modern Football", *International Journal of the History of Sport*, 17, 1 (2000), 135-143.

Harris, Jonathan, "The Early History of Association Football in Breconshire", *Brycheiniog*, XXVIII, (1996), 127-135.

Harvey, Adrian, " 'An Epoch in the Annals of National Sport': Football in Sheffield and the Creation of Modern Soccer and Rugby", *International Journal of the History of Sport*, 18, 4 (2001), 53-87.

Harvey, Adrian, " 'The Curate's Egg Put Back Together: Comments on Eric Dunning's Response to 'An Epoch in the Annals of National Sport' ", *International Journal of the History of Sport*, 19, 4 (2002), 192-199.

Harvey, Adrian, "Curate's Egg Pursued by Red Herrings: A Reply to Eric Dunning and Graham Curry", *International Journal of the History of Sport*, 21, 1 (2004), 127-131.

Harvey, Adrian, "The Oldest Rugby Football Club in the World?", *Sport in History*, 26, 1 (2006), 150-152.

Hignell, Andrew, "Alexandra Park – Cardiff's First-Ever Purpose-Built Sports Ground", *Morgannwg*, 57, (2013), 103-119.

Holt, Richard, "Working-Class Football and the City: The Problem of Continuity", *British Journal of Sports History*, 3, 1 (1986), 5-17.

Huggins, M., "The Spread of Association Football in North-East England, 1876-90: The Pattern of Diffusion", *International Journal of the History of Sport*, 6, 3 (1989), 299-318.

Huggins, Mike, "Second-Class Citizens? English Middle-Class Culture and Sport 1850-1910: A Reconsideration", *International Journal of the History of Sport*, 17, 1 (2000), 135-143.

Hutchinson, John, "Sport, Education and Philanthropy in Nineteenth-century Edinburgh: The Emergence of Modern Forms of Football", *Sport in History*, 28, 4 (2008), 547-565.

Johnes, Martin, "Eighty Minute Patriots? National Identity and Sport in Modern Wales", *International Journal of the History of Sport*, 17, 4 (2000), 93-110.

Johnes, Martin, " 'Poor Man's Cricket': Baseball, Class and Community in south Wales c.1880-1950", *International Journal of the History of Sport*, 17, 4 (2000), 153-166.

Johnes, Martin and Garland, Ian, " 'The New Craze': football and society in north-east Wales, c. 1870-90", *Welsh History Review*, 22, 2 (2004), 278-304.

Kennedy, David and Kennedy, Peter, "Ambiguity, Complexity and Convergence: The Evolution of Liverpool's Irish Football Clubs", *International Journal of the History of Sport*, 24, 7 (2007), 894-920.

Lile, Brian and Farmer, David, "The Early Development of Association Football in South Wales, 1890-1906", *Transactions of the Honourable Society of Cymmrodorion*, (1984), 193-215.

Livingston, J., "Football", *St Paul's Church Sketty: A Souvenir* (1910), 22-24.

Martens, James W., " 'To Throttle the Hydra': The Middle Class and Rugby's Great Schism", *Canadian Journal of History of Sport*, XXII, 1 (1991), 52-76.

Martens, James W., " 'They Stooped to Conquer': Rugby Union Football, 1895-1914", *Journal of Sports History*, 20, 1 (1993), 25-41.

Metcalfe, Alan, "Football in the Mining Communities of East Northumberland 1882-1914", *International Journal of the History of Sport*, 5, 3 (1988), 269-291.

Metcalfe, Alan, "The Control of Space and the Development of Sport: A Case Study of Twenty Two Sports in the Mining Communities of East Northumberland, 1880-1914", *Sports Historian*, 15, (1995), 23-33.

Morgan, Gareth, "Rugby and Revivalism: Sport and Religion in Edwardian Wales", *International Journal of the History of Sport*, 22, 3 (2005), 434-456.

Morgan, R.H., "The Development of an Urban Transport System: The Case of Cardiff", *Welsh History Review*, 13, 2 (1986), 178-193.

Prescott, Gwyn, "Competitive Rugby in Cardiff Before the First World War", *Touchlines (Rugby Memorabilia Society)*, 46, April (2010), 5-9.

Rivington, R.T., "W. Webb Ellis and Ashbourne Football", *International Journal of the History of Sport*, 8, 1 (1991), 133-9.

Roese, H.E., "Cardiff and its Port Facilities", *Morgannwg*, 39, (1995), 50-71.

Russell, David, " 'Sporadic and Curious': The Emergence of Rugby and Soccer Zones in Yorkshire and Lancashire, c 1860-1914", *International Journal of the History of Sport*, 5, 2 (1988), 185-205.

Seward, Andy, "Cornish Rugby and Cultural Identity: A Socio-Historical Perspective", *Sports Historian*, 18, 2 (1998), 78-94.

Smith, David, "People's Theatre – A Century of Welsh Rugby", *History Today*, 31, March (1981), 31-6.

Swain, Peter, "The Origins of Football Debate: The 'Grander Design and the Involvement of the Lower Classes', 1818-1840", *Sport in History*, 34, 4 (2014) 519-543.

Tranter, N.L., "The Social and Occupational Structure of Organized Sport in Central Scotland during the Nineteenth Century", *International Journal of the History of Sport*, 4, 3 (1987), 301-314.

Williams, Gareth, "Community, Class and Rugby in Wales 1880-1914", *Society for the Study of Labour History Bulletin*, 50, Spring, (1985), 10-11.

Williams, Gareth, "The 1905 All Blacks Tour of Great Britain", unpublished paper presented to the *"All Blacks and the 'Mother Country', 1905-2005"* conference, Museum of Rugby, Twickenham, 12 September 2005.

Theses

Croll, Andrew J., "Civilizing the Urban: Popular Culture, Public Space and Urban Meaning, Merthyr c.1870-1914" (Ph.D. thesis, University of Wales, Cardiff, 1997).

Evans, Kenneth, "A Historical Study of the Formative Years of the Welsh Rugby Union 1870-1900" (M.Ed. thesis, University of Liverpool, 1981).

French, Carl, "The History of the Welsh Schools Rugby Union 1903-1939" (M.Ed. thesis, University of Wales, Cardiff, 1991).

Hickey, J.V., "The Origin and Growth of the Irish Community in Cardiff" (M.A. thesis, University of Wales, Cardiff, 1959).

Hignell, Andrew K., "Suburban Development in North Cardiff, 1850-1919: A Case Study of the Pattern and Processes of Growth in the Parishes of

Llanishen, Lisvane and Whitchurch" (Ph.D. thesis, University of Wales, Cardiff, 1987).

Johnes, Martin, "That Other Game: A Social History of Soccer in South Wales c.1906-39" (Ph.D. thesis, University of Wales, Cardiff, 1998).

Rickus, Jack S., " 'A Fair Field of Spectators' The Development of Rugby Football in the Swansea, Neath and Llanelli Region, 1864-1900" (M.A. thesis, Swansea University, 2011).

Stroud, Raymond J., "The Landscape of Popular Recreation in Newport, Monmouthshire, 1888-1914" (M.A. thesis, University of Wales, Cardiff, 1993).

Websites

Cricket Archive: http://cricketarchive.com

National Library of Wales, Welsh Newspapers Online: http://newspapers. library.wales

Welsh Rugby Union: http://www.wru.co.uk

Audiovisual

DVD: *The Lost World of Mitchell and Kenyon*, (BBC, 2005).

Index

St David's Press

Also by Gwyn Prescott

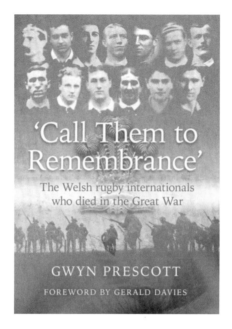

'These pages contain an unexplored and untold tale which, from the deepest anguish of the suffering born of their unquestioning bravery, pierces the heart...This book is [an] acknowledgment of the sacrifice made by 13 Welshmen....Theirs was a sacrifice which needs to be told....Gwyn Prescott, with meticulous and sympathetic attention to detail, tells the story. This narrative is an essential record'.
Gerald Davies, from the Foreword

'From the boisterous singing and exhilarating cheers of Cardiff Arms Park to the deafening roar of artillery shells and gunfire, these humbling stories describe thirteen individual journeys which began on muddy yet familiar Welsh playing fields but ended in the unimaginable brutality of the battles of the First World War.'
Dan Allsobrook, www.gwladrugby.com

'This is a book which moves as well as informs.'
Huw Richards, Associate Lecturer in Sports History, London College of Communication

978 1 902719 375 - £14.99 - 175pp - 120 illustrations/photographs